Ben West

RETIRING
ABROAD

CADOGANguides

Contents

About the author

Ben West has written on property, health, travel and numerous other subjects for many newspapers and magazines including the *Guardian*, the *Independent*, the *Daily Telegraph*, *The Times*, the *Daily Mail*, the *Evening Standard*, *Vogue* and *Readers' Digest*. He was chief property correspondent of the *Daily Express* and the *Sunday Express* from 1999 to 2001, and currently writes a weekly property column for the *Daily Express*. His books, *London for Free* (1996), *Fun for a Fiver in London* (2002) and *Fun for a Fiver in Amsterdam* (2002), were published by Pan Books. He has also written *Buying a Home: The Virgin Guide* (2003) and *Cameroon: the Bradt Travel Guide* (2004). He has written a short film, *Gertrude*, featuring Prunella Scales, which was filmed in 2004.

Conceived and produced for Cadogan Guides by **Navigator Guides Ltd**, The Old Post Office, Swanton Novers, Melton Constable, Norfolk NR24 2AJ, UK
www.navigatorguides.com
info@navigatorguides.com

Cadogan Guides
Network House, 1 Ariel Way, London W12 7SL, UK
info@cadoganguides.co.uk
www.cadoganguides.com

The Globe Pequot Press
246 Goose Lane, PO Box 480, Guilford,
Connecticut 06437–0480, USA

Copyright © Cadogan Guides 2004

"THE SUNDAY TIMES" is a registered trade mark of Times Newspapers Limited

Cover design: Sarah Gardner
Cover photographs: © Tomas del amo / Alamy, Images Etc Ltd / Alamy, Ingram Publishing / Alamy, Comstock Images / Alamy, Dynamic Graphics Group / Creatas / Alamy, Eyebyte / Alamy
Editor: Antonia Cunningham
Proofreader: Anna Amari-Parker
Indexing: Isobel McLean

Printed in Italy by Legoprint

A catalogue record for this book is available from the British Library
ISBN 1-86011-125-4

The author and publishers have made every effort to ensure the accuracy of the information in this book at the time of going to press. However, they cannot accept any responsibility for any loss, injury or inconvenience resulting from the use of information contained in this guide.

Please help us to keep this guide up to date. We have done our best to ensure that the information in it is correct at the time of going to press. But places are constantly changing, and rules and regulations fluctuate. We would be delighted to receive any comments concerning existing entries or omissions. Authors of the best letters will receive a copy of the Cadogan Guide of their choice.

Introduction

Every year, thousands of Britons say goodbye to dark, cold winters, traffic jams, cancelled trains and hospital queues to retire abroad, often in the sun. Indeed, the number of British pensioners living abroad currently hovers around the one million mark. Retirees are fitter than ever before, ready to enjoy life to the full in their new country, and medical advances mean that any health problems that crop up can often be dealt with far more effectively than in the past.

Yet without sufficient planning, a long, happy, relaxing retirement is a dream that can easily turn into a nightmare. From pension payments and tax regimes to property prices and medical costs, it is vital to carry out thorough research before embarking on such a life-changing adventure. A big headache for many buyers of properties abroad now is the huge spectrum of choice, and deciding exactly where they should focus on.

This book describes in an accessible, easily readable way the pros and cons of retiring in a wide range of countries, to help the buyer decide exactly where they might find their dream home abroad. It is designed to guide you all the way, from selecting a country to retire to, through choosing a property and the buying process, to the big move itself. The book contains hundreds of contacts, from embassies and estate agents to lawyers, financial advisers, tourist offices, useful organisations and informative websites. The buyer is directed step-by-step through the practicalities of viewing and buying, the legal and fiscal implications, the logistical considerations and the numerous things to look out for before you commit to buy. There are also tips on selling and letting your property as well as sources of further information on a wide range of subjects.

Whether you are primarily guided by price or by climate, by a love of water or winter sports, by a desire to experience the buzz of vibrant cities or relax in the countryside, we hope that this book will steer you through the maze of buying property abroad, avoiding the pitfalls and exploiting all the benefits along the way.

First Steps and Reasons for Buying

We need a new word for 'retirement'. The term conjures up images of the aged and decrepit, yet longer life expectancy and ever-improving healthcare mean that many retirees are healthier and more active than their predecessors.

A greater spread of affluence, as well as a general move away from the idea of retiring at the age specified by the government, means that many people retire considerably younger than their counterparts in previous generations.

Retirement brings lots of advantages. No longer governed by a work routine, you are likely to have the freedom to spend your time much more as you would like. You probably also have the freedom to travel, even to live in a different country. Not content simply to stay in the UK, more and more retirees are doing just that.

More people are retiring abroad

In 2005, more than 18 million people in the UK will be over 60 years of age. The relatively high value of property in the UK means that many of them will have the option of selling up and buying a very pleasant property abroad and still having money left in the bank. Others have inherited wealth from their parents or have substantial occupational pensions or efficient investments. Generous city bonuses have become more common, and many city workers have decided to take the money and run. Indeed, downshifting has mushroomed in popularity across the whole salary scale as people decide to jettison material acquisition and career status for a more relaxed, more rewarding way of life.

Even those without healthy bank accounts and high-value UK property are likely to find retiring abroad very tempting, as many countries offer not only an attractive, healthy climate, but also cheaper property prices and a cost of living far lower than that of the UK. Long gone are the days when owning a property abroad was a distant dream for most people, enjoyed by a smattering of film stars and tycoons, and precious few others. Nowadays you often don't need a Lottery win or inheritance to buy a villa on a sun-kissed beach or farmhouse deep in the unspoilt countryside to escape the grey skies of Britain.

In 1994, only 250,000 Britons owned properties abroad. Ten years later, the number, according to a survey by *Saga Magazine*, has reached 1.38 million. It is reckoned by one recent survey that one in 10 Britons will own a home abroad by 2008. It is no surprise that recent research by the Royal Bank of Scotland found that buying a home abroad was the main wish-list achievement for British people.

Reasons for retiring abroad

A survey by the UK's *YouGov* in 2002 found that 55 per cent of participants had seriously considered settling in another country, often because of discontent with the state of Britain. A 2004 survey found that 52 per cent of Britons want to leave their homeland, with 20 per cent wanting to relocate to Australia, 16 per cent to Spain and 11 per cent to the USA. Data from the Office for National Statistics shows that in 2001 some 159,000 Britons emigrated or moved to work overseas for at least a year.

Just a decade ago, it was still quite unusual for someone in Britain to have a home abroad, and even then that property would almost certainly be in Spain or France. Today, the market for homes abroad has changed beyond recognition and people are setting up home in the most remarkable places, including even ex-war zones only in very recent years vacated by soldiers, and an increasing list of countries that few people could find easily on a map.

A whole raft of factors have collided to cause a mass migration of Brits to other shores. These include increased general affluence, plunging international travel costs, a sustained period of low rates of borrowing and property values soaring in many areas of Britain that has been allowing many homeowners to release equity in their homes at a time when property prices remain low in many other areas of the globe. An unprecedented ease of access has been rapidly established by ridiculously low air fares and obscure new air routes, enabling potential homeowners abroad to search for properties quickly, easily and cheaply, and allowing them to move abroad happy in the knowledge that their children and grandchildren will be able to visit frequently.

The huge growth in foreign travel has encouraged a spirit of adventure and led many retirees to look beyond our nearest neighbours on the continent and consider more unusual or more exotic countries to inhabit – especially when, while on holiday perhaps, they see the low price tags of properties in many of these countries. There has also been a strong trend for people to retire earlier, with giving up work at 55 or so – something that was almost unheard of 20 years ago – becoming more and more common. This means active, fit, adventurous retirees looking for an interesting new phase of life rather than a general 'winding-down'.

High property prices in the UK, while benefiting many, have prevented others from buying property in the UK, causing them to look elsewhere to retire. Widespread disappointment with disastrous pension and endowment plans have increasingly encouraged older members of the population to search for other ways to create wealth for their senior years. Couple this with widespread disillusionment with the UK's crime and health records, as well as a challenging, often wet and cold climate, and the huge surge in numbers of people retiring abroad becomes easier and easier to understand.

A wider choice

Britons are the largest group of overseas buyers in Europe and have confidently moved on from choosing to locate only in familiar destinations like Cyprus, Florida, France, Portugal and Spain. Now a bewildering and adventurous choice of countries has emerged, all of which are sensible options to choose from – exotic territories as varied as Croatia, Dubai and Morocco. Agents, developers, lawyers and other professionals and organisations have swiftly sprung up, geared to making the task of searching and buying a home relatively enjoyable, secure and easy.

In response to these developments, this book covers a greater choice of countries suitable for buying a property abroad than any similar such book available (as far as the publishers are aware).

It is no surprise that more and more buyers are looking further afield than the familiar few countries so popular in the past, considering that much of the coast from Portugal all the way through Spain to France, the Greek Cypriot coast and swathes of Florida are made up of concrete, often high-rise, developments. Some people are even buying properties in several countries, casually flitting between them on the mushrooming choice of bargain air routes, plugging into the huge extension of global communication links along the way.

More affordable housing abroad

With the price of an average home in Britain standing at £160,565 in August 2004 according to HBOS plc, clearly many buyers are having to look further afield to buy. Properties in countries like rural Italy and Greece start at around £5,000, although at that price they may be little more than a glorified pile of rubble, and small town houses and remote cottages ready to move into but in need of renovation are still available for less than £30,000.

In some parts of London, £50,000 may buy you little more than a cupboard or parking space these days, but cross the Channel and you can take your pick from a fabulous range of beautiful villas, rustic farmhouses and beachside apartments. Just focus on unfashionable rural areas and keep well away from the more glamorous and recognised resorts. Cap d'Antibes is unlikely to be a possibility, but Carcassonne maybe; Chiantishire's Arezzo no, but Le Marche's Ascoli Piceno, yes.

What you get for your money differs surprisingly from country to country. Prices tend to differ least in big cities, with the biggest bargains emerging the more rural you go. In April 2004, the *Daily Telegraph* compared the price of a similarly sized two-bedroom flat in comparable trendy and exclusive neighbourhoods in various capital cities around the world and found the costs for them to be £550,000 in London, £570,000 in New York, £463,000 in Tokyo, £358,000 in Paris, £171,000 in Berlin and £120,000 in Cape Town.

For what you get property-wise, France, for example, remains generally substantially cheaper than neighbouring Spain, which in turn is substantially cheaper than Portugal on the whole. Similarly, Belgium and the Netherlands are generally not only notably more costly than neighbouring France, but very few agents are geared to the UK market and language difficulties can greatly hinder your search in such places. Whereas you can do much research at home on the Internet for France or Spain, for other countries it will be likely to be in person and therefore costly and time-consuming.

You have to be prepared to research carefully to find the bargains, especially as homeowners in many countries have woken up to the profit potential of turning neglected properties into retirement or holiday homes. And even smaller properties available at lower price ranges often need a considerable amount of work, which can be tricky to price, organise and oversee if your main home is in Britain.

Better, cheaper transport options

For many retirees, relocating abroad is proving very attractive because transport is now so much easier, quicker and cheaper, which makes it much easier than it used to be to keep up with friends and family in the UK. There are vastly improved transport links, including the Eurotunnel's 35-minute Channel crossing, fierce competition from ferry companies, bargain-basement fares offered by the 'no-frills' airlines (and now standard airlines also), better motor-ways and an expanding high-speed train network right across the Continent. All these developments are making house-hunting and owning abroad quick, cheap and easy and allowing buyers to look further and further afield for their dream retirement or holiday home abroad.

Even so, 2004 saw the beginnings of a threat to the era of low-cost airfares. In April and May alone, easyJet announced falling profits, Ryanair axed several routes, and Birmingham airline Duo went out of business. Some destinations are summer-only or winter-only as far as airlines are concerned. It is a stark warning not to buy a property simply because a low-cost airline has launched a service there.

The golden era of cheap borrowing

A long period of enticingly low lending rates have made house-hunting abroad even more attractive, and a number of UK lenders now have branches on the Continent to cope with the increased demand. They can often offer cheaper mortgages and loans there when interest rates are lower than in the UK.

High UK property prices have allowed many homeowners awash with equity gained from their UK properties to extend their UK mortgage to fund a property abroad, perhaps a holiday home at first with plans to live there on retirement, and some younger retirees are taking on bigger projects, such as buying a big house abroad to live in and a couple of cottages nearby to let out for income.

Making the right choices

If retiring abroad appeals to you, where do you start? There are lots of questions to answer in the search for the ideal place to retire. Dreaming of retirement in a sunny climate where the lifestyle is relaxed and the living easy and cheap is certainly a pleasant occupation, yet the goal is unlikely to be reached simply without some hard research.

There is a huge choice of countries that can be considered to buy in for retirement now or later, which throws up many tempting possibilities. Should you buy a brand-new property that with any luck is maintenance-free, or buy an elderly, rambling farmhouse in need of extensive renovation? Is it better to buy inland or on the coast?

It is imperative to research the options thoroughly before you commit yourself. As well as selecting the ideal region, lifestyle and culture, you need to know how to buy the property legally and safely using the best form of finance and lessening, as far as possible, any adverse effects of exchange rate fluctuations.

Vitally, when you come to buy you need to be represented legally by an experienced, independent lawyer. The maze of conveyancing laws around the world opens up considerable potential pitfalls for the ignorant and unwary. You should have the necessary safeguards in place to prevent you buying a property with no title, one with no or inadequate planning permission, one which has been sold to someone else or is subject to debts or even that maybe does not even exist, as numerous unfortunate buyers of properties abroad have done.

Whatever decision you make, take your time making it. Before making a decision that you may later regret, explore all the options to ensure that you buy exactly the property you want in the place that you want it to be. So many people move abroad in a rush, taking none of the precautions they would in their own country, intoxicated by the pleasures of a short holiday but without investigating the possible alternatives, pitfalls and disadvantages. If possible, it's a good idea to try a country out for a few months by renting before committing or keeping a base in the UK if you can afford it, in case the dream turns sour.

What do you want from the property?

Do you yearn for a better climate, clean fresh air, to get away from the crowds? To move back to an area where you have emotional ties, or perhaps to be nearer family? Is cost the overriding factor, or language? Do you want a holiday home for now, a place to retire immediately, or possibly a home that can also bring in income, such as offering a bed-and-breakfast arrangement or being available for letting out?

If you want the home for holidays initially, choose somewhere too far and weekend breaks are out. Is it vital that the property can be easily maintained?

With advancing years will you want to be saddled with the extra responsibility a foreign home brings – or a second home if you intend to keep a base in the UK?

If you wish to indulge in a sport, such as golf, skiing or sailing, that will narrow choices down considerably. If this is to be a second home, and you have pets and don't wish to put them in kennels frequently, that is another major factor that will influence your choice of location.

Do not assume that, just because your UK property has appreciated well in recent years, the same will happen abroad and you will make a quick profit should you wish to sell. In many countries, properties increase annually in value by under 5 per cent, if at all, which means that the costs of buying will probably not be covered for at least three years. And capital gains taxes, should you come to sell, can greatly reduce any profits that you do make. Buy principally for the pleasure a foreign home can bring, rather than for financial gain. Generally the people who make significant financial gains are developers, housebuilders and those running successful holiday rentals businesses.

Sources of information

Guidebooks, travel magazines and websites can give plenty of background information, and there are an increasing number of UK magazines geared to all aspects of a country, such as France, Italy and Spain, giving the lowdown on anything from cuisine to culture, and property to transportation. See pp.269–71 for a list. Tourist offices can help a lot too.

If you make an initial exploratory trip, pick up some of the local papers, which can give a lot of information about an area, especially the local property market. Embassies and consulates (listed under each country in **Country Profiles**) can help with many specific enquiries and give up-to-date information on such things as visa requirements and residency regulations. Until you are absolutely sure of what and where you want to buy, it is a good idea to rent for a period so that you become more familiar with the region.

Look before you leap

Be sure to consider all the pitfalls of retiring abroad. Living in a foreign country is very different from being on holiday, and when the tourists have gone home and the village has all but closed down for the winter, things may look very different from the heady days of summer. At such a time, the attractions of Britain – such as a stroll down the local lane, dinner with friends or an evening in the pub – may become more attractive than ever. On the positive side, keeping active mentally and physically, and taking on new challenges, such learning a new language, integrating into a new neighbourhood and making new friends, is a good way of keeping well.

If you're considering buying in a resort community, bear in mind that resorts are geared to the short-term visitor and may not have the right infrastructure for a full-time resident. It may be difficult to establish a social life with people disappearing at the end of each holiday season, or if hobby or sports clubs are few and far between. You may find it frustrating if there is a dearth of galleries, theatres and concert halls.

Check out the climate at every time of year. Many regions boast invitingly warm summers yet winters can be far more harsh than you imagined. A hot climate may be overwhelming week after week and attract unwelcome guests like mosquitoes and other troublesome insects. Incessant sun, with little variety, may become dull over time.

What about the local lifestyle? Are you at ease with the way of life at your proposed destination? Could you easily fit in if everything shuts down each afternoon for a siesta, or everyone eats before 6pm or not until after 10pm?

Beware of buying in a remote area away from essential facilities. Rural living can be very attractive when you are in good health, but when elderly and frail, long, gruelling drives on bumpy tracks to shop, socialise or visit the dentist can be no joke. An *urbanización* near a town may be far more practical. Also, the property and location may be idyllic, but will there be enough there to stimulate and distract you? Many people retire to a beautiful spot only to find after the initial excitement that they are bored out of their minds and that a life lounging by the pool week after week lacks purpose. What about transport and local health provision? You may want the option to study, volunteer or possibly work part-time. Are there any opportunities there?

Being separated from friends and family may affect you more strongly than you expect. And although you may start retirement active, independent and affluent, you need to consider how you would cope if your health begins to deteriorate and you become increasingly dependent on someone else or if your partner dies. Would there be adequate support from a relative or are there suit-able welfare facilities such as sheltered housing or residential homes? In many countries abroad, such support can be rare.

If you decide that you would return to the UK if you become frail, bear in mind that this can have its pitfalls, too. Moving home, especially to another country, is a major upheaval at any time of life, especially if you are elderly. You may have trouble selling your property abroad in the timeframe you are restricted to and leaving a close circle of friends you have made abroad may be more of a wrench than you bargained for.

Before committing yourself to purchasing, ensure that you are satisfied that you can actually afford it. The costs may seem affordable now, but the economy and your personal circumstances may be very different in a few years' time. Also, although a property abroad may seem very cheap by UK standards, the final amount can swiftly go up once the purchasing costs are added, which can be far higher than in Britain, not to mention the ongoing running costs, from local taxes to possibly a gardener and someone to regularly clear the pool.

In addition, you need to have a good idea of the likely stability and security of a country, and ease of access to the UK should you need it.

Your knowledge of the local language is also important. If you plan to spend your days with other Brits in a gated development within an overwhelmingly English resort or village, an ability to speak the local language is not so vital, but if you plan lengthy renovations of your property requiring much interaction with builders, architects and suppliers, good knowledge of the local language may be almost essential.

Also ask yourself whether your partner likes the idea of a property abroad as much as you. If one partner is attracted to a property because of the nearby golf course, in which the other has no interest, or one partner wants the bright lights and a lively social life while the other wants the solitude of a remote village, it is obviously a good idea to come to some compromise before buying. You should also seriously consider what both of you would feel and how you would cope after the death of either partner – do you speak the language and understand the bureaucracy well enough to cope alone if necessary?

Some buyers try a new life abroad to try and improve or save a troubled union, but, instead of taking focus away from the negative, emigrating can put so much stress on a relationship that the partnership is irredeemably damaged, possibly only to fall apart, rather than be salvaged.

If you plan to live abroad full-time, what kind of property would you need that would have everything you require? The type of home you choose is especially important – a remote farmhouse may not be the ideal choice in later years, and instead a place in or near a town with a management company may be far more suitable. Do you love the area sufficiently that daily life will always be a pleasure? If you have always loved travelling, will owning a property abroad use up all your spare cash and prevent you from visiting other lands?

It can be such an enticing idea, when you're struggling with everything from traffic jams to the rain and bitter cold of a British winter, to picture upping sticks to some foreign field in the back of beyond in a gorgeous sun-drenched villa or farmhouse. Yet some people find that the grass isn't necessarily greener on the other side and within months return to the UK because they find the rural bliss interminably boring, they miss their friends and family and such British pleasures as local food, and feel isolated by the incomprehensible language and culture differences of their new country of residence.

Those who tend not to stick it out speak little or none of the language, have unrealistic goals and struggle to integrate, while those who manage to survive tend to arrive with a realistic view of the limitations and of how they intend to spend their days in their new country.

Friends and family

If you want to stay in touch with friends, family and business colleagues, the availability, efficiency and cost of communication, whether telephone, mobile phone, mail or e-mail, should be a consideration. While this may not be such a problem in a country like France or America, it may be a crucial issue in a less developed country. International mobile phone tariffs can vary greatly, for instance. Fortunately, technological advances and widespread competition in recent years have generally brought down prices and improved quality of service greatly for all forms of communication.

Many people who emigrate underestimate how much they will miss family and friends when they go abroad. People you leave in the UK may not visit anything like as much as they initially planned to as the complications of life plus time and money pressures take their toll. And when they do stay, it can sometimes seem as if you are running an hotel, where instead of being paid hotel rates you receive a box of chocolates and a bottle of wine.

Older buyers especially often find that they underestimate what a wrench leaving the country can be, even for their young adult children – instead of welcoming independence, they can feel rather abandoned. It is important to assess how easy it will be to visit family and friends back in the UK in years to come. This may not be difficult when in your 60s and mobile, but may be more problematic 15 or 20 years later, when you may be more frail.

Consider the implications of a move on your dependents. Is your partner as keen as you to move abroad? Would being separated from family and friends cause her or him considerable anguish? Do you have elderly parents or other relatives who rely on you? Would they be happy to move abroad also, perhaps in the future, or would someone else be able to take over the role that you have played in their lives, both practical and emotional?

Alternatives to retiring abroad

While retirement abroad works out for the majority of those who make the move, some retired people unfortunately greatly regret doing so. Yet often the mistakes they made could have been avoided by careful forethought and planning. Many of these people did not seek good advice concerning financial issues, such as taxation, pensions or acquiring a property overseas, or find that their financial position worsens if health problems accumulate.

If you're not entirely sure of where you want to retire, why not try **roaming**? You could travel around on a cruise or by rail, in a boat or a camper van, renting along the way when it takes your fancy. You could stay in a hotel for an extended period off-season. During the British winter, many hotels in countries like Spain, Portugal, Cyprus and Tunisia attract residents by offering extremely low rates. You could try a **home exchange** for a limited time, either with someone you know abroad who may be interested in doing the same thing, or using one of the home exchange agencies that match people wanting to swap homes for a while (*see* p.234 for more information and some addresses).

If your finances allow it, you could **buy in more than one location** (especially feasible in the many countries where property is a fraction of the cost of that in the UK). Maintaining more than one property certainly brings additional responsibilities, but you get to enjoy greater variety and could settle in each location where you have a home when the climate there is ideal.

Another solution, if it is possible, may be to **keep a home in the UK and abroad**, which could allow you to escape the British winter, returning to the UK for spring and summer. The extra cost of such an arrangement could be offset somewhat by letting out either property in your absence. This may your only option if you wish to buy, for example, in Florida, where you may not be able to get a visa for more than 6 months per year. Downsides are the extra responsibility and the fact that you may not feel a true resident in either place if you opt for this arrangement. If you need to let the property, you will have ongoing pressure to find tenants, and when you are absent from the property there may have the worry of the ongoing maintenance or that a neighbour will telephone because of a calamity like flooding or burglary. You may have to consider enlisting a paid minder to oversee the property while you are absent. The commitment of a second home also means that you are far less likely to make trips to pastures new as you will feel obliged to visit your home abroad as much as possible to realise value for money.

Where to retire to?

In 2004, according to Prudential UK, the top 10 dream retirement destinations in order of popularity are Spain, Australia, France, America, Canada, Portugal, Italy, New Zealand, Ireland and, surprisingly, Germany. The top 10 destinations that retirees in reality currently move to are, in order again, Spain, Australia, France, America, Canada, South Africa, Cyprus, New Zealand, Jamaica and Italy.

Relocating can be much more problematic in some countries than others. For example, obtaining a residence permit for New Zealand, Australia or Canada can be very difficult, and America does not issue visitor residence permits to retirees, although they are entitled to stay for six months at a time as visitors. Switzerland has restrictions on the number of foreign owners of property it allows, which varies from *canton* to *canton*.

Unless you've entirely made up your mind of where to move to, consider various options before taking the plunge. Whether you want to settle in a place that will stretch your budget, somewhere that is culture-rich or exotic, or whether you simply want a better climate or somewhere that is English-speaking, we hope that this book will help you come to the all-important decision with relative ease. It covers a wide range of countries, describing the positive and negative aspects of retirement in each, and setting out many vital details, from taxation rates to property prices and buying procedures.

Retiring abroad is simplest if you select a country that is within the European Union (EU) or European Economic Area (EEA). British nationals have the right to live, work and retire in any EU country, although a residence permit may have to be applied for. In late 2004, the **European Union** consists of 455 million citizens in Austria, Belgium, Cyprus (although EU law does not generally apply in the northern part, it being under Turkish control), the Czech Republic, Denmark, Estonia, Finland, France, Germany, Greece, Hungary, Ireland, Italy, Latvia, Lithuania, Luxembourg, Malta, the Netherlands, Poland, Portugal, Slovakia, Slovenia, Spain, Sweden and the United Kingdom.

Bear in mind that some countries in the EU have territories far away from Europe, but these still count as part of the EU. For example, Spain extends to the Canary and Balearic Islands, while France includes such places as Guadeloupe and Martinique in the Caribbean. Other French territories are French Guiana on the coast of South America and Réunion in the Indian Ocean. Portugal extends to the Azores and Madeira in the Atlantic Ocean.

The **European Economic Area** includes Iceland, Liechtenstein and Norway.

You may also wish to investigate countries that may soon be candidates for **future EU membership**, such as Turkey, which in October 2004 was recommended for consideration by the European Commission.

The Practicalities of Living Abroad

Red tape and costs

Do you need a visa or permit?

Before even considering buying in a specific country, ensure that you will be able to use the property as you wish. You can do this by checking with the embassy or consulate of the country concerned. In some countries, the rules change regularly and so it is important to get up-to-date details.

In the USA, for example, non-residents can buy a property, but cannot stay for more than six months per year unless they have an appropriate visa or permit. And the other way round, Americans may not be allowed to retire in some EU countries. EU nationals can live and work in other EU countries, but cannot retire unless they can show they reach the minimum income level required.

For embassy contact details, *see* under each country in **Country Profiles**.

Fees

Another important thing to consider is the associated costs of buying a home abroad. In many foreign countries the fees involved with buying are proportionately far higher than in Britain. They may include a valuation and/or surveyor's fee, estate agent's fee, notary's fee, title search fee, mortgage tax, value added tax, insurance, transfer tax, property registration fees, conveyancing fee and utility connection fees.

Before committing to buy, make sure you have details of all fees payable in writing. Most of these fees are paid by the buyer, but some fees, such as for the estate agent, are paid for by the vendor or shared by both parties.

The emigration application itself may be costly, and may involve an application fee to the immigration authorities, proof of assets, medical fees, legal fees and other such costs.

Insurance

Various insurances are particularly important when you have a property abroad, such as household (both buildings and contents), motor, holiday and travel, and/or health insurance (*see* below). If you need to make a claim, you have to report the incident to the police, often within 24 hours.

For more on insurance, *see* **Moving In and Settling Down**, pp.256–9.

Health

The health benefits of a warmer climate

Many Britons buy homes abroad to escape the cold, grey weather of Britain. Hot weather and sun are well known to make people feel healthier and happier, and sunlight and a dry climate also help eradicate conditions such as arthritis, eczema, psoriasis and asthma.

Healthcare facilities and health risks

Healthcare facilities vary greatly from country to country and it is worth investigating them before deciding which country to buy into. In some areas it may be vital that you take out private health insurance, and in others, decent health facilities may be free but a long distance away.

Potential health problems may also be very different from those in your home country, ranging from an added risk of sunburn to serious tropical diseases like malaria. Provision for the disabled may be considerably lacking compared with services in the UK.

Some countries, especially in the tropics, have strict entry requirements where certain inoculations are mandatory. For example, a jab for yellow fever is necessary to enter certain African countries. In many countries, there are medical precautions that are advised but not mandatory; ignoring them could be fatal (in the case of malaria, for example) and therefore it is advisable to research the medical risks of the country you are going to. Even countries not thought of as being particularly high risk may pose significant medical dangers not seen in the home country.

Get a copy of the Department of Health's leaflet *Health Advice for Travellers*, from any post office or by calling t 0800 555 777, or online at **www.dh.gov.uk/ travellers**.

Travel clinics

If you are considering investing in a property in a country that is less developed than your home country, has inferior medical facilities or significant health risks, it is worth visiting a travel clinic to assess the possible health risk of the country you are considering. A list of travel clinic websites worldwide is on the **International Society of Travel Medicine's** website, **www.istm.org**.

For other journey preparation information, consult **Travel Health Online**; **www.tripprep.com**.

Also, **www.traveldoctor.co.uk** contains a list of UK clinics.

UK

• **British Airways Travel Clinic and Immunisation Service**, 213 Piccadilly, London W1J 9HQ, **t** 0845 600 2236; **www.britishairways.com/travelclinics**.

• **Hospital for Tropical Diseases Travel Clinic**, Mortimer Market Centre, 2nd floor, Capper St, London WC1E 6AU, **t** (020) 7388 9600; **www.thehtd.org**.

• **MASTA (Medical Advisory Service for Travellers Abroad)**, London School of Hygiene and Tropical Medicine, Keppel St, London WC1 7HT, **t** 09068 224100; **www.masta.org**. Has details of clinics around the UK.

• **www.fitfortravel.scot.nhs.uk**: the **NHS travel website** provides country-by-country advice on immunisation and malaria, plus details of recent developments, and a list of relevant health organisations.

• **www.doh.gov.uk/traveladvice/index.htm** and **www.nhsdirect.nhs.uk**: also have medical travel advice.

• **Travel Health Online, www.tripprep.com**. Journey preparation info.

Irish Republic

• **Tropical Medical Bureau**, Grafton Street Medical Centre, Grafton Buildings, 34 Grafton St, Dublin 2, **t** (01) 671 9200; **www.tmb.ie**.

USA

• **Centers for Disease Control and Prevention**, 1600 Clifton Rd, Atlanta, GA 30333, **t** 800 311 3435; **www.cdc.gov/travel**.

• **International Association for Medical Assistance to Travelers (IAMAT)**, 417 Center St, Lewiston, NY 14092, **t** (716) 754 4883; **www.iamat.org**.

Canada

• **International Association for Medical Assistance to Travelers**, Suite 1, 1287 St Clair Ave W., Toronto, Ontario M6E 1B8, **t** (416) 652 0137; **www.iamat.org**.

• **Travel Doctors Group**, Sulphur Springs Rd, Ancaster, Ontario, **t** 905 648 1112; **www.tmvc.com.au**.

• **www.travelhealth.gc.ca**: details of travel clinics in Canada.

Medical insurance

Possible medical costs need to be factored in when you retire. In countries within the EU, to obtain cover from a reciprocal health agreement, you usually need to complete **form E111**, which you can get from your local post office, social security office or the Department of Social Security, Overseas Department, Newcastle-on-Tyne NE98 1YX, before leaving home. This covers UK residents for up to 90 days each trip, and emergency treatment will also be covered, but it does not cover all costs, nor repatriation, and you will often have to pay up front.

Once you receive your state pension, in most EU countries you are entitled to use the health service in the same way that local pensioners can by completing the **E121 form**. Yet the healthcare will not necessarily be free and an expatriate may still have to pay a large percentage of the costs. In France, for example, the E121 form covers around two-thirds of costs but the remainder has to be paid by the individual; local people have private insurance for this.

Private medical insurance may therefore be advisable within the EU, and in countries outside the European Economic Area nothing may be free and therefore insurance is essential. This can vary greatly in price, anything from around £1,000 or so annually for a couple living in Europe to over £10,000 a year for America or Canada.

Numerous other countries provide *emergency* treatment only for visitors under reciprocal health agreements. In spite of this, usually health insurance should also be arranged, not only because often the national health service or compulsory health scheme in the country is inadequate, but because as a foreigner you may not qualify for these. And you can still be saddled with a large bill even when there is a reciprocal health agreement. Many countries do not have reciprocal agreements even for emergency treatment, including the USA, Canada, Switzerland. Turkey, Mexico and Japan. The Department of Health's leaflet *Health Advice for Travellers*, available from any post office or by calling **t** 0800 555 777, or online at **www.dh.gov.uk/travellers**, lists countries with reciprocal agreements.

Private health insurance will allow you to be treated by an English-speaking doctor in a country where this would otherwise probably not be possible. The cost and extent of cover can vary greatly so take care when selecting a policy.

The Department of Work and Pensions in the UK publishes a useful leaflet, SA29, *Your Social Security, Benefits and Healthcare Rights in the European Economic Area*, available from **www.dwp.gov.uk**.

Expatriate insurance providers

- **Blue Cross** (France), **t** (00 33) 1 42 81 98 76.
- **BUPA International** (UK), **t** (01273) 208181; **www.bupa-intl.com**.
- **Dave Tester Expatriate Insurance Services**, 18a Hove Park Villas, Hove BN3 6HG (UK), **t** (01273) 703469.
- **ExpaCare** (UK), **t** (01483) 717800.
- **Goodhealth International Healthcare**, 5 Lloyds Avenue, London EC3N 3AE (UK), **t** 0870 442 7376; **www.goodhealth.co.uk**.
- **International Health Insurance Danmark** (UK), **t** (01624) 677412.
- **Lloyds Expatriate Protection Plans** (USA), **t** 800 399 3904.
- **Medibroker International** (UK), **t** 0800 980 1082.
- **PPP International** (UK), **t** (01892) 512345.

- **Private Health Associates** (UK), **t** 0870 770 0946.
- **Private Medical Intermediaries** (UK), **t** (01606) 352035.

Pets

Check the latest regulations for taking pets abroad, not just for your destination, but for any countries you may pass through if travelling overland. Shipping companies and airlines may have restrictions and impose specific requirements.

Some countries require a period of quarantine and you may need to organise health and vaccination certificates and other documentation.

Pet passport schemes are now operated by a number of countries and have allowed many animal-lovers to consider buying a home abroad who previously would have been unhappy with putting their pets into kennels. Pets on such schemes are typically required to be microchipped, or sometimes tattooed, for identification, and to be administered anti-rabies inoculations and various blood tests. Some dog breeds are not permitted pet passports. More information on the subject is available at **www.petsabroad-uk.com** and from the **Department of the Environment, Food and Rural Affairs** (**t** 0845 933 5577).

Bear in mind that there may be additional potential dangers and diseases for a pet abroad. Health insurance for pets should be considered, especially as veterinary care can be very expensive.

Language

If the language spoken in your chosen country is not your own and you plan to spend considerable time there, then obviously the more you can understand and speak the local language the easier and more rewarding the whole experience will be. Although many foreign buyers get by in English-speaking enclaves, such as on the Spanish or southern Portuguese coast, obviously you are going to have considerable problems if you are not at all acquainted with the local language in an area where only the native tongue is likely to be spoken, such as the wilds of rural Lithuania. Also, if you plan to restore a property or run a local business, some command of the local language is going to be more necessary than if you are buying a holiday home for infrequent visits in a tourist area.

Language skills are more important in some countries than others. Generally, the Spanish are more relaxed if you do not speak the language, while in France it is expected that you should do so, and your not doing so can cause resentment, especially if your shopping trips normally consist of pointing feverishly, waving your arms and shouting in English without even a *bonjour*.

Not only will you find it easier to integrate into the local community if you speak the local language, but the cost of living will reduce as you will be able to do more, more quickly, without possibly involving outside paid help, and the endless routine things like deciphering bills, reading instruction manuals or taking a parcel to the post office will become quick and easy. Living full time in a country where you do not understand anything from the road signs to the local newspaper is at best infuriating, at worst isolating and depressing.

There's even less excuse not to learn the language considering the wide range of language course options available now, whether on CD or computer, video or evening course. But don't underestimate the time and effort necessary to learn one, especially as many languages, such as French, are more structured than English and therefore need sustained study. Whichever way you learn, becoming fluent can take time, but is invariably well worth the effort in the end.

Cost of living

With the drawing of a salary coming to an end, the cost of living becomes more crucial than ever. Even if you have a good idea of how much money you have to buy a property abroad, do you have enough to cope with unexpected extra costs, possibly a higher cost of living in some or even all respects, currency fluctuations and foreign taxes, as well as the property itself? Will you have a contingency fund set aside for unforeseen problems, and would you be able to cope financially if your pension is frozen, which happens in many countries, while the cost of living rises?

When you look at the British cost of living – a cappuccino can be around £2 a shot and parking in some areas over £10 an hour – it is easy to assume that retiring abroad will be cheaper. Yet the cost of living in some retirement hotspots is actually much higher than in Britain. When researching a new country, don't just look at the cost of properties and everyday items like groceries. Other expenses may be far higher than you imagine, such as local taxes, taxis, healthcare and costs of anything from a visit by an electrician to going to the cinema.

According to a survey by the Prudential in 2004, the cost of living in the 10 most popular retirement destinations, as measured by the cost of 10 commonly bought goods, runs as follows with the most expensive first: Cyprus (Greek), Canada, Australia, France, Jamaica, Italy, USA, Spain, New Zealand and South Africa. The UK sits in the middle of these.

Financial discrepancies with locals

If you buy in an expensive area, will it be a struggle to keep up? If the house prices are high, the cost of everything else, from local services to local taxes, is likely to be equally costly. Likewise, if you buy into an area where the prices are a fraction of where you're coming from, how will the discrepancy in income and costs affect things? If you are living like a lord while all around you are on the poverty line, this may cause problems with both your conscience and your social life.

Education overseas

If you are retiring early in life and have school-aged children, find out if there would be adequate educational provision for them. Are there good English-speaking schools in the locality; could you teach your children yourself; or would you consider a boarding school in the UK? If your children are resident abroad, it is unlikely that they would be able to receive subsidised student loans in the UK should they wish to continue in higher education there. Fortunately, most countries have at least an adequate choice of educational options for children of people relocating abroad and in some countries, notably in most of Europe, there is both a good choice of private English-speaking schools and colleges, as well as local state ones.

Education abroad offers children an early introduction to the international scene and can broaden horizons greatly. Young children educated in a foreign country can also often benefit from becoming bilingual quite effortlessly.

For further information, the **European Council of International Schools** (21 Lavant Street, Petersfield, Hants GU32 3EL, UK, **t** (01730) 268244; **www.ecis.org**) publishes an international schools directory, and the website **www.ibiblio.org/cisco/schools/international** lists international schools.

Payment of the UK state pension and other benefits abroad

The UK state pension, as well as widow's and bereavement benefits, can be paid in full anywhere in the EEA, and rises each year with inflation, as in the UK. In addition, there are 20 more countries where the retirement pension is paid in full and index-linked each year. This list, which looks rather arbitrarily compiled, is made up of Alderney, Barbados, Bermuda, Bosnia and Herzegovina, Croatia, Federal Republic of Yugoslavia (Serbia), Gibraltar, Guernsey, Isle of Man, Israel, Jamaica, Jersey, Kosovo, Macedonia, Mauritius, Philippines, Sark, Switzerland, Turkey and the USA. More such social security agreements could be made in the future. If the country you are considering is not on this list, it may be worth consulting the Benefits Agency in the UK.

In every other country in the world, the UK state pension can be paid but is frozen, which means it does not increase each year with inflation. Such countries include Australia, Canada, New Zealand and South Africa, and this illogical rule causes around 500,000 British expatriates to suffer frozen pension payments. This means that some people who retired abroad 40 years ago are receiving less than £3 per week. If your pension is frozen but you return to the UK, fortunately you will receive your pension at the prevailing rate.

War pensions are paid in full in any country in the world but virtually all other social security benefits are not paid to those people who live permanently outside the UK. This includes disability payments. Instead, residents abroad are entitled to the social assistance provided for other citizens of that country, which may not be as generous as those in the UK.

Retired or working EU citizens have the right to use the health service of other member states in the same way that a citizen of that country can (*see* pp.17–19). Equally, residents of other countries are subject to their tax regulations.

The winter fuel payment provided by the UK government, which is currently £200 tax-free for individuals or couples over the age of 60, can sometimes be paid to people living outside the UK. Although entitlement is a complicated issue, generally speaking, if you are 60 or over and permanently resident in the UK during the qualifying week in late September, you are entitled to the payment in subsequent years if you move within the EU, EEA, Gibraltar or Switzerland. (This may seem illogical considering that the winter temperature in many of these countries is far higher than that of the UK!) To further complicate things, payment is not made to residents of the Channel Islands or the Isle of Man as they are outside both the UK and the EU.

More information on state pensions for those living abroad is available from the **Pension Service International Pension Centre (t** (0191) 218 7777).

Taxation and savings

As many retirees have found the hard way, after rushing into retirement abroad after being seduced by a two-week holiday, the financial side of such a move requires careful thought. You need to make a realistic assessment of how far your pension and any savings will stretch and take into account future currency fluctuations. This is all often most effectively done by taking professional advice.

Taxation

Although it may be tempting to skimp researching taxation, it is vital to look into the local taxes, as a country's system of income tax, inheritance tax, gift tax, capital gains tax and/or wealth tax, and its laws, could seriously affect your pocket and might affect your decision about which country to move to. It may be beneficial that you keep your assets protected elsewhere, such as by keeping them in the UK.

If you decide to keep a home in the UK as well as a property abroad, you may be liable to pay UK tax as well as tax abroad. Only thorough research and the help of a suitably qualified expert will lead you to the best way. Most countries will levy tax on any income earned in the country, but others may also tax an individual's worldwide income or capital gains, or administer punitive inheritance tax on their estate when they die.

Whether you are 'resident' or 'domiciled' in a country can have a significant impact on your tax bill. To remain **resident** in a country in the European Union you need to be physically present in the country for at least 183 days of the tax year. The Inland Revenue also considers you to be a UK resident ('**ordinarily resident**') and therefore liable for UK tax if you spend on average more than 90 days a year in the UK over a period of four years or if you have accommodation in the UK. An individual's **domicile**, however, refers to the country the individual considers to be their permanent home, and is not easily changed from their country of birth.

To establish non-resident status, you need to show the Inland Revenue that your intention is to live abroad for at least one tax year. If you do this successfully, you obtain provisional non-resident status, and therefore no liability for UK tax on income arising outside of the UK, although you will still be liable to pay tax on income arising in the UK. UK income is any income from a source in the UK. Examples include interest from a UK bank or building society account, interest paid by a UK company, dividends from a UK company, interest on UK government securities (gilts), income from property in the UK, such as from rentals, UK pensions or annuities and royalties.

Fortunately, in many countries, tax paid on income starts at a higher income level than in Britain and therefore expatriates often find that they do not pay income tax if they live in one of them. Yet many countries have other taxes to claw in government income, such as property taxes, foreign resident's tax, higher VAT rates and wealth tax. A specialist tax adviser or the embassy of the country concerned should be able to supply the current tax rates.

Of course, if you pay tax to both the Inland Revenue in the UK and in a foreign country, the possibility of paying tax twice on the same income or capital is possible. Fortunately, the UK has double taxation agreements with a number of countries around the world to prevent or at least partially prevent this, although the terms of these agreements, available for inspection at the Inspector of Foreign Dividends or the Inland Revenue Library at Somerset House in London, can vary.

Countries with which the UK has double taxation agreements currently are: Antigua and Barbuda, Argentina, Australia, Austria, Azerbaijan, Bangladesh, Barbados, Belarus, Belgium, Belize, Bolivia, Botswana, Brunei, Bulgaria, Burma (Myanmar), Canada, China, Croatia, Cyprus, Czech Republic, Denmark, Egypt, Estonia, Falkland Islands, Fiji Islands, Finland, France, Gambia, Germany, Ghana, Greece, Grenada, Guyana, Hungary, Iceland, India, Indonesia, Ireland, Israel, Italy,

Ivory Coast, Jamaica, Japan, Kazakhstan, Kenya, Kiribati, Latvia, Lesotho, Lithuania, Luxembourg, Macedonia, Malawi, Malaysia, Malta, Mauritius, Mexico, Mongolia, Montserrat, Morocco, Namibia, Netherlands, New Zealand, Nigeria, Norway, Oman, Pakistan, Papua New Guinea, Philippines, Poland, Portugal, Romania, Russia, St Kitts and Nevis, Sierra Leone, Singapore, Slovakia, Slovenia, Solomon Islands, South Africa, South Korea, Spain, Sri Lanka, Sudan, Swaziland, Sweden, Switzerland, Thailand, Trinidad and Tobago, Tunisia, Turkey, Tuvalu, Uganda, Ukraine, USA, Uzbekistan, Venezuela, Vietnam, Yugoslavia, Zambia and Zimbabwe.

The Inland Revenue website, **www.inlandrevenue.gov.uk**, has links that explain tax rules in different countries. If you go to live or retire abroad, you should complete **form P85** ('Residence or Employment Abroad'), obtainable from your UK tax office, and return it to that office when you leave the UK.

See also pp.240–42.

Making a will

It is almost always wise to make a will in the country you are buying into, as the alternative, using your UK will, can cause sizeable costs and tax disadvantages. Having no will at all is obviously even costlier still.

The decision of whether you, you and your partner, your children, you and your children, a company or trust own the property should be carefully considered and discussed with a suitably experienced lawyer or financial adviser as the wrong one could be very costly in tax implications.

Who you leave your property to can also lead to expensive tax implications. Those in second marriages or who live together but are unmarried can further complicate matters. There can be restrictions; in France, for example, you cannot leave your property to whoever you want as certain relatives have automatic priority claims to it. A lawyer experienced in the property laws of the country concerned should be consulted before purchase, as you can solve this problem in advance by careful choice of ownership of the property – sole or joint ownership, putting some of it it the name of your children, buying it in the name of a company you set up – but they all have different tax consequences.

See also pp.240–42.

Savings

Address the practical and financial implications of such a move many months in advance. For example, note that savings and investments obtained in the UK may not qualify for the same tax breaks in the country that you are planning to emigrate to.

An independent financial adviser and/or an accountant may be able to advise you how to protect savings and transfer them abroad tax-efficiently. Dual arrangements mean tax is only paid once rather than twice when investments are assessed.

Savings may benefit from being left in a UK deposit account, in which case you will need an Inland Revenue **IR85 form**, available from banks and building societies. This form allows for tax-free interest payments for the non-resident. Savings can also be put into offshore bonds to benefit from tax-free growth. Those planning to emigrate should also check whether life and critical illness insurance premiums, income protection plans and similar insurance will still be covered abroad. *See* also p.242.

Working abroad

If you are considering perhaps working part-time to supplement your pension, check that you are permitted to work in your country of choice. It is often easier to obtain a residence permit as a retiree than it is a work permit, as you will not be taking a job from a local. Even if you are, is there enough demand for the qualifications, experience and skills you have to offer? There may be plenty of work in the ugly, heavily industrialised part of the country, but opportunities are likely to be far fewer in the beautiful, rural region you may picture yourself being in. And are the local rates of pay high enough to make working financially worthwhile? Another thing to consider seriously is whether your grasp of the language is strong enough to enable you to take a job, or handle the bureaucracy involved in running a small business such as a B&B..

Dying abroad

The trauma of the death of a partner can be even worse abroad. Apart from anything else there are lots of decisions to be made, including whether the deceased should be buried or cremated abroad or the body be taken back to the UK, which is expensive and can be problemmatic. Burial abroad can be very expensive in localities where burial space is very limited. It may be most practical for the body to be cremated locally and the ashes returned to the UK.

Most countries require a death to be registered within a few days at the local births and deaths register office. As well as next of kin and an undertaker, other people and authorities need to be informed of a death abroad. These include the deceased's lawyer, any applicable local authorities, and the British consulate in the country of residence, which will notify the UK's General Register Office so that a death certificate can be issued. Administrators of the pension fund of the deceased, as well as insurance companies holding any life insurance policies, the deceased's bank and the social security office, should all be informed.

Travel to your selected country

Even if you plan to stay at your home abroad all or the majority of the time, the speed, cost and ease of transport to and from the country may still be a very important consideration if you wish to keep regular links with the UK. Will you or your visitors be able to go effortlessly door-to-door by train, or does the trip involve a myriad connections by train, ferry and taxi, or aeroplane and bus? Do transport services operate adequately throughout the year and do prices remain similar from season to season?

Before purchasing a property, research transport options thoroughly. Study timetables: many routes operate only at the most popular times, such as from May to October, rather than all year round. Study price structures: if the only low-cost flights are available at inconvenient times and for only a few days in the depths of winter, and summer prices are astronomical, think again. Also, often outgoing and incoming flights, trains and ferries can vary enormously in price, causing any bargain to evaporate. Ideally there should be more than one option offering affordable fares a comfortable distance from the property to cover the possibility of a route being discontinued or carrier or ferry operator going bust.

Don't forget to check what the journey to and from airports is like. If the flight is cheap and quick, but travel from home and to the property takes several hours, the property is unlikely to be suitable for repeated short breaks.

By air

Where easy access to a ferry port was once crucial in determining where to retire abroad, now proximity to an airport is increasingly the deciding factor.

With the recent huge growth in bargain air flights, commonly from under £35 return to an ever-expanding array of destinations and now with more than 50 low-cost airlines across Europe, today's purchasers abroad can cast their nets further than ever before. Indeed, today it is often easier and cheaper to fly abroad than catch a train in the UK to many other places in Britain. Now a second home for weekends in the south of France or maybe an Italian city is an affordable, practical reality, and the only problem is in selecting which country or region to opt for.

But beware of allowing the existence of a budget flight to an airport near your preferred destination to strongly influence your decision to buy. A number of budget routes have been discontinued in recent years, and in February 2004 a European Commission ruling banned Ryanair from receiving subsidies to fly to Charleroi, in Belgium, which could accelerate the closure of further routes in Europe in months to come. Such a development would probably cause a surge in British-owned property coming on to the market at lower prices.

Certainly subsequent developments in 2004 indicate that it certainly is not a good idea to buy a property simply because a low-cost airline has launched a service there. In May, easyJet's share calculation fell 20 per cent and it admitted 'unprofitable and unrealistic pricing' while Ryanair axed three French routes, Reims, Clermont-Ferrand and Brest, after an earlier profit-warning. In addition, Birmingham airline Duo went out of business, the ninth European airline to fail from September 2001 to May 2004. More closures of both airlines and routes seem likely at the time of writing.

How much of a bargain are the bargain air fares?

The amazing fares being offered by the so-called bargain airlines are well-known, and an increasing number of travellers have even managed to buy tickets at crazy prices – or even been given tickets for free, with only the taxes to pay. But if you cannot be very flexible over flight timings, are the prices offered by no-frills airlines really significantly lower the majority of the time?

An extensive survey of airfares conducted by the author in 2002 showed that at popular times the bargains offered by the no-frills airlines often disappear, especially when taxes and surcharges are added, or if you don't book weeks in advance. Generally, the low-cost airlines increasingly live up to their name the further the distance you fly. A number of fares were monitored for four weeks, for a weekend break – taking Friday and Sunday afternoon or evening flights – with flight timings as similar as possible. If a flight became unavailable, the fare of the next available flight was checked until none was being offered for the departure dates. These were the results:

- The cost of a **British Airways London Heathrow** to **Glasgow International** flight on 24 May 2002, returning on 26 May 2002, varied in cost from £114 to £268.30 during the month before departure.

- Around the same time on the same dates, return **easyJet** flights from **London Luton** to **Glasgow International** varied from £65 to £225 during the month before departure.

- **Ryanair's London Stansted** to **Glasgow Prestwick** flights varied from £113.16 to £193.16 during the month before departure.

- **British Airways** flights from **London Heathrow** to **Nice** and back on these days varied very little, from £569.30 to £570.

- **EasyJet's** flights from **London Luton** to **Nice** varied in cost from £244.59 to £364.59 during the month before departure.

- Return flights with **BMIbaby** from **East Midlands** to **Nice** varied from £195.00 to £245.00 during the month before departure.

Opting for a low-cost carrier can leave you using an inconvenient departure airport, enduring significant delays, and spending time and money at the other end getting from an obscure rural airport to the centre of town. You also forgo complimentary snacks. Most bargain airlines do not offer child discounts and apply hefty charges for excess luggage.

If you are prepared or able to take the least popular flights offered by no-frills carriers, typically very early or late in the day and outside the summer and school holidays, and happy to use one carrier one-way, another for the return (which could mean returning to a different airport), then your chances of low ticket prices increase. Travellers able to be flexible over airports are of course even more likely to land a bargain, although it can be inconvenient when you arrive. Ryanair flies to Glasgow Prestwick, for example, although it really should be called Ayr airport as it is adjacent to that city, an hour's drive from Glasgow.

Yet if you cannot be flexible and want to fly at a popular time then there can be surprisingly little difference in price, whichever airline you choose.

Airlines and where they fly to

European destinations are shown below for those airlines that offer flights from various airports in the UK. Only European destinations are shown. Many of the airlines included offer further flights from the destinations shown.

• **Aer Arann, t** 0800 587 2324; **www.aerarann.ie**.
Cork, Kerry, Waterford, Derry, Donegal, Galway.

• **Aer Lingus, t** 0845 084 4444; **www.aerlingus.com**.
Dublin, Cork.

• **Aeroflot, t** (020) 8577 9570; **www.aeroflot.co.uk**.
Moscow, St Petersburg.

• **Air Baltic, t** (021753) 685020; **www.airbaltic.com**.
Riga.

• **Air Berlin, t** 0870 738 8880; **www.airberlin.com**.
Berlin, Dortmund, Hamburg, Hanover, M'Gladbach, Munster, Nuremberg, Paderborn, Vienna.

• **Air Europa, t** 0870 240 240 1501; **www.aireuropa.com**.
Madrid, Palma.

• **Air France, t** 0845 0845 111; **www.airfrance.com**.
Numerous destinations.

• **Air Malta, t** (020) 8785 3199; **www.airmalta.com**.
Various destinations.

• **Air Polonia, t** 48 22 575 0000; **www.airpolonia.com**.
Warsaw, Gdansk, Poznan, Katowice, Slupsk.

• **Air Scotland, t** 0141 848 4990; **www.air-scotland.com**.
Alicante, Barcelona, Fuerteventura, Girona, Gran Canaria, Tenerife.

• **Air Slovakia, t** (020) 7436 9009; **www.airslovakia.sk**.
Bratislava.

- **Alitalia, t** 0870 544 8259; **www.alitalia.co.uk**.
Various destinations.

- **Austrian Airlines, t** (020) 7766 0300; **www.aua.com**.
Bratislava.

- **Basiq Air, t** (020) 7365 4997; **www.basiqair.com**.
Amsterdam, Rotterdam.

- **BMIbaby, t** 0870 264 2229; **www.bmibaby.com**.
Alicante, Amsterdam, Barcelona, Brussels, Cork, Dublin, Faro, Geneva, Ibiza, Jersey, Málaga, Milan, Munich, Murcia, Nice, Palma, Paris, Pisa, Prague, Toulouse.

- **British Airways, t** 0870 850 9850; **www.ba.com**.
Alicante, Almeria, Amsterdam, Athens, Barcelona, Belgrade, Berlin, Bilbao, Bologna, Bordeaux, Brussels, Bucharest, Budapest, Cologne, Copenhagen, Dublin, Dubrovnik, Düsseldorf, Faro, Frankfurt, Fuerteventura, Geneva, Genoa, Gibraltar, Girona, Gothenburg, Gran Canaria, Hamburg, Hanover, Helsinki, Istanbul, Jerez, Kiev, Knock, Krakow, Lanzarote, Larnaca, Lisbon, Luxembourg, Lyons, Madeira, Madrid, Málaga, Malta, Marseille, Menorca, Milan, Montpellier, Moscow, Munich, Murcia, Naples, Nice, Oporto, Oslo, Palma, Paphos, Paris, Pisa, Prague, Pristina, Riga, Rome, St Petersburg, Seville, Shannon, Sofia, Stockholm, Stuttgart, Tenerife, Toulon, Toulouse, Turin, Valencia, Venice, Verona, Vienna, Warsaw, Zürich.

- **British Midland (bmi), t** 0870 607 0555; **www.flybmi.com**.
Alicante, Amsterdam, Berlin, Brussels, Cologne, Copenhagen, Cork, Dublin, Düsseldorf, Esbjerg, Frankfurt, Gothenburg, Hanover, Jersey, Madrid, Milan, Nice, Oslo, Palma, Paris, Stockholm, Stuttgart, Tenerife, Toulouse, Venice.

- **Cirrus Airlines, t** 0845 773 7747; **www.cirrusairlines.de**.
Leipzig.

- **Croatia Airlines, t** (020) 8563 0022; **www.croatiaairlines.hr**.
Various destinations.

- **Czech Airlines, t** 0870 444 3747; **www.czechairlines.com**.
Various destinations.

- **easyJet, t** 0870 600 0000; **www.easyjet.com**.
Alicante, Amsterdam, Athens, Barcelona, Basel, Bilbao, Bologna, Budapest, Copenhagen, Faro, Geneva, Ibiza, Ljubljana, Lyon, Madrid, Málaga, Marseille, Milan, Munich, Naples, Nice, Palma, Paris, Prague, Rome, Tallinn, Venice, Zurich.

- **Finnair, t** (020) 7408 1222; **www.finnair.com**.
Helsinki.

- **Flybe, t** 0870 567 6676; **www.flybe.com**.
Alicante, Bergerac, Bordeaux, Chambéry, Cork, Dublin, Faro, Geneva, Ibiza, Lyons, Málaga, Milan, Murcia, Nantes, Paris, Perpignan, Prague, Salzburg, Shannon, Toulouse.

- **German Wings, t** (020) 8321 7255; **www.germanwings.com**.
Cologne.

- **Germania Express, t** (01292) 511 060; **www.gexx.de**.
Berlin.

- **Hapag-Lloyd Express, t** 0870 606 0519; **www.hlx.com**.
Cologne.

- **Helios Airways, t** (020) 8819 8819; **www.helios-airways.com**.
Larnaca, Paphos.

- **Iberia, t** 0845 601 2854; **www.iberia.com**.
Various destinations.

- **Iceland Air, t** (020) 7874 1000; **www.icelandair.co.uk**.
Reykjavik.

- **Iceland Express, t** 0870 850 0737; **www.icelandexpress.com**.
Reykjavik.

- **JAT, t** (020) 7627 2007; **www.jatlondon.com**.
Belgrade, Tivat.

- **Jet2, t** 0870 737 8282; **www.jet2.com**.
Alicante, Amsterdam, Barcelona, Faro, Geneva, Málaga, Milan, Nice,
Palma, Prague.

- **Jetmagic, t** 0870 1780 135; **www.jetmagic.com**.
Cork.

- **KLM, t** 0870 5074 074; **www.klm.com**.
Various destinations.

- **LOT Polish Airlines, t** 0845 601 0949; **www.lot.com**.
Warsaw.

- **Lufthansa, t** 0845 7737 747; **www.lufthansa.co.uk**.
Various destinations.

- **Luxair, t** (01293) 596 633; **www.luxair.lu**.
Luxembourg.

- **Maersk Air, t** (020) 7333 0066; **www.maersk-air.com**.
Aarhus, Athens, Copenhagen, Oslo, Stockholm.

- **Malev Hungarian Airlines, t** (020) 7439 0577; **www.malev.hu**.
Budapest.

- **Monarch, t** 0870 040 5040; **www.fly-monarch.com**.
Alicante, Barcelona, Faro, Gibraltar, Málaga, Menorca, Palma, Tenerife.

- **MyTravelLite, t** 0870 156 4564; **www.mytravellite.com**.
Alicante, Almeria, Amsterdam, Barcelona, Faro, Knock, Málaga, Murcia, Palma,
Pisa, Tenerife.

- **Olympic Airways, t** 0870 606 0460; **www.olympic-airways.gr**.
Various destinations.

- **Portugalia, t** (0161) 489 5049; **www.pga.pt**.
Lisbon, Oporto.

- **Ryanair, t** 0871 246 0000; **www.ryanair.com**.
Aachen, Aarhus, Alghero, Ancona, Baden-Baden, Bergerac, Berlin, Biarritz,
Brescia, Brussels, Carcassonne, Cork, Dinard, Dublin, Düsseldorf, Eindhoven,
Esbjerg, Forlí, Frankfurt, Friedrichshafen, Genoa, Girona, Gothenburg, Graz,
Gröningen, Haugesund, Jerez, Kerry, Klagenfurt, Knock, La Rochelle, Leipzig,
Limoges, Lübeck, Maastricht, Málaga, Malmö, Milan, Montpellier, Murcia,
Nimes, Oslo, Ostend, Palermo, Paris, Pau, Perpignan, Pescara, Pisa, Poitiers,
Rodez, Rome, Salzburg, Shannon, St Etienne, Stockholm, Tampere, Tours,
Treviso, Trieste, Turin, Västerås.

- **SAS Scandinavian Airlines, t** 0870 607 2772; **www.scandinavian.net**.
Various destinations.

- **Scot Airways, t** 0870 606 0707; **www.scotairways.co.uk**.
Amsterdam.

- **Sky Europe, t** (020) 7365 0365; **www.skyeurope.com**.
Bratislava, Budapest.

- **SN Brussels Airlines, t** (020) 7559 9787; **www.flysn.com**.
Various destinations.

- **Swiss Airlines, t** 0845 601 0956; **www.swiss.com**.
Various destinations.

- **Tap Air Portugal, t** 0845 601 0932; **www.tap-airportugal.co.uk**.
Various destinations.

- **Thomson, t** 0870 1900 737; **www.thomsonfly.com**.
Ibiza, Málaga, Marseille, Naples, Nice, Palma, Pisa, Rome, Valencia, Venice.

- **Turkish Airlines, t** (020) 7766 9300; **www.turkishairlines.com**.
Various destinations.

- **VLM Airlines, t** (020) 7476 6677; **www.vlm-airlines.com**.
Antwerp, Brussels, Luxembourg, Rotterdam.

- **Volare, t** 0800 032 0992; **www.volareweb.com**.
Cagliari, Rimini, Venice.

- **Wizz Air, t** 48 22 500 9499; **www.wizzair.com**.
Katowice, Budapest.

By car

You've found that dream home abroad, a romantic little cottage immersed in a landscape straight from an Impressionist painting – all for the price of a second-hand car. There must be a catch.

Unfortunately, there often is. One reason why some properties abroad go for a song is because they are so far from a good port and fast road that getting there can seem only slightly easier than finding ancient Rome with a London street map. Access from the property to good roads is even more of an issue if you are retired.

By ferry

Almost two million Britons took a ferry to the Continent in 2003. This may partly be because the low-cost airlines do not look so attractive after a delay or cancellation or when the bargain fares evaporate just at the time you want to go. Ferries are often the cheapest and most convenient option once you've compared the cost of taking a ferry with the price of the air fares coupled with extras like airport parking and use of a hire car. To get an idea of driving times and distances from port to destination, check out one of the route-planning websites, such as **www.theaa.com**, **www.rac.co.uk**, **www.mappy.com** or **www. viamichelin.com**.

Prices can vary surprisingly throughout the year so investigate them carefully. For example, the return price for two adults, two children and a car from Dover to Calais was £38 in May 2004 and £394 in August with Hoverspeed, and £40.18 in May and £315.92 in August with P&O. Increased competition should reduce the high prices at peak times. For example, launching in May 2004, SpeedFerries plans to drastically undercut established operators like P&O, SeaFrance, Hoverspeed and Eurotunnel, starting with an £80 return crossing in August for a car, two adults and two children, compared with prices ranging from £293 to £394 with the other companies.

Midweek crossings and those at unsocial hours are usually cheapest. Some ferry companies offer attractive incentives such as early-booking offers and frequent user programmes. Check out sailing times and the facilities on board too – increasingly important the longer the trip. The larger vessels offer such facilities as cinemas, swimming pools, children's clubs, discos, gyms and casinos.

Note that although the Dover–Calais route is the shortest and quickest to the UK, and has good road links, it will not necessarily be the most convenient service if you are heading west of Paris. Norfolkline's Dover–Dunkirk service is good for Belgium, Holland and northern Germany. St-Malo and Dieppe are among the more attractive ports.

The website **www.ferrybooker.com** contains useful information and pricing from all of the ferry operators.

Ferry operators

Note: not all of these services operate throughout the year.

• **Brittany Ferries, t** 0870 366 5333; **www.brittanyferries.com**
Plymouth–Roscoff (France): 6hrs (day); 7hrs (night).
Plymouth–Santander (Spain): 18hrs.
Portsmouth–St-Malo (France): 9hrs (day); 10hrs 45mins (night).
Portsmouth–Cherbourg (France): 4hrs 30mins.
Portsmouth–Caen (France): 5hrs 4mins (day); 7hrs 15mins (night).
Poole–Cherbourg (France): 2hrs 15mins or 4hrs 15mins (day); 6hrs 15mins (night).
Cork (Ireland)–*Roscoff* (France): 11hrs.

• **Condor Ferries, t** 0845 345 2000; **www.condorferries.com**
Weymouth–St Malo (France): 4hrs 30mins.
Poole–St Malo (France): 4hrs 30mins.
Portsmouth–Cherbourg (France): 6hrs 30mins.

• **DFDS Seaways, t** 0870 533 3111; **www.dfdsseaways.co.uk**
Newcastle–Gothenburg (Sweden): 25hrs 30mins.
Newcastle–IJmuiden/Amsterdam (Netherlands): 15hrs.
Harwich–Esbjerg (Denmark): 17hrs.
Harwich–Cuxhaven (West Germany): 18hrs 15mins.

• **Fjord Line, t** 0191 296 1313; **www.fjordline.co.uk**
Newcastle–Bergen via Stavanger, Haugesund (Norway): 18–25hrs.

• **Hoverspeed, t** 0870 240 8282/0870 460 7171; **www.hoverspeed.com**
Dover–Calais (France): 1hr.
Newhaven–Dieppe (France): 2hrs.

• **Irish Ferries, t** 0870 517 1717; **www.irishferries.com**
Rosslare (Ireland)–*Roscoff* (France): 18hrs.
Rosslare (Ireland)–*Cherbourg* (France): 18hrs.

• **Norfolkline, t** 0870 870 1020; **www.norfolkline.com**
Dover–Dunkirk (France): 2hrs.

• **P&O Ferries, t** 0870 520 2020; **www.poferries.com**
Dover–Calais (France): 75–90mins.
Portsmouth–Le Havre (France): 5hrs 30mins (day); 7hrs 30mins (night).
Portsmouth–Caen (France): 3hrs 25mins.

Portsmouth–Cherbourg (France): 2hrs 45mins or 4hrs 45mins (day); 5hrs 30mins (night).
Portsmouth–Bilbao (Spain): 35hrs (outbound); 29hrs (return).
Hull–Rotterdam (Netherlands): 10hrs.
Hull–Zeebrugge (Netherlands): 12hrs 30mins.

• **SeaFrance, t** 0870 571 1711; **www.seafrance.com**
Dover–Calais (France): 70mins.

• **SpeedFerries, t** (01304) 203000; **www.speedferries.com**
Dover–Boulogne (France): 90mins.

• **Stena Line, t** 0870 400 6748; **www.stenaline.com**
Harwich–Hook of Holland (Netherlands): 3hrs 40mins (day); 6hrs 15mins (night).

• **Superfast Ferries, t** 0870 234 0870; **www.superfast.com**
Rosyth–Hook of Holland (Netherlands): 17hrs 30mins.

• **Transmanche Ferries, t** 0800 917 1201; **www.transmancheferries.com**
Newhaven–Dieppe (France): 4hrs.

By train

Journeys from the UK to all European destinations start at the Eurostar terminals at London Waterloo or Ashford International in Kent. The first main transport hubs for destinations further into Europe are Paris, Lille and Brussels, the latter being 2hrs 20mins from London. Overnight services go to such destinations as Nice, Avignon, Barcelona, Madrid, Florence, Rome and Venice.

The French Motorail sleeper service can whisk you and your car from Calais to Avignon, Biarritz, Bordeaux, Brive, Narbonne, Nice and Toulouse. Prices start at £185 per car and cabin. Further details are available from **Rail Europe**, 34 Tower View, King's Hill, West Malling, Kent ME19 4ED, UK, or the travel centre at 178 Piccadilly, London W1, UK, **t** (01732) 526 700/08702 415415; **www.raileurope.co.uk**.

The **Eurotunnel service** (**Eurotunnel, t** 0870 535 3535/0870 243 0892; **www.eurotunnel.com**) to Calais is fast and convenient, as long as it is working without hitches, though you pay extra for it. You enter from the M20 near Folkestone and emerge in France on the A16 after being cocooned in your vehicle in a metal tube for 35mins. There are up to four departures per hour at peak times. For retirees wishing to make regular trips back to the UK, Eurotunnel operates a Property Owners' Club where, for an annual fee of £35 and a one-off registration fee of £30, substantial savings are made when you book between five and 50 tickets.

Travel within your selected country

It is no good selecting a property abroad that is impossible to travel around. The roads or drivers may be much worse than you are used to and parking spaces in town almost nonexistent.

Before buying a property, investigate the state of local public transport: are trains non-existent and buses almost so? Is there an excellent service during the summer months but just a skeleton one at other times?

Driving abroad

Be fully prepared for driving abroad. If you have a foreign-registered car, your nationality plate or sticker must be displayed. You may need to produce an array of car-related documents, such as the car registration, insurance and MOT certificates at any time. Be prepared to comply with the regulations; you may by law need any or all of the following items:

- **an international driving licence or translation of your UK one**
- **beam deflectors to be fitted to your headlights**
- **a warning triangle (Spain specifies two)**
- **a first-aid kit**
- **a fire extinguisher**
- **adequate breakdown cover and insurance**

Make sure you have local currency for such things as tolls, petrol and possible fines. In some European countries, where you have an international driving certificate (a **green card**), you can in most cases extend your vehicle insurance, but the time limit is usually around three months and longer stays are likely to need local insurance. Legal protection insurance may also be strongly recommended in some countries.

Be aware that vehicle crime may be far higher in the country you are buying into, compared with the UK. The legal blood level limit varies greatly from country to country, and can be as low as nil, for instance in Turkey. Study local traffic rules before setting off, especially if you will be driving on the other side of the road from that to which you are accustomed. There can be some quirky rules: for example, some countries, such as Norway, require low-beam headlights to be on day or night when driving. A motoring organisation like the **AA** (**t** 0870 600 0371; **www.theaa.com**) or **RAC** (**t** 08705 722 722; **www.rac.co.uk**) will be able to advise of up-to-date regulations.

Country Profiles

Andorra

Why retire here?

More people could probably find the Lost City of Atlantis than place the tiny landlocked country of Andorra on a map. Along with Austria, France, Germany, Italy, Spain and Switzerland, Andorra is one of the key countries to focus on if you enjoy skiing. Sandwiched in the eastern Pyrenees between Toulouse in France to the north and Barcelona in Spain to the south, this mountainous country has seven excellent winter ski resorts, with drops of 3,000ft and runs of a couple of miles or more.

In spring and summer, when the snow and ice has melted, the resorts are transformed into beautiful mountain holiday destinations with hot summers, unrivalled air quality, wonderful walking country and unspoilt villages. Horse-riding, mountain-biking, fishing, hiking and hunting are popular, and there is an 18-hole golf course just across the border in Spain. There are beautiful streams, lakes, waterfalls, forests and meadows.

Andorra's popularity is further boosted by its being a tax haven. There are no income, capital gains, inheritance, sales or value-added taxes.

Downsides

Andorra's small size and exclusivity make it significantly more expensive to buy in compared with neighbouring France and Spain. It suffers from very bad traffic aggravated by seasonal and holiday visitors as well as air pollution in the valleys caused by the country's incinerators, and by lorries travelling to and from Spain and France.

Property types

Housing is not cheap, and many properties are on plots hewn from the side of a mountain. Apartments in the ski resorts are most popular with foreign buyers, and town houses and chalets are also widely available.

Where to retire

The most popular area for foreigners is the parish of La Massana (pop. 6,000) in the northeast of the country. Good locations include the outskirts of the town and the nearby villages of Anyos, Sispony, L'Aldosa, Pal, Erts, Xixerella and Arinsal. The smaller parish of Ordino, adjacent to La Massana, is also popular, but few properties are available and prices are high.

Currency and exchange rate

Euro (€); £1 = €1.50.

Property prices

Andorra's size, tax-haven status and strict controls on building ensure that property prices are among the highest in Europe. Apartments in one of the ski resorts would typically cost more than £100,000, and commonly £200,000. Chalets are typically £700,000 plus. In the La Massana area, the minimum asking price for a detached house is about £150,000 and some hover around the £1 million mark. Low-rise apartment buildings are common, especially in Arinsal. Small apartments here are available for less than £60,000.

Local mortgages

Andorran banks offer loans in euros, but better terms may be available in the UK. Local banks typically offer mortgages up to 25 years for 60–70 per cent of the purchase price.

Access to and from the UK

Andorra enjoys the excellent transport options available in neighbouring southwest France and northern Spain.

Legal restrictions

Foreigners may own only one property, with surrounding land not exceeding 1,000 square metres.

The buying process

When both parties agree on the purchase price, typically a non-refundable deposit of 10 per cent is paid to the vendor and official permission to buy is sought from the government. The purchase contract is signed in front of a notary, who duly issues the deeds to the property.

Costs of buying

On top of the 1 per cent (maximum) fee for the notary, a property transfer fee of up to 2 per cent of the purchase price is payable. Although a small fee is payable for applying for government approval of the sale, no stamp duty or land registry fees are charged.

Is property a good investment?

Andorra's political stability, steady property market and enduring demand for both summer and winter holiday rentals (on which there are no restrictions) make property generally a good, safe investment.

Living in Andorra

Around a quarter of the 70,000 population of this 486 square kilometre country are native Andorrans, with the remainder principally coming from France and Spain. The official language is Catalan, with French and Spanish also commonly spoken.

The granting of a residence permit (*residencia*) is subject to strict financial conditions concerning income and requires a financial deposit to be paid. Foreigners wishing to be full-time residents (technically, more than 90 consecutive days in any one year) fall into two categories: retirees and those wanting to work or start a business. Unless you're an EU national, it is almost impossible to get a work permit.

Foreigners are permitted to own a property and spend more than 90 days in the country without a residence permit provided they can prove that it is their second rather than their main home.

Residents enjoy both a low cost and a high standard of living, boosted by there being virtually no taxes. A nominal annual property tax is payable, however. Work permits are rare.

The crime rate is low and medical facilities are good, although private health insurance should be taken out.

Selling

As Andorra is a tax haven, no capital gains tax is payable on selling.

Inheritance tax

As Andorra is a tax haven, there is no inheritance tax.

Further information

- **Andorra: t** (00 376)
- **Andorra Delegation**, 63 Westover Road, London SW18 2RF, UK, **t** (020) 8874 4806.

Estate agents

- **Servissim** (Andorra), **t** 73 78 00; **www.servissim.ad**.
- **www.propertyandorra.com**: a good search resource.

Australia

Why retire here?

Currently around 10,000 Britons a year leave to live in Australia, and in 2001 around 1,000 Brits applied to buy property compared with about 700 the year before. That is unsurprising, considering Australia's high quality of life, relaxed outdoor lifestyle, fabulous climate, pristine environment and huge geographical diversity. Prices have been especially attractive to British buyers in recent years with sterling performing well against the weak Australian dollar.

A wide range of sports are popular and there are many national parks as well as natural wonders like 1,100ft Ayers Rock and the Great Barrier Reef.

Downsides

It can be very difficult to retire to Australia permanently if you do not have family resident there who can sponsor your application for a visa. Even so, it is possible.

If you want to keep in touch with family and friends in the UK, obviously the long distance makes visits difficult. And Christmas isn't quite the same in the blazing heat of summer.

Property types

There is a wide range of property available, as can be expected of a prosperous first-world country. Many buyers purchase a plot of land and have a home built on it. Many homes are spacious when compared with those in the far more densely populated UK.

Where to retire

Sydney is eternally popular with foreign buyers. The inner-city Sydney suburb of Paddington, 20mins from the centre, has charming convict-built period terraced homes. Modern loft-style apartments are located at Woolloomoolloo. Glebe, Randwick and Birchwood boast grand old mansions, and Potts Point contains splendid Art Deco apartments.

Australia's second city, Melbourne, is busy and vibrant but also has pleasant parks and Victorian architecture. The neighbourhood of Toorak has some of the country's most expensive real estate. Nearby, but far cheaper, is Melbourne's answer to London Docklands, Port Melbourne. St Kilda is ideal for the beach.

The modern city of Brisbane enjoys a subtropical climate and, with it being near the Great Barrier Reef, the beaches are great. The suburbs of Ascot, Hamilton and Clayfield, a short drive from the city, are popular with expatriates.

Adelaide is attractive, with its charming parks, residential and shopping areas. It has a good arts festival. Areas popular with foreign buyers include Dulwich, Hawthorn, Burnside and Belair.

Currency and exchange rate

Australian dollar (A$); £1 = A$2.60.

Property prices

Prices are significantly lower than in the UK. In most city suburbs, two-bedroom apartments and houses are available from under £40,000, with Sydney property, generally the most expensive in the country, costing at least four times as much, although central one-bed apartments are still available for less than £150,000. Three-bedroom suburban bungalows start at £60,000 or so. Terraced homes in Paddington, Sydney, are available for less than £300,000. Melbourne is also expensive, but not by London standards; properties in Toorak, however, top the £1 million mark.

Many newspapers carry property auction statistics, allowing potential buyers to track the property market in their locality.

Local mortgages

British banks do not offer mortgages for Australian property, but mortgages from local lenders are generally straightforward to arrange. There is a large choice available, up to 100 per cent.

Access to and from the UK

Mile for mile, air fares to Australia are comparatively cheap. There are numerous carriers offering a wide choice of special offers including tempting stopovers in places like Singapore to break the long journey.

Legal restrictions

Only foreign nationals in possession of a permanent visa are permitted to purchase residential property otherwise they can only buy new property off-plan. Foreign buyers living in Australia are required to sell the property if they leave. Although most property and land is freehold, in Canberra (the Australian Capital Territory) land is sold on a 99-year lease.

The buying process

If you are planning on permanent residence, it is advisable not to start looking at properties until you are in possession of a visa. Foreign nationals, unless they have permanent resident status, are required to seek approval from the Foreign Investment Review Board before buying a property.

Buying and selling is very different from the process in the UK. Most property is sold by auction. The property is typically open to the public for viewing the three weekends preceding the sale on the fourth weekend. The auction is usually held in the property itself, unlike in the UK where a succession of properties are sold at a neutral venue. The auction system can be nerve-racking as the buyer can so easily lose out and the seller may not raise the price wanted. At least it is straightforward and quick, and eliminates gazumping, although there have been problems with dummy bidders driving prices up. State governments intend to stop this by introducing a purchaser registration system.

Costs of buying

These average around 5 per cent of the purchase price and includes legal fees, stamp duty, which varies from region to region, and a small land transfer registration fee.

Is property a good investment?

Australia's property market is quite stable. Waterside property, especially, is likely to appreciate well because such homes are generally in short supply.

Living in Australia

The climate is tropical in the north and temperate in the south; summer is from December to February and winter from June to August.

Australia is sparsely populated, politically very stable, the people very hospitable, transport good and cheap and the crime rate relatively low.

The cost of living is rather lower than that of northern Europe, although some items are considerably more or less costly when compared with the UK. For example, a good restaurant meal would only be around £5 to £10, yet cars cost as much as double the amount as in North America.

Bear in mind that UK state pensions are not indexed in line with prices if you go to live in Australia (see pp.22–3), and therefore income can drop substantially over some years.

Medical facilities are very good, although there are no reciprocal agreements with the UK. Residents contribute 1.5 per cent of taxable income to the national health scheme, Medicare, which covers most medical costs. Non-residents and the retired may not be covered and will require private medical insurance.

Property taxes can vary greatly from region to region. Income tax is payable by those remaining in the country for more than six months a year and ranges from 17 per cent on incomes of £2,300 to a maximum of 47 per cent on incomes above £23,000. Australian residents are taxed on their worldwide income.

There are various ways to emigrate to Australia including around 80 types of entry visa with strict guidelines. For example, you can marry or live with an existing Australian citizen. You would be required to prove that your relationship is genuine and has lasted for a minimum of a year, demonstrating this through such things as a joint bank account and other examples of shared commitments. Australia also runs a **Retirement Visa Program**, which enables those aged over 55 who can support themselves financially to emigrate to Australia. Initially the visa lasts four years, with visas for further stays normally granted for two years at a time. The visa allows holders to work part-time.

If you are over 55, have no dependent children and sufficient assets and/or income, you can also obtain residency if you can show that you have A$870,000 (around £350,000). The amount is reduced to A$800,000 if you have a non-dependent child in the country; or you may have A$350,000 plus a pension or other annual income totalling at least A$50,000 annually, or A$315,000 and A$50,000 annually if you have a non-dependent child in the country.

Selling

Capital gains tax is not applicable on a taxpayer's main residence. It is paid at 33 per cent on gains on properties by non-residents.

Inheritance tax

None is payable.

Further information

- **Australia: t** (00 61)

- **Australian Consulate**, 19th floor, Century Plaza Towers, 2049 Century Park East, Los Angeles, CA 90067-3238, USA, **t** (310) 229 4800.

- **Australian Embassy**, 1601 Massachusetts Avenue, NW, Washington, DC 20036, USA, **t** (202) 797 3000; **www.ausemb.org**.

- **Australian High Commission**, Australia House, Strand, London WC2B 4LA, UK, **t** (020) 7836 7123; **www.australia.org.uk**.

- **Australian Tourist Commission**, Gemini House, 10–18 Putney Hill, London SW15 6AA, UK, **t** (020) 8780 2227; **www.australia.com**.

- **Australians Abroad; www.australiansabroad.com**: relocation information.

- **Commonwealth Bank of Australia** (UK), **t** (020) 7710 3990; **www.migrantbanking.co.uk**: caters to the needs of migrants from the UK and the rest of Europe.

- **Council on the Aging; www.cota.org.au**: information on retirement homes in Australia.
- **Foreign Investor Review Board**, Treasury Department, Parkes Place, Parkes, ACT 2600, Australia, **t** 02 6263 3795; **www.firb.gov.au**: information on property purchase by non-residents.
- **Southern Cross Group, www.southern-cross-group.org**: general expatriate advice.
- **www.fed.gov.au** and **www.immigov.au**: government websites with details about immigration
- **www.customs.gov.au**: explains Australian customs
- **www.emigrate-to-australia.co.uk** and **www.where2retire.com.au**: information on emigration to Australia.
- *Getting a Job in Australia*, Nick Vandome (HowToBooks, £10.99)

Emigration advisers

- **Amber Collins** (UK), **t** (020) 7371 0213; **www.ambercollins.com**.
- **Concept Australia** (UK), **t** (020) 8467 8521; **www.conceptaustralia.co.uk**.
- **Emigration Group** (UK), **t** (01244) 321414; **www.emigration.uk.com**.
- **Four Corners** (UK), **t** 0845 841 9453; **www.4-corners.com**.
- **Global Visas** (UK), **t** (020) 7009 3800; **www.globalvisas.com**.
- **Migration Bureau** (UK), **t** (020) 8874 2844.
- **Migration Expert; www.migrationexpert.com**.
- **Overseas Emigration Visas; www.overseas-emigration.co.uk**.

Estate agents

These estate agents are all in Australia.

- **Century 21 Australia, t** 28 295 0601; **www.century21.com.au**.
- **First National, t** 29 240 6165; **www.firstnational.com.au**.
- **L.J. Hooker, t** 29 283 5511; **www.ljhooker.com.au**.
- **Laing and Simmons Real Estate, t** 29 223 4888; **www.laingsimmons.com.au**.
- **McGrath, t** 29 568 0811; **www.mcgrath.com.au**.
- **Raine and Horne, t** 29 258 5400; **www.raineandhorne.com**.
- **Ray White, t** 29 262 3700; **www.raywhite.com.au**.
- **www.realestate.com.au**: a good search tool.

Austria

Why retire here?

Austria is not an obvious choice for foreign buyers, yet has lots to offer. Set at the heart of Europe, it is central to much else, containing such gorgeous cities as Salzburg and Vienna, with others like Prague, Venice and Budapest nearby. It is rich in culture and past distinguished citizens include Mozart and Strauss.

Although it is landlocked, more than half of the country is situated within the eastern Alps, offering stunning mountains and beautiful valleys. Much is forested. The winter sports season is generally from December to early April, although the higher ski resorts are active until May. Other distractions include skating, sailing, tobogganing, horse-riding, cycling, scuba-diving, hang-gliding, thermal baths, cable-cars, mountain railways and horse-drawn sleigh rides.

Downsides

As it is landlocked and has a milder climate than the Mediterranean countries, Austria isn't for beach-lovers or sun-worshippers; and, if you are not strong on languages, the national language, German, may be a problem.

Property types

A wide mix from studio apartments to large detached chalets.

Where to retire

The ski resorts are the most popular for foreign buyers, and are excellent in summer for outdoor pursuits like hiking. It is best to avoid the resorts frequented by package tours, which though lovely for a holiday, are geared to mass tourism. The resorts further afield represent the true Austria and are far better for residency. The swankiest areas, such as Kitzbühel in Tirol, should only be considered if you have a budget of over £600,000 but prices reduce around such towns as Zillertal, Zoll, Scheffau, Kufstein and Worgl. Salzburg is a popular destination, and elegant Vienna is ever-popular, too.

Currency and exchange rate

Euro (€); £1 = €1.50.

Property prices

Compared with France and Spain, where property prices have risen substantially in recent years, property has fallen relatively in price over the past few years, stabilising in 2004.

The capital, Vienna, unsurprisingly has the highest prices, with asking prices in excess of £80,000 for a one-bedroom apartment common. A large detached chalet would start in the region of £600,000. On the outskirts of the city, three-bedroom houses are available for around £150,000.

Local mortgages

Local banks offer mortgages to foreign buyers and rates are generally lower than UK mortgages. They can generally be fixed up in a few days. Typically, local lenders require a 40 per cent deposit and lend over 10 or 15 years.

Access to and from the UK

Various airlines, including Austrian Airlines, British Airways and Air Berlin, fly to Vienna, while Ryanair, BMIbaby and Flybe have daily flights to Salzburg. In addition, there are many flight options in neighbouring countries, and motorway access through Germany is straightforward and efficient.

Legal restrictions

Each province (*Bundesland*) imposes restrictions on ownership (whether by an Austrian or foreigner) of property, and in some regions, such as the Tirol, it is almost banned completely for holiday use (*Zweitwohnsitz*). Buyers are required to have their purchases approved by the appropriate *Grundverkehrsbehörde* – part of the local authority.

The buying process

Conveyancing is usually administered by the same lawyer for buyer and seller. A deposit, usually of 10 per cent, is usually but not always payable and then a purchase agreement is drawn up and signed by both parties. As this is in German, a translation may be required.

Neither purchaser nor vendor can back out, which prevents gazumping and means the finance must be in place before making an offer. The lawyer draws up the sale contract on behalf of both parties. Registering the title typically takes between three and six months. The lawyer acting for the sale then pays all the necessary taxes and fees and the balance owing to the vendor.

Costs of buying

Conveyancing fees average around 3 per cent of the purchase price, and there is an additional property transfer tax of 3.5 per cent, and stamp duty, land registry and title registration costs of around 2 per cent. Estate agents' fees are controlled by law and typically cost both buyer and seller 3 per cent. VAT at 20 per cent is payable on fees.

Is property a good investment?

The property market is stable and because of the scarcity of properties available prices are unlikely to go lower. Property in the ski resorts is attractive to renters all year round and there are no restrictions on holiday letting.

Living in Austria

Austria has a mild, pleasant climate, although this can vary greatly around the country. It is a very clean country, from the hotels, restaurants, trains and roads to the fresh, clean water of the rivers and lakes. Almost the entire population of eight million speaks German, although many Austrians speak some English, especially in the resort areas and cities. Austria is politically stable, with a low crime rate, excellent public transport and very good medical care. The cost of living in Austria is similar to the UK.

Income tax ranges from 15 to 50 per cent and there is an annual property tax of 0.8 per cent on the assessed value of a property. EU nationals as well as non-EU ones are required to register for a residence permit, although this is essentially a formality. Austria has an excellent national health service available to anyone paying social security in the country, although private health insurance is recommended for foreigners.

Selling

Capital gains tax is set at 50 per cent on the profit of a sale, and main residences are not liable for the tax after 10 years of ownership.

Inheritance tax

There is an inheritance tax ranging from 15 to 50 per cent.

Further information

- **Austria: t** (00 43)
- **Austrian Embassy**, 18 Belgrave Mews West, London SW1X 8HU, UK, **t** (020) 7235 3731.
- **Austrian Embassy**, 3524 International Court, NW, Washington, DC 20008, USA, **t** (202) 895 6700; **www.austria-emb.org**.
- **Austrian Tourist Office**, PO Box 2363, London W1A 2QB, UK, **t** (020) 7629 0461; **www.austria.info/www.austria-tourism.at**.

Estate agents

- **Euroburo** (Austria), **t** 6137 20099; **www.euroburolimited.co.uk**.
- **www.homesbyweb.co.uk**: Features Austrian properties.

Bulgaria

Why retire here?

This largely rural country is approximately the size of England yet has a population of only around 8 million. Its lack of development and rural tranquillity provide a glimpse of life which has long since disappeared in most of Europe. Bulgaria has the mass market appeal that Spain had many years ago. It is relatively near to the UK, has a great climate (clear blue skies and temperatures of 30–35°C in the summer) and fabulous coast, a low cost of living and very low property prices. It also has a wealth of historic towns, unspoilt villages, castles, churches and monasteries, and unchanged traditions.

There is increasing interest from foreign buyers in investing in the areas popular for skiing and other winter sports as well.

Bulgaria is set to join the EU by 2007, and this would undoubtedly do much to secure the property market and increase property values. Until then, the European Union is been investing millions of pounds in upgrading the country's roads, airports and other infrastructure.

Downsides

Most buyers are focusing on the coast, but as this is not a long stretch, it is likely to become increasingly like that of Spain, with overdevelopment and high prices. Also, the Slavonic language takes a considerable effort to get to grips with. Although Bulgaria has very much left behind its Communist past, some grim buildings, including some towering grey hotels in popular resort areas, still remain. It has some problems with crime and corruption, although the present government is relatively stable.

In recent years the country has undergone numerous economic problems, including the devaluation of its currency and a struggling economy. Although many Bulgarians welcome foreign buyers, whom they see as regenerating neglected rural areas, others resent them. While £10,000 houses are very cheap by UK standards, they are not to Bulgarians, who earn an average of around £1,000 per year.

Until the low-cost airlines launch rumoured routes to Bulgaria, getting there is expensive.

Restrictions on foreigners buying property with land, which includes anything with a garden, remain. Setting up a company, which can be arranged by agents, solves this, but is an added complication.

Property types

These vary from apartments and villas in new-build developments to larger, older, run-down rural properties.

Where to retire

Although on the eastern part of the Balkan peninsula, Bulgaria has the feel of the Mediterranean. Bulgaria's Black Sea riviera is especially popular, at Sunny Beach, Golden Sands and Bourgas, and the resort city of Varna. But there are some stretches scarred by unsympathetic development. Inland, there are beautiful Dordogne- or Tuscany-like hilltop towns, such medieval Veliko Turnovo. Shabla and Durankulak are tranquil rural communities north of Varna.

Bulgaria has several magnificent mountain ranges: the Rila, Balkan, Sredna Gora and Prini. The ski areas in the Rhodope Mountains in the south of the country are increasingly popular, and in summer these mountainous areas are ideal for trekking, climbing and discovering the many traditional villages, monasteries, national parks and rich wildlife.

There are attractive properties along the Danube, on Bulgaria's northern border with Romania, and the Danube towns have much to offer, not least historic Ruse, with its splendid architecture.

Culture vultures will appreciate the numerous museums and galleries of Sofia, Plovdiv and Veliko Turnovo.

Currency and exchange rate

Lev; £1 = 2.95 LEV.

Property prices

Although Bulgarian property is among the cheapest in Europe, like most Eastern European destinations it is beginning to see an upsurge in foreign investors in some areas and in 2003 prices rose by around 20 per cent, with signs of rises of around 25 per cent in 2004. Bargains still exist, but the last year or two have seen phenomenal interest from bargain-hunters, and really cheap property is becoming rarer and rarer. A new apartment on the coast would cost around £35,000, although Black Sea villas are still available for half that cost or £50,000 new. Three- or four-bedroom rural houses in need of renovation are still widely available for less than £20,000, sometimes under £5,000.

Local mortgages

The local lending market is undeveloped and using a UK lender is preferable.

Access to and from the UK

Direct international flights are available to the capital, Sofia, all year round, while direct charter flights to the Black Sea at airports at Varna and Burgas are available during the spring and summer months. A number of budget airlines are planning routes in response to the increasing tourism in this country.

Legal restrictions

You need to set up a local private limited company to buy property with land (for example, a garden), and this can usually be arranged by the estate agent or property consultant. The process costs around £600 and is likely to be abolished as EU membership draws near.

The company you set up will be subject to tax in Bulgaria but also corporation tax has to be paid in the UK on any company profits (i.e. when you sell, or from rental income). Currently UK corporation tax is 23.75 per cent on profits of between £10,000 and £50,000. However, tax paid on the property overseas can usually be offset against your British tax bill.

The buying process

After reserving the property with the agent, the first thing to do is to determine whether the sale is with land. If it is, a company needs to be incorporated to hold the land. If not, no company is required. There are also strict zoning restrictions that need to be adhered to.

When a sale is agreed, a notary draws up a purchase contract, which is similar to 'sold subject to contract' in the UK and which is in the form of a notary deed. The notary will require various documents certifying such things as the ability of the buyer to pay for the property, the ownership rights of the vendor, and the vendor's declaration that all fiscal obligations to the state have been paid. Details about the status of buyer and seller and proof that the property is unencumbered are also required.

The buyer's lawyer should make the necessary checks on the property. These include examination of title documents, licences and permissions, any debts on title, and the terms of the contract. When everything is seen to be in order, the vendor and purchaser sign the contract of purchase in front of a notary.

The notary registers the notary deed in the local court's land registry.

Costs of buying

Both purchaser and vendor pay commission to the estate agent, with charges typically ranging from 3 to 6 per cent. Stamp duty is a further 2 per cent of the price. Agents typically charge several per cent extra for such costs as legal and translation costs and the cost of setting up a company to buy the property (around £600).

The buyer is usually responsible for paying the notary tax for the deeds and land tax of 2 per cent.

Is property a good investment?

Upcoming EU membership, house prices the cost of a good kitchen back home and a healthy rise in tourism make Bulgaria a good bet for the future. However, the risks are considerable, as in other emerging eastern European states, with legal and financial issues, the property market and the physical infrastructure all not as solidly in place as many other countries in Europe.

Living in Bulgaria

The cost of living is very low, with a typical three-course meal with wine costing just £3 or so, a beer 50p, and a coffee 20p.

UK passport-holders do not require a visa in order to visit Bulgaria for a period of up to 30 days. Long-term visas are obtainable from the Bulgarian embassy in London. Visa control has been considerably relaxed between the UK and Bulgaria.

The health system has changed from tax-orientated to insurance-based, and so private health insurance is essential for foreigners at present.

Selling

Non-resident investors pay 15 per cent tax on rentals and capital gains.

Inheritance tax

This varies depending on individual circumstances.

Further information

- **Bulgaria: t** (00 359)
- **Bulgarian Embassy,** 186–188 Queen's Gate, London SW7 5HL, UK, **t** (020) 7584 9400; **www.bulgarianembassy.org.uk.**
- **www.sofiaecho.com, www.bulgariaski.com** and **www.travel-bulgaria.com**: have information about Bulgaria.

Estate agents

- **Avatar International** (UK), **t** 08707 282827; **www.avatar-international.com.**
- **Balkan Ski Chalets** (Bulgaria), **t** 889 633 086; **www.balkanskichalet.com.**
- **Barrasford and Bird** (UK), **t** (01566) 782642; **www.barrasfordandbird.co.uk.**
- **Bulgarian Dreams** (UK), **t** 0800 684 8502; **www.bulgariandreams.com.**
- **Stara Planina,** (Bulgaria) **t** 887 203364; **www.staraplanina.com.** As well as a source for properties, at a cost of around 10 per cent more than the cost of the property, Stara Planina can organise the necessary legal work, accounting, translating and logistics.

Canada

Why retire here?

Although Canada has a reputation for extreme cold weather, in many regions the climate is terrific. The north has Arctic conditions, with temperatures below freezing for much of the year, but Ottawa has a severe winter for four months of the year but also has excellent long, hot summers. Vancouver has warm summers and mild winters.

Foreign property-buyers attracted to Canada are largely lovers of 'the great outdoors'. Canada, a country the size of Europe, is sparsely populated and has vast areas of natural beauty, good infrastructure and a comparatively wealthy society – with the attendant lack of social problems.

The very varied topography includes forests, mountains, polar desert and more lakes and inland waters than any other country, including four of the world's largest. Its mountains provide excellent skiing conditions and its cities are cosmopolitan.

Downsides

Not only is the cost of living significantly higher than in the USA, but becoming a resident can present considerable difficulties. If you need easy access to the UK, to visit family and friends, for example, the lengthy flight time from Canada can deter visits. Much of Canada experiences harsh weather, which can be a significant factor for retirees, especially in more remote areas.

Property types

A great variety, from apartments to large detached buildings, old and new.

Where to retire

Properties in cities such as Toronto and Ottawa are popular with foreign buyers, as are lakeside, forest and ski resort properties. British buyers are increasingly being lured by new developments in the Rockies and other areas. Calgary is the country's sunniest spot, with an average of more than 320 days of sun annually.

Montréal, in Québec Province, has a distinctly French flavour, and the attractive old town in the centre of the city has a more multicultural mix than other neighbourhoods.

Vancouver in British Columbia is popular with retirees, offering wonderful scenery, tranquillity and a temperate climate. Popular spots include the Okanagan Valley and its towns such as Kamlopps and Kelowana. There is plenty of opportunity for gentler outdoor activities like golf and sailing.

Currency and exchange rate

Canadian dollar (C$); £1 = C$2.50.

Property prices

These vary greatly in such a large country and are generally substantially lower than in the UK. In 2003 the average cost of a home in Canada was C$207,699 (£83,000) according to the Canada Real Estate Association. According to Royal LePage Real Estate Services, low interest rates and a confident market caused prices to rise in most areas of the property market in the first three months of 2004 and the average price of a detached bungalow was C$241,190 (£98,847) while a standard condominium stood at C$172,072 (£70,520).

Small city flats typically cost from about £45,000 and a detached three- or four-bed city home would typically be in excess of £80,000. Building plots and simple accommodation in remote areas cost a small fraction of that.

Prices have recently been rising fastest in Winnipeg, Montréal, Victoria, Vancouver and in St John's, Newfoundland. A large three-bedroom flat in the centre of Vancouver would cost about £70,000 while out of town luxury six-bedroom homes are available for less than £200,000.

Local mortgages

Mortgages up to 75 per cent (but normally 65 per cent or so for foreign buyers) of the property value are available, but strict lending criteria are applied with proof of income and expenditure required. Interest rates are historically low and often there is the option of long-term fixed rates.

Access to and from the UK

There are plenty of daily flights from the UK to Canada. British Airways, for example, has a daily flight to Vancouver alone, from £350 return. Cut-price carrier Zoom has begun flights for less than £300 return from Stansted, Gatwick and Glasgow to Vancouver.

Legal restrictions

There are generally no restrictions concerning foreign ownership, although there are some exceptions, such as Banff, where only those who live or work in Banff may buy.

The buying process

This is speedy and efficient when compared with the UK. Each province has its own conveyancing laws and the process is in English except in the province of

Québec, where it is conducted in French. Once your offer to buy is accepted, you cannot be gazumped (beaten by a higher offer from another buyer). The searches can be completed within a week, whereas in the UK this can take several weeks.

Sellers usually provide a property condition disclosure statement, which provides basic information about the property. Purchasers usually impose conditions when making an offer, for example, that the property has an accept-able survey report. The buyer, along with their solicitor, often visits the municipal hall before buying to ensure that such things as the lot size, maximum building size and occupancy permit are in order.

If you pay cash, the whole deal can be completed within a couple of weeks. It is a good idea to use a buyer's broker who acts on your behalf.

Costs of buying

This typically represents about 3 per cent of the purchase price made up of land transfer tax (0.5 to 2 per cent), conveyancing costs (1 per cent), survey costs, title registration and a compliance certificate. In some provinces, newly built homes attract a 15 per cent harmonised sales tax.

Realtors (estate agents) typically charge 6 per cent on the first £45,000 of the purchase price and 3 per cent thereafter.

Is property a good investment?

The property market is generally stable and there are no restrictions on holiday letting. New tax residents can use an immigrant trust to shelter non-Canadian source income and capital gains for a maximum of 5 years. After 5 years, this can be transferred from the trust without attracting tax.

Living in Canada

Canada is particularly multiracial with three-quarters of the population of British or French origin and the remainder German, Dutch, Hong Kong, Ukrainian and other nationalities. English and French are the official languages.

Politically stable, the country enjoys a very high standard of living coupled with a cost of living lower than that of much of western Europe. Several times in recent years the United Nations has voted Canada as having the best stand-ard of living in the world. This doesn't mean it's wildly exciting, though. Currently around 4,000 to 5,000 Britons move from the UK to Canada annually.

Both federal and provincial income taxes are payable by residents, as well as annual property taxes, all of which vary greatly from region to region. It is important to pay your council tax on time: in Montréal, for example, those failing to pay have their name and address published in the newspaper, their home is seized and auctioned off to the highest bidder.

The crime rate is low and medical facilities very good and free to those covered by the national health scheme. Those not covered should have private health insurance in place.

Full-time residence is difficult to obtain. Close family ties are generally required for those wanting a residence permit. Skills as a linguist, age, level of education and ability to adapt to a new country are all taken into account. Retirees are required to show such documents as bank statements, pension records and social security details to prove they have sufficient income to support themselves.

Note that UK state pensions are frozen if you become a resident in Canada (*see* pp.22–3), which will have a significant long-term effect on your income.

An application to emigrate currently involves the following approximate charges: application fee to the Canadian government (£245), right of permanent residence fee (£435), birth certificate reissue (£25), medical fees (£150), language exams (£165), legal fees (£500).

Selling

Capital gains tax is payable on the purchase or sale of assets other than a main residence.

Inheritance tax

None.

Further information

- **Canada: t** (00 1)
- **Canadian High Commission**, 1 Grosvenor Street, London W1X 0AB, UK, **t** (020) 7258 6600; **www.canada.org.uk**.
- **Canadian High Commission**, 501 Pennsylvania Avenue, NW, Washington DC 20001, USA, **t** (202) 682 1740; **www.cdnemb-washsc.org**.
- **Canadian Real Estate Association**, 334 Slater Street, Suite 1600, Canada Building, Ottawa, ON K1R 743, Canada, **t** (613) 237 7111.
- **Canada Online; www.canadaonline.about.com**.
- **Canadian Tourist Commission; www.travelcanada.ca**.
- **Canadian Government**; **www.canada.gc.ca**.
- **Canadian Association of Retired Persons; www.50plus.com**: information concerning retirement homes and developments in Canada.

For details about different regions, log on to **www.halifaxinfo.com** for Greater Halifax, **www.tourism-vancouver.org** and **www.islands.bc.ca** for Greater Vancouver, and **www.gov.nb.ca** for New Brunswick.

Emigration advisers

- **Amber Collins** (UK), **t** (020) 7371 0213; **www.ambercollins.com**.
- **Emigration Group** (UK), **t** (01244) 321414; **www.emigration.uk.com**.
- **Four Corners** (UK), **t** 0845 841 9453; **www.4-corners.com**.
- **Global Visas** (UK), **t** (020) 7009 3800; **www.globalvisas.com**.
- **Migration Bureau** (UK), **t** (020) 8874 2844.
- **Migration Expert; www.migrationexpert.com**.
- **Overseas Emigration Visas; www.overseas-emigration.co.uk**.
- **Workpermit.com** (UK), **t** (020) 7842 0800; **www.workpermit.com**.

Estate agents

- **Chesterton International** (UK), **t** (020) 7201 2070; **www.chesterton.co.uk**.
- **Premier Resorts** (UK), **t** (020) 8940 9406; **www.premierresorts.co.uk**.
- **Canadian Real Estate Association; www.mls.ca**.
- **International Real Estate Digest; www.ired.com/int/canada/**: features lists of estate agents around the country.

The Caribbean

Why retire here?

Britons are increasingly waking up to the benefits of buying a dream retirement home in the Caribbean rather than the sunnier climes of Europe. Plunging air fares and sunshine 365 days a year, which peaks during the depth of the UK winter, in what is often thought the world's premier tropical paradise, with glorious powder-white sands and turquoise seas are all behind the property boom. The official language on many of the islands is English. The political stability on many islands is good.

The Caribbean consists of thousands of islands, with two main chains of islands, the Greater and the Lesser Antilles, and extends nearly 4,000km (2,500 miles) from the Bahamas, off the coast of Florida, to Trinidad, off the coast of Venezuela. The islands are characterised by white sandy beaches, warm, clear blue seas, rainforests and mountains.

Downsides

Strong sea breezes and the tropical weather can result in high maintenance and gardening bills. Some islands have been badly hit by hurricanes.

The most popular islands are increasingly becoming the victims of their own success. Barbados, for example, is becoming increasingly crowded, while traffic jams are becoming more and more of a regular occurrence on the pricey Cayman Islands.

Property types

These vary from ocean-front villas and apartments to townhouses and rural farms. There are a wide range of luxury homes on many islands. Newer detached homes usually have a swimming pool, and developments often have extra facilities such as a management service, tennis courts, swimming pools and other sports facilities, as well as restaurants and shops.

Where to retire

Developments are now being constructed on many of the islands. The most popular islands with the British are the ones people can get to easily, like Trinidad and Tobago (pop. 1.3 million), Antigua and Barbuda (pop. 80,000), Barbados (pop. 260,000), St Lucia (pop. 150,000) and the Bahamas (pop. 290,000). But these are also the most expensive. Barbados (pop. 250,000), for example, is often reckoned number one in sophistication and investment potential, but this image is reflected in its prices.

The **Turks and Caicos Islands** (pop. 10,000), however, very much remain a tropical paradise. Consisting of a small archipelago of eight major islands and 40 small cays southeast of Florida, they boast plenty of deserted beaches and unspoilt areas. A 90-minute flight from Florida, they enjoy the lowest crime rate by far in the Caribbean and are a wonderful destination for sailing and diving among the coral reefs. They've become a popular haunt for celebrities: Cindy Crawford, Richard Gere, Bruce Willis, Donatella Versace, Paul McCartney, John Galliano, Brad Pitt and Demi Moore have all visited in recent years.

The third-largest Caribbean island, **Jamaica** (pop. 2.5 million), was ranked the ninth most popular retirement destination by the Prudential in a 2004 survey. Although it is indeed often considered the most beautiful Caribbean island because of its beautiful beaches and 7,000ft Blue Mountains, this ranking may seem surprising, as it is known for its economic instability and crime problems – Kingston has a high crime rate, and grilles and bars on windows are a common sight. Indeed, the Foreign and Commonwealth Office advises that residents should employ a security guard. The most sought-after areas of the island are the northern coastal resorts of Ocho Ríos and Montego Bay, as well as Negril in the west.

Antigua has 365 beaches, and is especially popular with the yachting fraternity. **St Barthélémy** in the French West Indies is seldom considered by British buyers despite being the Caribbean's answer to St-Tropez.

An upsurge in holidaying Brits has led to increased interest in the **Dominican Republic**, a 49,000 square kilometre island with a population of 75,000, making up the eastern two-thirds of Hispaniola (the remainder being Haiti) and one of the prettier of the Greater Antilles. Not only does the island possess the highest peak in the Caribbean at 3,175 metres, but also fertile valleys, desert, and palm-tree-fringed beaches. Resorts started appearing from the 1970s and one of the newest – and largest in the Caribbean – is the luxurious Cap Cana, which features 8km of beach. When completed, it will feature around 5,000 homes, including beachside and golfside apartments, three golf courses, and a marina large enough to take 500 boats.

Other islands that are particularly popular with foreign buyers include **Puerto Rico** (pop. 4 million) and **Guadeloupe** (pop. 350,000). Guadeloupe and Martinique are French and therefore EU regulations will apply.

Currency and exchange rate

There are numerous currencies, but US dollars ($) are widely accepted and are the official currency on some islands.

Property prices

The Caribbean is largely not for the budget property-buyer: whether you want an old colonial-style home with verandas or a new villa, you are likely to pay in excess of £500,000 for starters, and many homes cost several million pounds.

Prices are relatively high in the islands as a whole, especially near the beach. Apartments generally start at around £200,000 and detached homes cost £280,000 plus. Properties at the livelier, more well-known islands generally cost the most, with properties at the quieter, less well-known ones costing less.

Two-bedroom villas in the Turks and Caicos Islands typically start at around £200,000 and one-bed apartments from £150,000 in the Grace Bay beach area, resort capital Providenciales' best beach and home to the majority of hotels and apartments. A four-bed, four-bath villa in one of the most select neigh-bourhoods boasting an ocean frontage would cost at least £700,000. If your budget doesn't stretch quite that far, cheaper houses on the islands start at around £90,000 in Blue Hills, one of Providenciales' original settlements.

On Barbados, the most popular properties with overseas buyers are £400,000–550,000 detached houses in secure developments, although colonial-style mansions are still available on the island for less than £150,000.

Property is clearly not cheap when compared with, say, France or Greece, but there are properties at cheaper developments being built all the time on many of the more popular islands. And prices have reduced significantly recently, generally by as much as 35 per cent lower in 2004 than in 2001.

Local mortgages

Local mortgages typically run for 15 to 20 years and are available for up to 80 per cent of the property, but usually for 50 or 60 per cent.

Access to and from the UK

Access is getting easier as flights to the islands increase. There are plenty of direct flights from the UK to the Caribbean, with daily ones to all Caribbean countries popular with the British. The cost ranges from around just £260–500, and flights take around 7–10hrs from the UK. Return flights are cheapest in the winter. Many visitors fly via Miami (under 2hrs' flight time), New York or Toronto.

Legal restrictions

Some islands restrict or forbid the export of local currency and some require foreign currency to be declared on entry and exit. In Barbados, foreign buyers are required to import all funds for the property purchase and register the funds with the Central Bank of Barbados. Almost always this is simply a formality, but permission to purchase must be obtained from the Bank.

There are numerous other restrictions: for example, on Antigua foreigners need an alien landholder's licence to buy a property. This costs 5 per cent of the property's value and can take six months to obtain.

The buying process

The buying process varies from island to island, as each island retains autonomy and has its own conveyancing system. Although usually things run smoothly, it is important to employ the services of an experienced local solicitor. The conveyancing process in the Caribbean can be slow.

Buying new property involves paying in stages: 10 per cent deposit, 10 per cent when the foundations are laid and so on.

The Turks and Caicos, for example, are a British dependent territory and therefore have an accountable legal and political system. There are no restrictions on foreigners buying property and no income or capital gains taxes to pay. The only taxes are stamp duty on your property at 9.75 per cent, a $15 (around £10) departure tax at the airport and on importing certain goods.

In the British Virgin Islands (pop. 15,000) , however, purchasers from overseas are required to obtain a non-belongers' land-holding licence from the government of the islands, supported by documents indicating your solvency and absence of a criminal record. A deposit of 10 per cent is commonly paid, purchaser and vendor sign a sale agreement drawn up by the vendor's solicitor and final payments are made when the land-holding licence is obtained.

Costs of buying

Conveyancing fees are generally around 3 per cent of the purchase price. In addition, many Caribbean countries levy transfer tax of 5–10 per cent and/or stamp duty at from 1 to 9.75 per cent. Estate agents fees also typically vary between 5 and 6 per cent.

In the British Virgin Islands, conveyancing fees average 2–3 per cent of the purchase price of the property, and stamp duty is 8 per cent. In Barbados, conveyancing fees average 2 per cent but property transfer tax of 10 per cent was removed in 2002.

Is property a good investment?

Numerous islands, notably the Bahamas (pop. 290,000), the Turks and Caicos Islands and the British Overseas territory the Cayman Islands (pop. 40,000), are an attractive investment proposition and have a strong rental market, being international tax havens, with no income, property, capital gains or inheritance taxes. The smaller islands retain a more exclusive cachet, but bear in mind that they are more likely to suffer from political instability.

Living in the Caribbean

The Caribbean has a large cultural mix including British, American, French, Dutch, Spanish and Afro-Caribbean cultures, and have many sports, art festivals, fishing and golf. Most islands have a sizeable population of British and American retirees and expatriates working in tourism and finance.

The climate is widely thought of as almost perfect. There is a rainy season, although it is seldom cold, and strong sun invariably follows any downpour. The hurricane season is officially from June to the end of October, but in reality damage-causing storms rarely occur outside mid-August to late October.

The crime rate is generally low, although it has increased on some islands in recent years, and the more populated ones like Jamaica, Trinidad and St Lucia have crime problems. Medical facilities are generally good, although lacking in facilities on less developed islands. Private health insurance is required.

The cost of living is comparable to that in western Europe, but higher than the USA, and many items are expensive as they have had to be imported. Income tax is usually either low or non-existent, but property taxes are common, usually 1 or 2 per cent of the assessed value of the home.

Residency rules vary from island to island. Permits are generally granted to those able to prove that they have adequate funds and who own a property valued at above a specified amount or who have invested to a certain level. Citizens of the UK and Ireland can stay in the Dominican Republic, for example, for a maximum of 90 days with a tourist permit (obtainable for $10 from a Dominican consulate when purchasing a ticket, or on arrival at one of the country's ports or international airports). In the British Virgin Islands, visitors can stay for a maximum of six months at a time.

Selling

Most islands have no capital gains tax.

Inheritance tax

Most Caribbean countries operate no system of inheritance tax.

Further information

- **Antigua and Barbuda: t** (00 1 268)
- **Bahamas: t** (00 1 242)
- **Barbados: t** (00 1 246)
- **Dominican Republic: t** (00 1 809)
- **Jamaica: t** (00 1 876)
- **Trinidad and Tobago: t** (00 1 868)
- **Turks and Caicos: t** (00 1 649)
- **High Commission for Antigua and Barbuda**, Antigua House, 15 Thayer Street, London W1M 5LD, UK, **t** (020) 7486 7073; **www.antigua-barbuda.com**.
- **High Commission for the Commonwealth of the Bahamas**, 10 Chesterfield Street, London W1X 8AH, UK, **t** (020) 7408 4488.
- **Dominican Republic Department of Immigration**, Avenida México esqu, 30 de Marzo, Edificio D, Santa Domingo, Dominican Republic, **t** 685 2535.
- **Embassy of Jamaica**, 1520 New Hampshire Avenue, NW, Washington, DC 20036, USA, **t** (202) 452 0660; **www.emjam-usa.org**.
- **Jamaican High Commission; www.jhcuk.com**: operates a Returning Residents' Facilitation Unit for Jamaican expatriates wishing to retire in their homeland.
- **Trinidad and Tobago Embassy**, 1708 Massachusetts Avenue, NW, Washington, DC 20036, USA, **t** (202) 467 6490.
- **Trinidad and Tobago High Commission**, 42 Belgrave Square, London SW1X 8NT, UK, **t** (020) 7245 9351.

Estate agents

General

- **Caribbean Property Services** (UK), **t** (020) 7622 6515; **www.caribbeanpropertyservices.co.uk**.
- **Prestigious Properties** (Turks and Caicos), **t** 946 4379; **www.prestigiousproperties.com**.
- **Sotheby's International Realty** (Caribbean), **t** 561 659 3555; **www.sothebysrealty.com**.

Antigua

- **Tradewind Realty** (Antigua), **t** 460 1082; **www.tradewindrealty.com**.

- **Waterside Properties** (UK), **t** (02380) 230 066; www.watersideproperties-worldwide.com.

Bahamas

- **Grand Bahama Realty** (Bahamas), **t** 373 9999; www.grandbahamarealty.com.

- **Shoreline Grand Bahama** (Bahamas), **t** 373 3174; www.shorelinebahamas.com.

Barbados

- **Big Mac Real Estate** (Barbados), **t** 423 5830; www.barbados.org/realest/bigmac.

- **Eugenie Smith International** (UK), **t** (01268) 685273; www.esi.barbados.com.

- **Hamptons International** (UK), **t** (020) 7824 8822; www.hamptons-int.com.

- **Knight Frank** (UK), **t** (020) 7629 8171; **www.knightfrank.com**.

Jamaica

- **C.B. Jamaica, www.cbjamaica.com.**

Tobago

- **Hamptons International** (UK), **t** (020) 7824 8822; www.hamptons-int.com.

- **Real Estate Tobago** (Tobago), **t** 639 5263; **www.realestatetobago.com**.

Turks and Caicos

- **Trade Winds Realty** (Turks and Caicos), **t** 941 3389; **www.twrealty.com**.
- **Turks and Caicos Realty** (Turks and Caicos), **t** 946 4474; www.tcrealty.com.

Croatia

Why retire here?

Often dubbed 'the new Tuscany', the Adriatic country of Croatia, with a population of 4.4 million people, is often compared to St-Tropez. As well as having breathtaking though seldom sandy beaches, it is a magnet for yacht-owners and has better sailing than Turkey. A very diverse country, it boasts beautiful, unspoilt scenery and Venetian-style towns and villages, 1,000 islands that rival those of Greece, and a cuisine that is on a par with Italy's.

A popular tourist destination in the 1980s, Croatia became independent in 1991 after the collapse of Yugoslavia but was immediately engulfed in the

Balkan Wars, which ended in 1996. It has recovered well, as it wasn't greatly affected by the conflict, and is set to become the 28th member of the European Union, possibly in 2007. Tourism is a key industry, and 170,000 Britons are expected to holiday here in 2004 alone. Robert de Niro, Clint Eastwood and Sharon Stone are all rumoured to have bought private islands in Croatia.

Downsides

Prices are high compared with other Eastern European countries. If you are buying on some of the islands, like Korcula, poor transport connections can mean that it takes more than a day to travel from London. And there can be a long wait for ferries when the tourist season is in full swing in August, while in winter the ferry schedules between mainland and islands reduce dramatically.

There have been cases of title-deed disputes and corruption in Croatia. For example, buyers are required to form a company to buy the land your property lies on. Having such a company requires purchasers to employ a receptionist who will answer the telephone on their behalf, but the employee also has rights of access to the owner's bank account, which could cause serious problems if the receptionist is dishonest.

There is always a concern about a resurgence of political instability, although Croatia's move towards EU membership should dissipate this.

The language barrier can be frustrating and means that contact with local builders, should your home need renovating, can be fraught with difficulty. Fortunately, younger Croatians are increasingly speaking English as well as German and Italian.

Property types

These commonly vary from beachside and city apartments to large, luxurious detached villas and rambling rural piles.

Where to retire

Most foreign buyers head for the long, unspoilt coastline. Much of the buying occurs on the sleepy, unspoilt, uncrowded Dalmatian coast, with its bustling town of Split and numerous tourist resorts, old walled towns, small villages and pine forests. Beach-lovers will enjoy the more pleasant resorts such as low-key Tucepi, Brela, Mlini or Cavtat.

The Istrian coastline is also worth considering. The largest peninsula in the Adriatic, Istria has strong ties with Italy and boasts a cosmopolitan atmosphere distinct from the rest of Croatia, as well as pine forests olive groves, vineyards and old stone houses. Resorts and areas worth checking out here include quiet, good-value Pula, the capital of the region, which is famous for its Roman amphitheatre and other remains, and Porec and the fishing port of Rovinj, whose Old Town is contained within an oval peninsula surrounded by forested hills.

The Croatian coast also boasts a huge variety of islands that are just a short boat ride away. Of the 1,000 or so islands, only 67 are inhabited. The island of Brac, the largest of the Dalmatian islands and a short ferry ride from Split, is popular. Another, Hvar, is noted for its vineyards and lavender fields and is good for views, beaches and exclusivity, as is Korcula.

Lovers of winter sports should consider the Slovenian Alps. Sea-kayaking, rock-climbing, white-water rafting, night-canoeing, canyoning, mountain-biking, hydrospeeding and boating are all possible in this region.

Many foreign buyers wanting to purchase in culture- and history-rich Dubrovnik head for the picturesque, rather cramped Old Town, which perplexes locals, as that is where the poorer local inhabitants live, and where property is largely run-down. Split is another city foreign buyers focus on, while stately Zagreb is reminiscent of Budapest and Vienna, with a pretty medieval section, an elegant 19th-century zone, and excellent museums and galleries.

Currency and exchange rate

Kuna; £1 = 11 Kuna.

Property prices

Prices rose by around 40 per cent in 2003 and spectacular rises are set to continue. Apartments in new developments on popular islands like Korcula and Brac, in the harbour of Milna, for example, currently range from between £50,000 and £80,000. Houses average £80,000–180,000, while apartments in Dubrovnik sell from £80,000. If you're looking for an island, £1m-plus should fit the bill, although one was recently for sale for under £300,000, and recent sales include a 17th-century castle 8 miles from Dubrovnik for around £375,000.

Local mortgages

The local lending market is in its infancy and simpler, better deals are available in the UK.

Access to and from the UK

Buoyant tourism ensures that there is plenty of choice. Czech Airlines, Aer Lingus and Croatia Airlines fly from several British airports, while British Airways has a scheduled service from London to Dubrovnik three times a week and an increasing number of charter flights are being launched. Other airports served by flights from the UK include Pula, Rijeka, Split and Zagreb. You can also get a budget flight to Trieste in northern Italy, which has frequent buses to Zagreb and the north Croatian coast; or to Ancona, Pescara or Bari on the Italian

Adriatic coast, which are a short ferry journey from Split, Dubrovnik, and many coastal islands. See **www.visitcroatia.co.uk** for extremely thorough details.

Legal restrictions

You need permission from the Ministry of Foreign Affairs to buy here, which can take 3–12 months. To speed things up, you can avoid the need to obtain permission by setting up a local company to buy property here, and this can usually be arranged by the estate agent or property consultant. The company is subject to tax in Croatia, and corporation tax also has to be paid in the UK on any company profits (i.e. when you sell or from rental income). Currently UK corporation tax is 23.75 per cent on profits of between £10,001 and £50,000. However, tax paid on the property overseas can usually be offset against your British tax bill.

The buying process

The estate agency sector is still evolving and it is well worth looking in shops and bars, where details of properties for sale may be on display. It is important to engage a bilingual lawyer experienced in Croatian conveyancing to safeguard you against possible pitfalls. There are two options for private investors: either to buy as a foreign national, which requires permission from the Foreign Ministry and typically takes around 6 months but can take 12, or to form a company in Croatia to buy the property on the buyer's behalf.

The buyer should check the legality of the sale, as estate agents in the country are unregulated. Establishing ownership can be complex, especially with older properties, as they may have been inherited by an extended family, all of whom are required to agree to the sale.

The buyer's lawyer draws up a contract that contains relevant details of the sale including price, buyer, seller, completion date and description of the property. There should be conditional clauses protecting the buyer in case there is an unforeseen problem such as with title or with obtaining a loan. The buyer pays a deposit, typically of 10 to 20 per cent of the price. If the purchase is not completed within the specified time, the buyer loses the deposit, while the vendor is required to pay back twice the amount of the deposit should she or he subsequently sell to another party. The buying process can drag on and involves a government-appointed notary who oversees the signing of the sale contracts. The local tax office must be informed of the sale within 30 days of completion; 5 per cent tax is payable after that.

Costs of buying

Estate agents charge around 3 per cent to buyer and seller; stamp duty is 5 per cent of the purchase price. Conveyancing costs average 2 to 3 per cent.

Is property a good investment?

Capital has been appreciating well in recent years. Prices rose between 20 and 30 per cent between 2002 and 2003 but the market is still young, so there is plenty opportunity for further price rises.

Living in Croatia

Croatia is one of the wealthiest parts of former Yugoslavia, with an average income in 2004 of £4,790 ($8,800). The crime rate is very low and people generally are very friendly. As well as speeding up a house purchase, forming a company makes it easier to open a bank account, own a car and so on.

Travelling around can be patchy. An extensive ferry network links 40 islands as well as 60 coastal resorts, but in winter the schedules are reduced. A new motorway is being built from Zagreb to Dubrovnik.

You are considered tax resident in Croatia if you stay for at least 183 days. The 183-day visit may overlap calendar years. You are tax resident in Croatia if you have accommodation there, whether owned or rented, for at least 183 days. Tax residents are usually taxed on their worldwide income, although there are significant exemptions. Foreign nationals wishing to stay longer than 3 months are required to obtain a residence permit, which takes about 2 months and can be done simply by mooring a yacht in a Croatian marina or renting an apartment. Proof of sufficient funds for living in Croatia are required. The residence permit is valid for a maximum of one year but can be renewed easily.

Income tax for residents varies on a rising scale from 15 per cent for annual income above around £2,500 to 35 per cent for incomes over about £6,000. Surtaxes and social security deductions can often increase the total tax burden to over 50 per cent. Pensions received from abroad, capital gains from trading financial assets, and interest payments on loans, investments and deposits with financial institutions are exempted from tax. The Croatian health system enables foreign citizens to have similar services as local people do; once you apply for a permanent residentship, you also apply for an inexpensive healthcare package, paid monthly. Many foreigners supplement this with private cover.

Selling

Capital gains tax is 35 per cent, charged as income tax on any profits made if the property is sold within three years. There is no capital gains tax payable on properties owned for more than three years or sold to your spouse or members of your immediate family.

Inheritance tax

Inheritance and gifts are exempted from taxation in the first line of succession, otherwise the rate is 5 per cent.

Further information

- **Croatia: t** (00 385)
- **Croatia Embassy,** 21 Conway Street, London W1P 5HL, UK, **t** 0870 005 6709/(020) 7387 1790; **www.croatiaembassyhomepage.com**.
- **Croatia Tourist Office,** 2 The Lanchesters, 162–4 Fulham Palace Road, London W6 9ER, UK, **t** (020) 8563 7979; **www.croatia.hr**.
- **www.visit-croatia.co.uk**: lots of information on many aspects of Croatia.

Estate agents

- **Avatar International** (UK), **t** 08707 282827; **www.avatar-international.com**.
- **Broker Nektretnine** (Croatia), **t** 21 547 004; **www.broker.hr**.
- **Croatia Estate** (Croatia), **t** 21 547 004; **www.croatia-estate.com**.
- **Croatian Sun** (Croatia), **t** 20 312 228/213 1602; **www.croatiansun.com**. An agency that specialises in dealing with British clients.
- **Homes in Croatia** (UK), **t** (020) 7502 1371; **www.homesincroatia.com**.
- **Passage Real Estate** (Croatia), **t** 52 811 403; **www.passage.hr**.

Czech Republic

Why retire here?

The Czech Republic, with a population of 10 million, is bordered by Germany, Poland, Austria and Slovakia and boasts forests, castles, spas, lakes and rivers. The Czech Republic is the most visited of the Eastern European countries and boasts one the most beautiful of Europe's capital cities, Prague, often compared to Paris for its beauty. The Czech Republic enjoys a relatively high standard of living coupled with a low cost of living, and European Union membership from May 2004 is already boosting the property market no end.

Downsides

There are restrictions on foreign ownership. The years of Communism blurred ownership in many cases and ownership disputes are not unknown.

Property types

Anything from newly renovated or new-build city apartments to rural villas and village houses.

Where to retire

Prague is a gorgeous city and an architectural delight, with buildings dating from the 11th century, including Art Nouveau, Art Deco, Cubism, Bauhaus and 18th-century Hapsburg grandeur. It has remained cheap compared with other European capitals, although prices are now steadily rising. Few expatriates stray far from Prague, but Pilsen is a good option, near enough the capital for day trips, while Brno, the second city, in Moravia, is pretty. with historic buildings.

Currency and exchange rate

Koruny; £1 = 48.21 Koruny.

Property prices

Prices in Prague rose by about 35 per cent from 2000 to 2004, although it is still possible to buy apartments for less than £40,000. Foreign buyers favour Prague's districts 1, 2 and 6.

The most expensive property is close to the historic Old Town (Staré Mesto) in district 1. District 1 also includes the Jewish Quarter (Josephov) and Lesser Town (Mala Strana), below the castle (Hradcany) district. A two-bedroom apartment in a traditional block would currently be around £200,000 and there is very little in the centre under £125,000, although studios are still available for half that. District 2 has a cheaper but pleasant residential neighbourhood, Vinohrady, while district 6 has the capital's most expensive property, with town houses and villas of £650,000 and more. This area is the most popular with expatriates.

Local mortgages

Typically, local banks will lend up to a maximum of 70 per cent of market value. UK mortgages are likely to offer more choice, flexibility and better rates.

Access to and from the UK

Prague is around 2hrs' flying time from the UK and there are several carriers, including low-cost ones.

Legal restrictions

You need to set up a local company to buy property here, and this can usually be arranged by the estate agent or property consultant. The company is subject to tax in the Czech Republic, and corporation tax also has to be paid in the UK on any company profits (i.e. when you sell or from rental income). Currently UK corporation tax is 23.75 per cent on profits of between £10,0001 and £50,000. However, tax paid on the property overseas can usually be offset against your British tax bill.

The buying process

The legal system is similar to that of Britain, and ownership is much more clear-cut than in some Eastern European countries, such as Croatia. Even so, there have been property disputes and therefore it is important to engage an experienced lawyer to ascertain title. Prague has a central registry of ownership known as the Kadastra to help do this. Many overseas buyers purchase in restored apartment blocks because these are generally not liable to ownership disputes. You also have to buy a limited company for about £1,000 to £1,500 to enable you to buy. The property registration process before a property can be lived in takes about six months. Documents are likely to be in Czech.

After buyer and seller have negotiated sale conditions, typically the purchaser lodges the purchase price in a notarial or escrow account, to which the seller will have access when the purchaser has been registered as the new owner.

Costs of buying

Estate agency fees vary: some charge the buyer, others charge the seller or both parties. The seller is liable for a property transfer tax of 5 per cent, which the buyer becomes liable for in the event that the seller does not pay.

Is property a good investment?

In Prague prices have doubled in the last five years and demand continues to outstrip supply, yet the property boom may soon be past its prime.

Living in the Czech Republic

The cost of living is low, with a meal for two at a good restaurant in Prague costing less than £12. The climate is continental – cool summers and cold, humid winters.

If the property has been acquired through a company then the company is subject to Czech corporation tax on net taxable income. The rate is currently 31 per cent.

The Czech Republic has relatively good standards of healthcare and qualified doctors, especially in Prague. Foreigners with a long-term visa or permanent residency in the Czech Republic may participate in the state healthcare system, the easiest and least expensive way to get quality care.

In addition, private medical insurance is strongly advised and emergency treatment is paid for up front. Medical insurance can be purchased from your provider at home or through the Czech state system, which costs about $35 per month. This is adequate for most people and usually far cheaper than using an international company like BUPA. The Czech health insurance company V.Z.P. (Vseobecna Zdravotni Pojistovna; **www.vzp.cz**) also covers expatriates with residence permits.

Note that Czech companies are required by law to provide medical care for employees (though not other family members) free or at a discount. Those with a business licence to work self-employed or operate their own company are required to pay a small fee to the Social Office and the Medical Office to cover health insurance.

Selling

Capital gains tax is payable according to the progressive personal income tax rate.

Inheritance tax

The rate is progressive and dependent upon the relation between donor and recipient.

Further information

- **Czech Republic: t** (00 420)
- **Czech Embassy**, 3900 Spring of Freedom Street NW, Washington, DC 20008, USA, **t** (202) 274 9100.
- **Czech Republic Tourist Office**, 320 Regent Street, London W1B 3BG, UK, **t** (020) 7631 0427; **www.czechtourism.com**.
- **Embassy of the Czech Republic**, 26 Kensington Palace Gardens, London W8 4QY, UK, **t** (020) 7243 1115; **www.czech.org.uk**.
- **www.czech.cz**; **www.czech-tourinfo.cz**; **www.czechsite.com**; **www.pragueaffair.cz**; and **www.timeout.com/prague/**. All have useful information.

Estate agents

- **Continental Realty** (Czech Republic), **t** 222 517 105; **www.continental.cz**.
- **Executive Housing Specialists** (Czech Republic), **t** 257 328 281; **www.ehs.cz**.
- **Hanex** (Czech Republic), **t** 224 217 648; **www.hanez.cz**.
- **Identity** (Czech Republic), **t** 627 3944.
- **Letterstone** (UK), **t** (020) 7348 6061.
- **Lexxus** (Czech Republic), **t** 224 812 611; **www.lexxus.cz**.
- **Orion Real Estate** (Czech Republic), **t** 225 167 88.

Dubai (United Arab Emirates)

Why retire here?

The Gulf state of Dubai, one of the seven emirates that constitute the United Arab Emirates in the Middle East, has emerged rapidly as a foreign property hotspot, undoubtedly helped by its tax-free status, very low crime rate and year-round sunshine. Some stunning new resorts are being built, with apartment blocks, villas, hotels, golf courses, shops and water parks all appearing out of the desert and the sea. It is aiming to be a sort of cross between Hong Kong, Miami and Barbados, or the new Caribbean.

Downsides

Sun-lovers will probably concede that the sun can get *too* hot: 47°C and 100 per cent humidity in mid-summer means typically an unbearably hot June, July and August. Also, with its being very much an artificial resort, there is precious little in the form of traditional culture.

There are complex ownership laws, and some things are very different, for example the criminal system, which is based on Sharia law.

Dubai may be comparatively stable, but is around 200 miles from Iran, 400 miles from Iraq, and as part of the United Arab Emirates is next to Saudi Arabia. It is, therefore, in a politically unstable region. It is politically and financially controlled by one family, the Maktoum family, which is fine at present in some respects if you disregard the lack of democracy and freedom of speech, but things could change considerably in such circumstances.

Property types

Many of the properties now coming available are apartments and villas being bought off-plan (before they have been built). Typically the developments will have swimming pools, children's clubs, gyms, room service and other features that you would normally expect at a luxury hotel rather than a private property.

Where to retire

In the next five years or so, the city state of Dubai is set to be the second fastest-growing metropolis in the world after Shanghai. By 2008 there should be an amazing 200 new skyscrapers and 250,000 new homes. Already a number of the England football team, including David Beckham and Michael Owen, and comedian Jim Davidson have put their names down for properties.

Many British buyers have been focusing on the extraordinary Palm Jumeirah complex, expected to be completed in 2005. This vast array of man-made palm-shaped islands reclaimed from the sea will house 2,000 apartments starting at around £165,000 and luxury villas costing up to several million pounds. It will feature 120km of sandy beaches.

An even bigger offshore development, Jebel Ali, is also currently being constructed, as well as Burji Dubai, set to become the world's tallest building.

Currency and exchange rate

UAE dirham; £1 = 6.76 dirhams. The dirham is pegged to the US dollar at 3.67.

Property prices

Properties start at around £50,000 for a sea-facing one-bedroom apartment, and three-bedroom villas start from £80,000. But more common are two-bedroom apartments from £140,000 or so and three-bedroom houses from £200,000, with five-bedroom houses nudging £500,000. These prices are relatively cheap compared to comparable properties in the Caribbean or Portugal.

Local mortgages

Muslims cannot pay or receive interest under Islamic law, but major banks like HSBC have local branches offering mortgages, typically for 10 to 30 years, with interest rates linked to the UK. Another local lender is Amlak Finance.

Access to and from the UK

Flights from London, with British Airways and Emirates, take around 7hrs and cost about £400.

Legal restrictions

The United Arab Emirates, of which Dubai is a part, have complex property ownership laws. Usually foreigners are forbidden from buying freehold property, although exceptions are being made in Dubai.

The buying process

Recent changes in property laws have meant that Dubai is the only place in the Persian Gulf where property can be bought freehold. Property contracts are based on British conveyancing laws.

Is property a good investment?

At present property seems to be a good investment, but with little investment history to go on and the instability of the region, and a virtual dictatorship running the country, in the long term investment potential may be very different. With so many properties being created, it is impossible to predict future rental yields or resale values. There are no restrictions on letting or resale.

Living in Dubai

This state on the Persian Gulf may be in the Middle East, yet security is good, crime is low, the cost of living in many respects is low, the economy is booming and there are few restrictions on day-to-day living. There are no taxes at all, including a local income tax. Although the local language is Arabic, English is widely spoken. The criminal system is based on Sharia law and therefore crimes and punishments are often very different from what westerners are used to.

Alcohol is permitted, and western dress is acceptable, although topless sunbathing is discouraged and homosexuality not tolerated.

New property-owners and their immediate family are given permanent residence visas providing that the owner visits Dubai at least once every six months. Visas are renewable every three years at a cost of around £1,000.

The healthcare system is of a very good standard but private health insurance is required by foreigners.

Selling

There is no capital gains tax.

Inheritance tax

There is no inheritance tax.

Further information

- **Dubai (United Arab Emirates): t** (00 971)

Estate agents and developers

- **Damac** (Dubai), **t** 4 390 8804; **www.damacproperties.com.**
- **Emaar** (Dubai), **t** 4 316 4608; **www.emaar.com.**
- **FPD Savills** (UK), **t** (020) 7022 0055; **www.fpdsavillspropertyoverseas.co.uk.**
- **Homes Dubai** (UK), **t** 08700 992400; **www.homesdubai.com.**
- **Nakheel** (Dubai), **t** 4 390 8804; **www.thepalm.ae.**
- **Oryx Real Estate** (Dubai), **t** 4 351 5770; **www.oryxrealestate.com.**

Estonia

Why retire here?

This lovely, if at times chilly, little Baltic state joined the EU in May 2004, and is one of the least costly and least spoilt countries in Europe. Property prices are exceptionally cheap owing to low levels of owner-occupation and years of a problematic, sluggish economy, as well as a troubled history. Yet EU membership in 2004 will change this former Soviet state rapidly, with large-scale EU investment improving infrastructure and mortgage finance becoming increasingly available to locals, causing prices to shoot up.

Downsides

As with the other Baltic states, Lithuania and Latvia, investment here is more of a risk than more familiar Eastern European countries like Poland, Hungary and Croatia. From October to March, the country is generally very cold and dark. The language is somewhat impenetrable for most outsiders.

Property types

Despite Estonia's small size, there is a wide variety of property types, from city apartment blocks to tall merchant houses, several thousand manor houses built in the pre-Soviet era, wooden homes in the forests and chalets by the sea.

Where to retire

Estonia's fairytale capital, Tallinn, will see the biggest boom. Although an ex-Soviet metropolis, it is a medieval gem, home to more than a third of the country's 1.5 million inhabitants. The very best restaurants charge £15 at most; superb opera and ballet costs around £6 a ticket; woodland boasting wolves, bears and elks; and unspoilt beaches are a 10min-drive away on the Gulf of Finland. The Old Town has cobbled streets, medieval and neoclassical merchant houses and well-preserved churches. Helsinki in Finland is a boat trip away, and St Petersburg a few hours away by car.

Currency and exchange rate

Krooni (EEK); £1 = 23.85 EEK.

Property prices

Although prices have already boomed in the capital, Tallinn, you can still pick up a studio flat from £12,000 to £18,000, a two-bedroom apartment for less than £30,000, and a four-bedroom home for less than £50,000. Conversely, a very good apartment in the Old Town can go for more than £1 million. Prices drop in the elegant, leafy suburbs, such as Kadriorg. In rural areas, run-down mansions can still be picked up for a song.

Local mortgages

The local lending market is still in its infancy, and for simplicity, flexibility and the best rates a UK lender would be best.

Access to and from the UK

There are daily flights to Tallinn from the UK.

Legal restrictions

None.

The buying process

Buying in Estonia can have its difficulties and it is important to engage an independent lawyer to protect your interests and ensure that you are obtaining true title. This is made more secure by there being an efficient land registry.

Costs of buying

Costs such as conveyancing, notary fees and a survey typically add around 15 per cent to the asking price.

Is property a good investment?

Currently Estonia is a good place to invest, with many undiscovered pockets and property prices rising rapidly. It is seen as a leading example of a country that has made a successful transition from Communism to capitalism.

There is no corporation tax and therefore, instead of being taxed on profits from investment, you can reinvest. But it is a complicated place, with many opportunities to be swamped by baffling bureaucracy or ripped off, and so care must be taken at every stage.

Living in Estonia

In 1991 Estonia quickly opted for a free market after independence from the Soviet Union and left annual inflation that had exceeded 1,000 per cent to now enjoy one of the fastest-growing and most stable economies in Eastern Europe. It enjoys a relatively high standard of living combined with a low cost of living. The climate can be harsh, with mild, warm summers and freezing winters. Reform of Estonia's health system began in the late 1980s, transforming it from a state-controlled system towards a decentralised one with private provider participation. In that time it has moved from a state-funded system to one based on health insurance. Private health insurance is very much recommended for foreign residents, especially as waiting times can be lengthy.

Selling

In most cases capital gains are added to an individual's regular income.

Inheritance tax

There is no tax on inheritance or gifts.

Further information

- **Estonia: t** (00 372)
- **Estonian Embassy,** 16 Hyde Park Gate, London SW7 5DG, UK, **t** (020) 7589 3428; **www.estonia.gov.uk**.
- **www.visitestonia.com** has information on the country.

Estate agents

- **Bristol and Stone** (UK); **www.bristolandstone.com**
- **Rime Real Estate** (Estonia), **t** 683 7777; **www.rime.ee**.
- **Raid and Co.** (Estonia), **t** 627 2080; **www.raid.ee**.
- **Ober Haus** (Estonia), **t** 665 9700; **www.ober-haus.ee**.

France

Why retire here?

After a relaxing holiday, it's easy to be seduced into retiring to France and buying a gorgeous villa or farmhouse with a price tag that is tiny when compared with the cost of a property in the UK – unless you're planning on moving to the Côte d'Azur or a fashionable address in Paris. Especially when French lifestyles are known to promote longevity.

Many of the disadvantages of relocating to France are associated with working life, and therefore retiring there is generally more attractive. Age is generally more respected in France than in the UK, and an indication of this is a French law requiring that children support their elderly parents. Retiring to France has been popular with UK residents for some years, not least because of the better climate in many areas. And the generally significantly lower cost of properties in France means that there may be funds to invest after selling a UK home, plus the lower cost of living allows pensions to stretch further.

France has magnificent beaches, spectacular countryside, culture for art-lovers and fine wines and cuisine. It also boasts good transport links with the UK with a good road network and plenty of cheap flights. The northwest of the country is convenient for ferry ports and therefore visiting the UK and visitors from the UK can easily come done by car.

Frustrations with a stressful, noisy, expensive life in Britain is what seems to cause many people to choose to live full-time in France. The UK bank Abbey estimates that more than half a million Britons now own homes in France , and one estate agent recently estimated that around 65 per cent of rural properties in Normandy are now bought by the British.

Although the popularity of Peter Mayle's *A Year in Provence* may have helped to price many buyers out of the south of France, there are plenty of other regions to consider. In some rural areas, £50,000 still goes quite a long way.

Downsides

We've all heard of people who supposedly bought a vast château for the price of a new Citroën. It's true, French property prices remain far lower than those in Britain, and genuine bargains do exist, but buying in France is very different and there can be many potential pitfalls to overcome.

Before you sign up for that beautiful barn ripe for conversion for the price you paid for the conveyancing on your British home, ask lots of questions. One fatal mistake is to underestimate restoration costs. Often it can be cheaper to buy a property that has already been restored. If you see something that's very cheap, ask why. First ask where it is. Check out the beach, airports and train stations. Many people see France in the summer and assume that the climate will be the same all year round. There's a small area where the weather is better, but prices are correspondingly high. The north may be convenient for the ferry ports, but you could have six months of mud. The south has lots of sun but is a very long drive or train ride from Britain. It seems romantic to live in a huge, rambling pile in the middle of nowhere, but wouldn't a modest, manageable home near a village be more practical?

Although much of France enjoys long, hot summers, the winter can be wet and freezing in many regions. Even Provence, despite harsh 95°F summers, can have winter nights well below freezing. The Mistral, a strong wind affecting the coast from Marseille to St-Tropez, should not be underestimated. It reaches force 10 at least once a year, peaking from November to April. There are also regular strong winds on the plains between Narbonne and Carcassonne in Languedoc.

The Brit invasion of recent years, where whole French villages are now dominated by British owners, has caused resentment and tensions in some areas. In early 2004, for example, English residents in Chamonix, in the French Alps and where 10 per cent of the 10,000 population are British, suffered slashed tyres and 'English go home' daubed on their cars or property.

At the same time, Bourbriac in Brittany, with a population of about 2,700 and where one in three properties sold is British, was subject to a rash of anti-British graffiti on roadsides and on the front wall of the village estate agent and local notary. Slogans included 'Brits out' and '*Anglais intégrés, oui. Colons, non*', which translates as 'Integrated English, yes. Colonisers, no.' Locals at Bourbriac resent the British pushing up property prices so far that locals cannot compete, especially as house prices have risen by 50 per cent or so in three years.

Some French nationals resent British home-buyers who make no effort to integrate, are unable to speak the language and create an enclosed all-Brit community. To make things worse, many Brits already in the country also resent hordes of newcomers from the UK. The best thing you can do to get the most out of France is learn the language and integrate as much as possible.

Property types

The whole range, from smart city apartments to townhouses to cosy village homes to manor houses to châteaux to working farms and isolated houses with outbuildings.

Where to retire

Often Brits who are considering buying a property in France first focus on the most familiar areas like Normandy, Brittany, the Dordogne and Provence. According to Abbey in 2003, the Côte d'Azur remains the most popular area with Brits. Yet France is a large country, with 95 *départements* (provinces) organised into 22 regions. Each has a charm of its own, and many are overlooked by UK buyers.

Hotspots in 2004 include areas north and east of the Dordogne, such as Limousin and the Auvergne, while Carcassonne and Bergerac have been boosted by low-cost airline routes. The Vendee on the west coast is being discovered as a region with an all-year mild climate, while Poitou-Charentes has cheaper, more rural properties than the Dordogne and Côte d'Azur.

It can be tempting to go for the bargains, which nowadays are usually in remote regions in the centre of the country. Yet these can be difficult to get to, isolated (think rural Scotland) and far from the distractions like lively towns and restaurants that so often make France so pleasurable. Retiring to remote regions is generally not a good idea anyway.

Prices begin to rise rapidly in fashionable coastal towns like Le Touquet, or the prettier ones like Deauville in Normandy and Dinard in Brittany. The Loire Valley near Angers has good access, with cheap airlines operating in the region, high-speed trains and good roads. People shy away from the Loire, thinking it's just château and vineyards, but there's a good choice of cheap properties.

The north is generally cheapest but the three things people always want are good access, climate and value for money, and central France is best for these.

Foreigners often underestimate the great variations in climate in France, which is the only European country to experience three distinct climates: maritime, Mediterranean and continental. Varied geographical factors create many further microclimates.

Limousin has good-value properties, as does Charente, though there is not such a choice of properties. Normandy and Brittany have similar prices to Limousin but a climate that is similar to England's, with mild winters and warm summers; in central France, you are unlikely to get a bad summer. The western Atlantic coast is reckoned to have the most favourable summer climate. South of the Loire is considered by many to be the point where the northern European climate begins to disappear to be replaced by the warmer southern one.

Brittany

Brittany (the departments of Finistère, Côtes d'Armor, Morbihan and Ille et Vilaine) has long been a favourite destination for those moving to France permanently. Access to the UK has become easier with the introduction of low-cost flights, the Eurotunnel, ferry services to St-Malo and road improvements from the Pas de Calais through Normandy to Brittany.

Brittany is the wettest region in France and can be windy, although the Gulf Stream warms things up slightly. Although you don't get the guaranteed hot summers of the south of France, in the north of Brittany the climate is generally a bit better than that of the south of England, and it improves gradually as you move southwards.

Brittany is reminiscent of Cornwall, with undulating countryside and sandy beaches and a dramatic granite coast always under an hour away. It has quiet country life and a bit more going on at the attractive coastal towns and ports like Dinan, Dinard and St-Malo. Fishing, horse-riding, sailing, boating, tennis, cycling and walking are all popular, and there is a good selection of golf courses.

Stone and granite cottages built using local stone abound and the more recently built properties in Brittany are usually built in keeping with the older styles. *Manoirs*, mill houses, *maisons de maitre* and châteaux are also often available. Many Brittany properties have less land than those in Normandy, probably because farming has never been as important here.

Poitou-Charentes

The southeastern Poitou-Charentes department of Charente, whose capital is Angoulême, is becoming increasingly popular as more and more buyers appreciate how transport improvements have made the area easier to access, and how prices compare very favourably with those elsewhere, especially next-door in the Dordogne.

The Charente is an area of rolling landscapes – vineyards, wooded river valleys, sunflower fields and scattered forests. The river Charente meanders through the region and is navigable from the town of Angoulême through to the coast. The region has a microclimate that makes it one of the warmest areas in France and it compares well with the Provence area. Buyers find that they can usually eat lunch outside from February to the end of October. The local people are friendly and welcoming, making you feel part of the community. The French retire here, too, and that's a good sign.

Access to Poitou-Charentes is supported by an excellent road system; Limoges and Bordeaux airports are less than 2hrs away by car, and the Eurostar train from London to Lille and then a fast TGV train to Angoulême takes 7hrs in total.

Charentais buildings are typically made from a lovely local light, sandy stone with orange-tiled roofs and many have courtyards and grand entrance gates. Interior features abound, including old stone sinks, stoves and fireplaces and charming little round windows.

The Charente-Maritime department, with its stretch of the Atlantic south of Nantes and north of Bordeaux, enjoys the second-sunniest climate in France after the Côte d'Azur. Despite this, it is little known to Britons compared with its expensive neighbours, Brittany to the north and the Dordogne to the south, and is relatively untouched by building or high property prices. Unrestored inland properties, of which there is a good choice, still start at under £40,000, and you'd be hard pressed to pay over £500,000 for the very best houses in top condition. There is a network of pretty waterways, and off the coast of the elegant 17th-century port of La Rochelle are some pleasant holiday islands with good, sandy beaches; the Ile d'Aix, reached by ferry; and the Ile d'Oléron and Ile de Ré, reached by toll bridge. Properties on the islands are substantially more expensive than on the mainland – a small village house on Ile de Ré would be £375,000 upwards. The resort of Châtelaillon-Plage, just south of La Rochelle, is very family-friendly with a good sandy beach.

Access to the UK is good: Ryanair operates a 75min direct flight to La Rochelle, while a journey by Eurostar and TGV from London takes about 9hrs with a two-hour stop in Paris. You can arrive by sea with Brittany Ferries to St-Malo, a three-hour drive away.

Rhône-Alpes

The Rhône-Alpes region consists of the *départements* of Ain, Haute-Savoie, Savoie, Isère, Drôme, Ardèche, Loire and Rhône. Many French Alpine communities have imposed restrictions on property development, which has caused prices to rise steadily and as much as 50 per cent from 2002 to 2004 in popular resorts like Mégève, Courchevel, Méribel, Val d'Isère and Chamonix,. Foreign buyers flock here, attracted to the all-year attractions of a chalet for skiing in the winter and hot summers in the mountains where mountain-biking, lake swimming and hiking are popular. Prices start at about £50,000 for a studio apartment to over £2 million for a spacious chalet in the best locations.

It is a good idea to view a property when the snow has melted, as this can show up such things as an ugly roof. The lower resorts, like Megève and Courchevel 1850, are more ideal for all seasons and mixed-ability skiers, while the higher ones like Val d'Isère are better for experienced skiers.

The Chamonix Valley, which lies at the foot of Europe's highest mountain, Mont Blanc, is a mecca for skiers and mountaineers from small children upwards as the range of activities includes skiing on the easiest green pistes, descending the north face of the 3,847m-high Aiguille du Midi, and ambling on the local golf course. Hang-gliding and paragliding, ice driving, rafting, canoeing, ice-skating, ice-hockey, mountain-biking, horse-riding and hiking are all popular here. There are plenty of restaurants, bars, casinos and nightclubs to while away the evenings.

Fortunately, there are many surprisingly inexpensive properties available in and around some of the smartest skiing areas, and in spring and summer, when the snow and ice has melted, many resorts are transformed into beautiful mountainous holiday destinations with hot summers, fresh air, wonderful walking country and unspoilt villages. Ice rinks are turned into tennis courts and open-air swimming pools are opened up.

Bear in mind that if you choose a detached home in a ski resort, heavy snowfall may greatly impede access and winters can be hard and long. Uncleared snow can result, once the temperature has risen and it refreezes, in a glacier forming around the property, causing access problems.

Paris

As gorgeous, romantic cities go, Paris is hard to beat. Access to the UK is easier than ever, with Eurostar trains whisking you there from London's Waterloo International station every hour or so and a good choice of bargain airlines.

The Parisian property market is very different from that of the rest of the country, and although there are great buys around, with apartments costing considerably less than their London equivalents, many are increasingly realising dizzying asking prices.

In a fashionable district like St-Germain, a two-bedroom apartment is likely to cost over £400,000, and even more near the Champs-Elysées. Move away from the centre of the city, however, and prices can plunge. Studio apartments in outer *arrondissements* are available for less than £50,000.

British retirees looking for a home in Paris with easy access to the UK would find the 9th and 10th *arrondissements* ideal, because they are good value as well as being close to the Gare du Nord railway station for the Eurostar to Britain. A two-bedroom apartment there is about £100,000, and 30 per cent less for a one-bedroom.

Pays de la Loire

Forget Paris and the Côte d'Azur if you want a bargain. The Mayenne, the northernmost department of the Loire, is a tranquil farming region well worth investigating, but it has been all but forgotten by British buyers, who instead flock to its neighbours Brittany and Normandy.

The typical stone houses are very attractive and the Devon-like countryside of rolling hills and lanes particularly peaceful. Village cottages start at about

£15,000, and you could get a group of farm buildings to renovate with ample land for double that. The drive from Caen or St-Malo (with Brittany Ferries from Portsmouth) is a manageable 90mins. The Mayenne is popular with Parisians as a location for second homes, as the high-speed train from the capital takes just 80mins.

There is an excellent service from London to Laval, but from there there are very few buses, taxis are inordinately expensive, and you are stuck unless you hire a car. For this area there is no country bus system. Once you are installed at your property, it is difficult to get about unless you have a car. But the property prices are among the lowest in France.

Aquitaine

The Aquitaine region in southwest France consists of the *départements* of Pyrénées-Orientales, Landes, Gironde, Lot-et-Garonne and Dordogne.

On the coast near the Spanish border around Biarritz, as long as you're not very close to the city itself, prices are reasonable. For example, a renovated farmhouse with land is around £100,000.

Moving northwards, the Gironde has stunning countryside and plenty of space as well as efficient transport, a vibrant cultural life and the city attractions of Bordeaux. Considerably cheaper than the Dordogne, and populated by far fewer British people, it is an area popular with writers, artists and publishers, and some British buyers are even taking on vineyards in the region. The Gironde's geographical position gives it an Atlantic climate – cold and windy at times, with quite severe winters.

Both the Pyrenees and Atlantic coast are easily accessible from Bordeaux, the fifth-biggest city in France. The climate is good and access is easy, with a TGV train service and choice of airlines flying to its airport. Much of the city has resembled a building site in the last few years, the result of an overambitious regeneration plan for the riverbank and centre. This has caused the city to be undervalued compared to similar-sized cities elsewhere in France, although prices should rise once the regeneration project is completed. Town houses in the city currently start at around £200,000, and £300,000 buys you a really fabulous home.

Entre-deux-Mers, east of the city, is a good region for country living. It is a beautiful hilly region with vineyards and very little new development likely. A good five-bedroom house here is around £500,000.

The Midi-Pyrénées

The Midi-Pyrénées region consists of the departments Haute-Garonne, Ariège, Hautes-Pyrénées, Gers, Tarn-et-Garonne, Lot, Aveyron and Tarn. The Midi extends from the Pyrenees to the Alps and enjoys a hot and dry climate, except for springtime, when there tends to be heavy rainfall.

The increasingly popular department of Gers is rich in rolling green countryside and, being agricultural and sparsely populated, is delightfully unaffected by modern development and free from traffic and mass tourism. It's dotted with ochre-coloured farms with terracotta roofs and fortified towns and villages with galleried arcades and market squares. Gers enjoys a temperate climate with mild winters and long summers and is close to some of France's principal wine-growing regions and to skiing resorts in the Pyrenees.

Locally there are concerts and music festivals, golf and many other leisure activities to enjoy. Auch, the capital of the Gers, has pedestrian shopping streets, pavement cafés and restaurants and a notable absence of heavy traffic or industrial development.

Housing is still excellent value for money. There's a wide range of building styles, including large farmhouses, elegant manors, country houses and historic châteaux. Many date from the late 18th century.

Good examples of five- or six-bedroomed properties start at around the £300,000 mark, but far cheaper properties abound in the region, and something like a three-bedroom village house with a terrace garden is relatively easy to find for less than £130,000.

Gascony is bordered by excellent roads and international airports, and the nearest TGV rail stations are at Toulouse, Tarbes, Pau and Bordeaux. The direct air links now provide easy access to the UK.

Another department of the Midi-Pyrénées worth considering is the Tarn, east of Toulouse, which is now easily accessible. Particularly in the area of Albi or Gaillac, the countryside is beautiful, with vineyards and attractive stone houses, and you can easily get to the Mediterranean coast. A stone house in good condition is £90,000 or so, and you can still find village properties for £50,000.

Provence-Alpes Côte d'Azur

If the climate is too dreary and unsettled and British presence too great in Dordogne, perhaps the south of France is for you, but you'll need a big wallet! Indeed, celebrities who have bought here include Elton John (Nice), George Michael and Joan Collins (St-Tropez). The south of France has a Mediterranean climate with mild winters and hot, humid summers.

The Côte d'Azur (or French Riviera), largely encompassing departments Var and Alpes-Maritimes, has some of France's most expensive real estate, especially around Nice, Cannes, Antibes, Cap-Ferrat, St-Tropez and St-Paul de Vence.

If the coast is too pricey, consider going northwards to neighbouring Alpes-de-Haute-Provence. Although many British people drive through it on the way to the Côte d'Azur, the region remains fairly undiscovered. It boasts many of the advantages of Provence yet with lower prices and a far smaller British contingent. The climate (over 300 sunny days per year and very mild winters) and terrain are similar to that of Provence, with farmland and pine forests, but with the added ingredient of imposing mountains as well. Properties vary from pretty wooden ski chalets to old stone houses and some new build too. Prices have risen by nearly 50 per cent between 2002 and 2004, pushed up by French buyers who can't afford the coast.

Languedoc-Roussillon

This region west of the Côte d'Azur consists of the *départements* of Aude, Hérault, Gard and Lozère. It is for those wanting to be near the Mediterranean but not wanting to pay St-Tropez prices. Pretty, old houses in hilltop villages an hour or so from the sea here can be picked up for about £80,000. Although Languedoc has hot, dry summers, the winters are much colder than on the Côte d'Azur, and snow is often present into May in the mountainous regions inland.

Currency and exchange rate

Euro (€); £1 = €1.50.

Property prices

On a general level, French property prices have risen by 50 per cent from 2000 to 2004. According to **www.primelocation.com**, in 2004 the average cost of a three-bedroom property was £107,000 in Pays de la Loire, £113,500 in Burgundy, £142,000 in Brittany, £175,000 in Midi-Pyrénées, £200,000 in Languedoc-Roussillon, £386,000 in Rhône-Alps, £598,500 in Provence, and £648,000 in Ile de France.

Prices continue to rise steadily in many areas and are increasingly putting affordability out of the reach of many, especially in cities and coastal areas. In the Côte d'Azur, prices rose by 9 per cent in 2003, and the average property there is now £232,000. In Paris, prices rose by 14 per cent in 2003 alone. But prices are generally still way below those in the UK. For example, in March 2004 British-based agents Domus Abroad were selling for £161,000 a four-bedroom 1850s house in a tranquil village 100km from Caen with four reception rooms set in 3.5 hectares (8.6 acres) with an attic ripe for conversion.

Inexpensive areas today now include Aveyron, a mountainous region 2hrs' drive from Toulouse (Ryanair flies to Rodez for access here) and Limoges in central France and northern Auvergne, where properties in good locations are still available for less than £50,000. EasyJet and Ryanair services have made £20,000 small town houses at Limoges in forested Limousin accessible. East of here, the Creuse region is rich in bargains, with cottages and small farms from £30,000, while to the northeast Allier in the Auvergne is cheaper still.

Normandy still has some bargains, too. A good area to focus on is the Calvados area in lower Normandy. Brittany still has some houses for renovation for sale at under £40,000. Between £40,000 and £80,000 two- and three-bedroom cottages with gardens and habitable village houses and apartments in good locations, such as near lakes, are available. From £75,000 to £150,000, you can choose between newly built four-bedroom houses and larger resale properties often requiring some remedial work. From £150,000 to £300,000, beautiful period stone houses with outbuildings, great views and land become available, as do newly built luxury homes. The £300,000 to £600,000+ price bracket gives you the choice of *manoirs*, châteaux, country estates and exceptional old stone-built houses. Properties in towns like Dinan, Dinard and St Malo are especially pricey. In Nice, Antibes and Cannes, £250,000 would generally only get you the most basic apartment.

Property prices in Poitou-Charentes generally range from under £40,000 to renovate, around £60,000 to £80,000 for something habitable, and from £100,000 for an impressive property that is completely ready to move into.

Local mortgages

French lenders require proof of income and a list of monthly outgoings. Most loans are on a repayment basis and granted with life cover also arranged. Unlike in the UK, remortgaging is relatively rare. Crédit Agricole is the largest French lender by far.

Numerous British lenders have set up shop in France in response to demand. Abbey, which has 10 branches in the country, saw mortgage demand in France rise by 42 per in 2003. It arranges loans of up to 85 per cent.

Access to and from the UK

The ferry ports have long been the traditional gateway to France, but bargain flights to a wide range of French airports have allowed buyers of retirement homes wishing to have easy access to Britain to infiltrate eastwards and southwards, where the climate is so much hotter.

The emergence of budget airlines has without question improved accessiblity in parts of France that were difficult to reach before, especially if you live north of Birmingham. Increasingly, the cheap airlines have meant that being nearer an airport has become more important than being near a ferry port.

Flights to La Rochelle are ideal for Vendée and the Charentes; Dinard is good for Brittany and Lower Normandy; and Carcassonne for Languedoc-Roussillon and the Pyrenees. These airports are small and therefore entry formalities are quick. In 2hrs, you can be in Biarritz, Toulouse, Carcassonne, La Rochelle or Poitiers. As a result, there is now interest in areas that until now have not been popular, such as the Basque Country east of Biarritz. There one has access to Spain, and wonderful surfing beaches. There's all the charm of Biarritz with its casino, restaurants and great nightlife, and just south is the fishing village of St-Jean de Luz, and skiing in the Pyrenees.

No country has been affected more by the air travel revolution than France, which is littered with little airports opening up whole new areas for Brits to buy in. Stansted has the best choice of flights. From here, Ryanair flies to Biarritz, Carcassonne, Dinard, St-Etienne, Nîmes, Montpellier and Perpignan. Ryanair's daily bargain flights from Stansted to Carcassonne and Perpignan have opened up the until-now-often-overlooked Tarn, east of Toulouse. Currently, Nice is the French airport best served by bargain carriers for buyers outside the southeast.

For really easy access not dependent on the airlines, of course, you can't beat a pad near Calais, with the 35-minute Eurotunnel service and ferries serving the Dover–Calais route, or in Lille, where the Eurostar stops – but you'll pay for it in the lack of hours of sunshine.

Legal restrictions

None.

The buying process

French property law is based on the *Code Napoléon*, introduced in 1804 and it shares similarities with the Scottish conveyancing system.

French estate agents (*agents immobiliers*) are regulated and subject to codes of practice. Sellers generally do not enter into exclusive contracts with agents and the same property may be with several agents at different prices and attracting differing fees. Therefore, look around first to see if you would get a better deal using a different agent. Note that in France it is also common for people to sell privately (*de particulier à particulier*) or '*PAP*') via newspapers and websites. Assume that any figures agents suggest for renovation are likely to be far below the true cost.

Make sure that the agent is professionally qualified and in possession of a current permit (*carte professionelle*) issued by the *préfecture*. Ideally the agent should be a member of the main trade association, FNAIM, but this is not absolutely necessary. Agents may try to get you to sign a contract to view (*mandat*) but try not to sign this, as if you see the same property with another agent and then buy it, the first agent will claim compensation.

The vendor is not legally obliged to point out any problems with the property and any structural defects found after the contract has been signed are the responsibility of the buyer. Therefore it can make sense to commission a survey. French surveyors (*experts immobiliers*) tend to specialise in one property type, such as industrial or residential, so it is important to make sure you have the right kind. A growing number of British surveyors well-versed in French property are becoming established in France.

Due to the complicated inheritance laws (*see* p.92), before committing yourself, you need to decide whether to buy the property in your name or your child(ren's) name(s) if applicable. There are various advantages and disadvantages to each and it is possible your heirs may have to pay inheritance tax at well over 60 per cent if you make the wrong choices. A suitably qualified lawyer or legal adviser should advise you of the most advantageous option.

Property purchase in France involves using the services of one of the nation's 7,800 notaries (*notaires*), who is a lawyer trained in property, family and corporate law. They are employed by the government to collect taxes payable to the state and ensure the sale is legal, that the title to the property is valid and that the contract represents the agreement reached between the buyer and seller. *Notaires* increasingly act to a limited extent as estate agents also.

The *notaire* will handle the conveyancing (*cession*) in the period between signing the preliminary agreement and the final deed of sale, (*acte de vente*). This usually takes about three months.

Use of a *notaire* is obligatory and almost always prevents any subsequent legal problems following a property purchase. You should also have your own lawyer to represent your interests.

Once the purchase price of the property has been decided, both buyer and seller sign the preliminary agreement, a legally binding document called the *compromis de vente*, which is comparable to an 'exchange of contract' in the UK. There are variants of the *compromis*, including the *promesse de vente*, *offre de vente*, *offre d'achat* and *échange des letters*.

The preliminary agreement contains such details as the full names and marital status of vendor(s) and purchaser(s), the agreed purchase price of the property, the method of payment and any extra costs, which could include registration taxes and any agency fees. The agreement usually includes the proposed completion date, when the final payments will be made, along with a deadline for completion. Agreement over payment for any necessary repair work should be made between the buyer and seller at this stage.

Explain to the *notaire* exactly what you intend to do with the property, for example, use it as a holiday home, for permanent residence, or convert. Clarify everything you are buying and if there is a plot of land confirm that it is included in the sale. Clarify rights of way. If you wish to buy the property in a trust or company name to avoid French inheritance tax, you will pay 3 per cent French tax annually to do so.

If the property is being bought using a mortgage, this must be included on the *compromis* as a conditional clause on which the sale is dependent. Other common conditional clauses are for obtaining planning permission, receiving acceptable survey results or confirmation of a tenant vacating the property.

When the preliminary agreement has been signed (either in the estate agent's offices, the *notaire*'s office or by post), the property is taken off the market. There is a seven-day 'cooling off' period to ensure that both parties wish to proceed with the sale before the deposit is paid to the *notaire* or estate agent, which is typically 10 per cent of the purchase price, and 5 per cent for new-build. An agent is required to be bonded to hold funds on a client's behalf and must display the amount of his financial guarantee (*pièce de garantie*).

At this stage, the buyer either decides to use the vendor's *notaire*, who is supposed to be neutral, or appoints his or her own also, or instead uses a UK solicitor experienced in notary practice. It is highly recommended that the buyer employ their own lawyer to scrutinise the sale and protect their interests.

If the buyer decides to cancel the sale after paying the deposit, the vendor keeps the deposit unless the sale cannot go ahead for reasons outside his or her control, for example if the mortgage is declined or the *notaire* finds problems with the title. The *notaire* checks such things as the identification of the property, buyer(s) and vendor(s), their place(s) and date(s) of birth, the legal right of the vendor to sell, that there are no outstanding loans or mortgages on the property, any planned restrictions or developments that would adversely affect the property, rights of way, common spaces, details of leases where a property is sold with a tenant in place, etc. The *notaire* ensures that the buyer is able to pay the purchase price, and registers the mortgage, if there is one, at the land registry (*conservation des hypothèques*).

The land registry then grants a certificate of free title and the local authority provides a *certificat d'urbanisme*, which declares the existing use of the land and any administrative restrictions or requirements imposed. As long as everything is in order the signing of the final deed of sale, the *acte de vente* (or *acte authentique*) drawn up by the *notaire* then takes place in his or her office. Buyers and sellers unable to attend can give power of attorney (*procuration*) to a relative, friend or clerk at the *notaire*'s office.

Before the *acte* is signed, the balance remaining for the property is paid to the vendor as well as the *notaire*'s fees, any outstanding loans or mortgages and estate agent's fees if applicable. On signing, the purchaser is responsible for third-party insurance and property taxes.

Costs of buying

Many Britons do not realise that it is often the buyer rather than the seller who generally pays the estate agent's fee in France, and this can run into thousands of pounds. If the fee is included in the purchase price, the letters 'FAI' are included in descriptions. *Notaires* also often act as estate agents. In this case, their fees are 5 per cent up to €46,000 and 2.5 per cent above that, plus VAT. There are also various taxes and a *notaire*'s fee, and prospective buyers, especially those on a tight budget, should be aware of all these extra costs before embarking on a purchase.

Transfer tax (stamp duty) is 7.5–13 per cent of the purchase price. VAT of 19.6 per cent is payable on new properties or the first sale within five years of completion. When VAT is due, the transfer tax is reduced to 0.6 per cent. The *notaire*'s fees, paid for by the purchaser, include such things as costs for requests for personal identification documents and planning information, and vary from 0.987 per cent to 5.98 per cent of the purchase price.

If you are taking out a mortgage, the *notaire* administers an extra charge for registering the lender's charge with the land registry.

Is property a good investment?

Long perceived by the British as a country with undervalued properties, France is now changing, and some areas are in the grip of rampant price inflation. In

2002 prices rose by an average of 7 per cent overall, and 11 per cent in 2003. The days of the fabled wreck for the price of an old Citroën are long gone.

For those who wish to own a property through an offshore company to avoid local taxes and inheritance laws, the Inland Revenue in the UK has in 2004 given notice that homes owned through a company structure may be taxed as a benefit in kind. The charge is based on an assumed value for the property and, therefore, the more it is thought to be worth, the higher the amount to pay. The Inland Revenue would assume a rateable value for the first £75,000 and charge what it calls the interest on beneficial loans on any excess amount. The rate is currently 5 per cent.

Living in France

France enjoys political stability, a high standard of living and a low cost of living compared with most of the EU. Except in rural areas, where rates are low, crime is at a similar rate to other European countries and has increased in recent years. Medical facilities are of a very good standard and there is a successful national health scheme for those making social security payments and retirees.

The transport infrastructure is also good. Rapid expansion of super-fast TGV routes throughout France has meant that train journey times are increasingly being shortened. The upgraded line from Valence to Marseille has cut journey times from Paris to just 3hrs. Because some areas of France are far better served by express services than others, some routes, despite serving areas that are considerably southern or eastern, are surprisingly quick – but slower lines relatively near to home can equally take an unexpectedly long time to get to. For example, to reach Charlesville-Mezières, northeast of Paris, takes around 7hrs from London, the same time that it takes to reach Grenoble in the far southeast.

If you do not have a car, it is vital to check the public transport options to your proposed property as these can be surprisingly limited outside main towns. For the Mayenne area, for example, there are very few buses and taxis are inordinately expensive.

There is no problem in having your state pension paid in France. If you have worked in France at some point you may qualify for a French pension, which is even better. Company pensions are paid wherever the pension scheme rules allow. If the funds cannot be paid straight into your French bank account, you will have to arrange for them to be transferred regularly from your UK account. By doing this only three or four times a year rather than monthly or weekly, you will save on bank transfer costs. Bear in mind that writing a cheque on an overdrawn account or post-dating a cheque is illegal. You can be banned from using French banks for 10 years for persistent banking misdemeanours.

While you are classed as retired in the UK when you reach 65 as a man or 60 as a woman, in France retirement for both sexes starts at age 60, when you are entitled to full use of the French healthcare system. Those economically inactive

French building works regulations

Unlike the UK, which has numerous well-applied building regulations, in France it can be difficult to ascertain who controls the regulations or find out exactly how they work. While a British builder has to check frequently that he is complying with the rules, in France the regulations are not treated with such importance. As a homeowner in France with building work that needs to be done, to protect yourself, in the first instance employ an insured, fully qualified structural engineer. For about 1 per cent of the total building cost, he or she will produce a structural design for the builder, backed up by insurance if anything were to go wrong. Regular inspections of the building works are required by your local French building regulations department, and your structural engineer should be able to carry these out for an additional fee.

– 'retired' below the age of 60 – are not entitled to this. UK government pensions, such as for the civil service, armed services or police, are taxed in the UK, but other pensions should be paid to you tax-free and therefore will be taxed in France.

If you are retired before leaving the UK, complete the Department of Security's form POD 708, available at their office in Newcastle-on-Tyne. This form allows the UK state pension to be paid into a French bank. The form also qualifies you to receive an E121 form, which entitles you to French state healthcare (although it does not cover all costs – private healthcare insurance covers the remainder) until you receive your permanent social service number.

Taxation is rather different in France. For example, families are taxed as a unit and each member is treated as earning a share of the household income. Personal taxation may be substantially less for a retired couple when compared with the UK, and tax on pensions and inheritance tax for children may also be significantly less.

You are a tax resident in France if you spend more than 183 days per tax year in the country or if your principal home (*foyer fiscal*) is there.

Income tax (*impôt sur le revenu*) is quite low (ranging from 7.5 to 52.75 per cent), but this is tempered by a high social security rate. If your gross income is less than €7,175 (or €7,780 if you are over 65), you pay no tax.

Property tax (*taxe foncière*) is paid annually, based on the assessed rental value as calculated by the land registry and can vary greatly from region to region. A further, smaller residential tax (*taxe d'habitation*) is payable by whoever lives at the property on 1 January. It is calculated by multiplying the notional rental value by the tax rate fixed in the locality.

Rubbish collection charges (*ordures*) are raised separately in some localities.

Wealth tax of between 0.55 and 1.8 per cent is payable on assets of more than €760,000. If you are domiciled in France, the value of your estate is based on your assets worldwide, but if you are resident in France but not domiciled there, the value of the estate is based on your assets in France only.

Work permits are not required by EU nationals but difficult to obtain by others. Obtaining residence permits is now a formality for EU nationals, although those not working need to prove sufficient financial resources to live in France without employment. Visitors may remain in the country for up to 90 days at a time although a number of nationalities require a visa to do so. Non-EU nationals must apply for a long-stay visa (*visa de long séjour*) if they wish to stay for more than 90 days.

Selling

Capital gains tax of 33.33 per cent is payable on profits made on the sale of a home that has been owned for less than two years; the percentage rate is reduced in subsequent years.

Inheritance tax

French inheritance law is very different from that in the UK and it is important to discuss the implications of it with a suitably qualified expert, especially if you have a significant amount of capital tied up in your property.

The tax is paid by individual beneficiaries rather than the estate, the rate payable, being dependent on the relationship between the beneficiary and the deceased. Immediate family (husband, wife, parents, children, adopted but not stepchildren) pay between 5 and 40 per cent, a brother or sister pays 35 to 45 per cent, relatives up to the fourth degree (such as uncles, cousins and nieces) pay 55 per cent and any other person pays 60 per cent.

There are also laws preventing you from disinheriting your children, which may mean you may not leave property entirely to your spouse. This is affected by your domicile status in France, and also by which 'matrimonial regime' you declare, or are assigned if you make no declaration. There is no one best solution; take advice before you buy.

It is wise to make a French will, as using your UK one can cause sizeable costs and tax disadvantages. Having no will at all is even costlier.

Further information

- **France: t** (00 33)
- **French Tourist Board**, 178 Piccadilly, London W1J 9AL, UK, **t** 0906 824 4123; **www.franceguide.com**.
- **French Embassy**, 58 Knightsbridge, London SW1X 7JT, UK, **t** (020) 7201 1000; **www.ambafrance.org.uk**.
- **French Embassy**, 4101 Reservoir Road, NW, Washington, DC 20007, USA, **t** (202) 944 4000; **www.info-france-usa.org**.
- **French National Association of Estate Agents**; **www.fnaim.fr**.

• **FrenchEntrée.com**; **www.frenchentree.com**. Guides to property and living in France.

• **Siddalls** (UK), **t** (01329) 288641; **www.siddalls.net**. Provides tax, pensions, inheritance and investment planning advice to British nationals living in France.

• **www.adventure-france.com**: gives an account of experiences of finding, buying and restoring a property in Calvados.

• **www.lamanche.com**: for information on La Manche, the *département* of Lower Normandy covering the Cherbourg peninsula.

• **www.francetourism.com**: for a map of France showing all the *départements* and regions, plus tourist information.

• *Buying and Renovating Property in France*, J. Kater Pollock (Flowerpoll, £8.95)

• *Buying and Restoring Old Property in France*, David Everett (Robert Hale, £10.99)

• *How to Renovate a House in France*, David Ackers, Jerome Aumont and Paul Carslake (Ascent, £25).

Estate agents

General

• **www.buyfrenchproperty.com**: properties for sale, advice and links covering finance, removals and legal matters.

Alps

• **Alpine Apartments Agency** (UK), **t** (01544) 388234; **www.alpineapartmentsagency.com**. Specialises in the French Alps, Swiss and Italian borders, the lakes near Geneva and Annecy.

• **Investors in Property** (UK), **t** (020) 8905 5511; **www.investorsinproperty.com**.

Bordeaux

• **European Property and Estate** (France), **t** 5 55 09 99 59; **www.epestate.com**.

• **Francophiles** (UK), **t** (01622) 688165; **www.francophiles.co.uk**.

• **French Property Services** (France), **t** 5 57 54 06 19; **www.french-property-services.com**.

• **Latitudes** (UK), **t** (020) 8951 5155; **www.latitudes.co.uk**.

• **Sarl Voilà**, **t** 5 53 807 213 (France); **www.sarlvoila.com**.

Charente

- **Cognac Property Services** (France), **t** 6 68 53 12 81;
www.cognacproperty.com.
- **Domus Abroad** (UK), **t** (020) 7431 4692; **www.domusabroad.com**.
- **Eclipse Overseas** (UK), **t** (0142) 275984;
www.french-property.com/eclipse.
- **North and West France Properties** (UK), **t** (020) 8891 1750;
www.all-france-properties.co.
- **VEF** (UK), **t** (020) 7515 8660; **www.vefuk.com**.

Charente-Maritime

- **Agence Delille** (France), **t** 5 46 47 02 45; **www.agence-delille.com**.
- **Baguelin Immobilier** (France), **t** 5 46 84 86 51;
www.baguelin-immobilier.com.
- **Century 21** (France), **t** 5 46 07 64 13; **www.century21france.fr**.
- **Eclipse Overseas** (UK), **t** (01425) 275984; **www.french-
property.com/eclipse**.
- **Turpin Immobilier** (France), **t** 5 46 56 02 03; **www.turpinimmobilier.com**.

Gascony

- **Purslow's Gascony** (France), **t** 5 62 67 61 50; **www.purslowsgascony.com**.

Haute-Provence

- **Eclipse Overseas** (UK), **t** (01425) 275984;
www.french-property.com/eclipse.
- **Francophiles** (UK), **t** (01622) 688165; **www.francophiles.co.uk**.
- **VEF** (UK), **t** (020) 7515 8660; **www.vefuk.com**.

Mayenne

- **Mayenne Properties** (France), **t** 2 43 04 36 80;
www.mayenneproperties.com.

Paris

- **Knight Frank** (France), **t** 1 43 16 88 88; **www.knightfrank.com**.
- **Paris Property Options** (UK), **t** (01424) 717281.
- **Philip Hawkes** (France), **t** 1 42 68 11 11; **www.luxuryrealestate.com**.
- **Propriété 'Direct' France** (France), **t** 1 40 07 86 25; **www.pdfparis.com**.

Provence

- **Hamptons International** (France), **t** 4 92 04 11 70; **www.hamptons.co.uk**.

- **Latitudes** (UK), **t** (020) 8951 5155; **www.latitudes.co.uk**.
- **Propriété 'Direct' France** (France), **t** 1 40 07 86 25; **www.pdfparis.com**.

Tarn

- **Agence Climex** (France), **t** 5 61 25 94 94; **www.climex.immo.com**.

Germany

Why retire here?

Comparatively few British people choose to relocate to Germany, for a variety of reasons. It is not known for its sunny beaches or scorching climate; there is a language barrier, as well as an uneasy history between the two countries; and few Britons have visited it anyway.

Even so, according to the Prudential in 2004, it is considered ninth in a list of dream retirement destinations. The Department of Work and Pensions pays pensions to nearly 29,000 expatriates there, which is nearly as many as in Italy, where it records 31,000. Possibly these people are seduced by such factors as the country's perceived high standard of living, good infrastructure and sound health service.

Germany boasts spectacular scenery, from gorgeous lakes and mountains to pretty, unspoilt countryside, a beautiful Baltic coastline, twee culture-rich towns steeped in history and vibrant, ultra-modern cities like Munich and recently transformed Berlin. Outdoor types keen on walking and cycling will love Germany, which is full of trails and bike paths. It is also a haven for skiers.

Downsides

It can take time to integrate, and German people generally, like many of those in the north of Europe, are not the most open on the continent.

There have been disputes over ownership of some older properties in former East Germany and therefore it is especially important to be completely clear about ownership there before committing yourself to purchasing. Furthermore, the quality of building in the east can be poor.

Bear in mind that, if you choose a detached home in a ski resort, heavy snowfall may greatly impede access, and winters can be hard and long.

Property types

Many Germans rent apartments in city suburbs but the properties most likely to be of interest to foreign buyers are either city-centre apartments or houses located in the pretty rural areas. The best value for money is in the former East German states and properties in need of restoration everywhere.

Where to retire

Berlin has been transformed in recent years, with huge building projects, and is an exciting, vibrant city. It has elegant boulevards, countless galleries, museums and theatres, as well as endless shopping and restaurants.

The cosmopolitan city of Munich is close to the mountains and Austria, Italy and Switzerland. Munich itself is possibly Germany's most beautiful large city.

More enterprising buyers may like to investigate pretty, culture-rich towns like Weimar and Erfurt. The area around the lakes is ideal for walking and cycling. Popular areas include the Rhine and Mosel valleys, Bavaria and the Black Forest. For skiing, the resorts of the German Alps are ideal.

Currency and exchange rate

Euro (€); £1 = €1.50.

Property prices

Property in Germany rose by a sober 0.5 per cent or so overall in 2002 and 2003, no doubt a reflection of the country's economic troubles in recent years. Prices are highest generally in the south of the country and here there are many more buyers than properties, which leaves little room for haggling or a relaxed purchase. To make things even more tricky, many vendors do not use agents as they know they will be able to sell quite easily by themselves.

Prices in and near the most popular cities like Berlin and Munich are relatively high. In a sought-after suburb of Munich like Pullach, for instance, expect to pay something like £500,000 for a spacious two-bedroom flat, although large houses further out at the River Wurm go for little more.

Local mortgages

German lenders generally require a larger deposit than UK ones and mortgages are less flexible and varied.

Access to and from the UK

Inexpensive direct flights from the UK are run by a large number of carriers, including easyJet, Ryanair, GermanWings, Hapag-Lloyd Express and Air Berlin, with single journeys from as little as £19.

Legal restrictions

None.

The buying process

Property sales are overseen by a government-appointed public notary or conveyancing lawyer, who carries out formalities, certifies the purchasing contracts and registers the title deed at the land registry.

Costs of buying

There is a transfer tax (*Grundwerbsteuer*) of 2 per cent of the purchase price. The estate agent's fee is comparatively large, as much as 6 or 7 per cent, and may be split between buyer and vendor. The notary's fee averages around 1.25 per cent.

Is property a good investment?

Properties in the booming major cities, popular resort areas and properties suitable for refurbishment are the best bet.

Living in Germany

Germany enjoys a high standard of living and a cost of living similar to the UK, France and Belgium. The crime rate is low; indeed, Munich was recently voted the safest city in Europe, although unification has caused rates to rise in recent years. Medical facilities are very good and for those paying social security, and retirees, treatment is free: residents (including foreigners) register with their local Allgemeine Ortskrankenkasse or Ersatzkasse, and are given an entitlement document, a *Krankenschein*, allowing them treatment. It is common to supplement the state scheme with a private one.

Although differences in climate inevitably occur in a country as large as 356,844 sq km (138,000 sq miles), Germany has a mild, temperate climate, with occasional periods when it can be very hot or cold.

As well as the official language, German, English is quite widely spoken, especially in the western half of the country. Though it is politically very stable, reunification in 1990 caused widespread economic and social difficulties, which are gradually being resolved.

Income tax ranges from 22 to 53 per cent and local authorities levy a land tax (*Grundsteuer*) of 0.5 to 1.5 per cent of a property's assessed rentable value.

Residence permits are a formality for EU citizens, although proof of sufficient income to support oneself is required by those not working. Work permits and visas are required by non-EU nationals, while visitors can stay for 90 days.

Selling

Income tax is payable on the capital gains made on property sold within two years of purchase.

Inheritance tax

Inheritance tax at 7–50 per cent is payable, depending on the relationship between the deceased and the beneficiary and the value of the property. Non-residents of Germany are only required to pay inheritance tax on property within Germany.

Further information

- **Germany: t** (00 49)
- **German Advice Centre; www.gac-online.org.uk**.
- **German Embassy,** 23 Belgrave Square, 1 Chesham Place, London SW1X 8PZ, UK, **t** (020) 7824 1300; **www.german-embassy.org.uk**.
- **German Embassy,** 4645 Reservoir Road, NW, Washington, DC 20007, USA, **t** (202) 298 4000; **www.germany-info.org**.
- **German Tourist Office,** PO Box 2695, London W1A 3TN, UK, **t** (020) 7317 0908; **www.germany-tourism.co.uk**.
- **German Tourist Office,** Chanin Building, 122 East 42nd Street, New York, NY 1068-0072, USA, **t** (212) 661 7200; **www.germany-tourism.de**.

Estate agents

Both are in Germany.

- **Casa Dimen, t** 865 995.
- **Engel and Volkers, t** 896 49 88 60; **www.engelvolkers.com**.

Gibraltar

Why retire here?

If you like a touch of Britishness coupled with the advantages of a Mediterranean climate of hot summers and mild winters, Gibraltar delivers on both counts, being a British dependent territory and Crown Colony since 1713. It is full of historical interest and charm. At the meeting place of the Mediterranean Sea and Atlantic Ocean, this small enclave (pop. 27,000 and just 4 square miles) is dominated by the 427m (1,400ft) Rock of Gibraltar, home of the colony's 300 Barbary apes. Its location, at the tip of southern Spain and just 20km (12 miles) north of Africa, is ideal for jaunts to both Spain and Morocco.

Downsides

There has been years of friction with Spain over ownership of the colony. There can be long delays at the Spanish border for those leaving or entering Gibraltar.

There is always the slight possibility that Spain will close the border, as it did in the 1980s.

Property types

Gibraltar's period property boasts an attractive mix of Maltese stonemasonry, Neopolitan *jalousies*, 18th-century wrought-ironwork and Portuguese tiling, but very little old property becomes available and the main market is in properties in newly built apartment blocks. In recent years, former boatyards have been transformed into marinas, and former naval and military buildings, including military barracks and officers' quarters dating back to 1760, have been redeveloped into imaginative apartment complexes.

Where to retire

Gibraltar is so small and, with not a huge choice of properties to choose from, most areas are good.

Currency and exchange rate

The official currency is the pound sterling (£), although there is also a Gibraltarian pound set at the same rate. Euros are also accepted widely, though the exchange rate may not be as good as in neighbouring Spain.

Property prices

Prices of residential property have almost doubled over the past decade. Prices are comparatively high as a result of the lack of building land available, although periods of uncertainty that flare up caused by British–Spanish tensions over the colony tend to help keep prices down.

A two-bedroom resale flat costs £65,000–85,000, while a small leasehold apartment in a new development is likely to cost in excess of £100,000, more typically £150,000 plus. (In Spain, in contrast, £150,000 would get you a house with a garage and garden.) Many of the luxury schemes have £500,000 apartments and the occasional villa nudging the £1 million mark.

Local mortgages

Branches of British lenders, like Barclay's and the Norwich and Peterborough Building Society, are present in Gibraltar, offering good rates of borrowing.

Access to and from the UK

There is a good choice of direct flights both to Gibraltar and neighbouring Spanish airports.

Legal restrictions

There are no restrictions on foreign ownership

The buying process

This is very similar to the British system, although a local lawyer should be used. There are no restrictions on foreign ownership.

Costs of buying

Stamp duty is 1.26 per cent of the purchase price, and there are nominal land registry and land title fees. Conveyancing fees average 0.5 to 1 per cent of the purchase price.

Is property a good investment?

Gibraltar's small size, coupled with an enduring sizeable number of people who wish to live there, ensures that the market is likely to stay buoyant.

There are generally no holiday letting restrictions and the letting season is year-round, unlike Spain, with a strong company-let market. Yields in recent years have hovered around 7 or 8 per cent.

Living in Gibraltar

Although Gibraltar is self-governing, a British-appointed governor representing Britain exerts executive authority and the UK is still responsible for defence and foreign policy. There are around 7,000 expatriates, including many ex-service people who returned after living on the island when it was an important military base.

English is the official language although native Gibraltarians, of which there are 20,000, also speak Spanish. Residents are swamped by visitors: 7.5 million of them descended on Gibraltar in 2002. The British feel is not only in the presence of British bobbies and bright red post and telephone boxes: the tacky souvenir shops along the main drag, Main Street, have been replaced by familiar UK retailers like Tesco, Topshop and Marks & Spencer.

Gibraltar boasts a Mediterranean climate. The temperature averages 19–27°C (66–81°F) in summer and 11–15°C (52–59°F) in winter.

The cost of living is low and similar to that of Spain. The crime rate is also low, although the smuggling of drugs and tobacco into Spain is widespread. Medical facilities are good, and free to those who pay towards social security and retirees. EU visitors have reciprocal health agreements.

Income tax varies but is comparatively low generally. EU residents do not require permission to live or work in the colony, but need to have sufficient living expenses, and if planning to work, need to find employment in the first six months. Work and residence permits for non-EU nationals are difficult to obtain for those who cannot show a minimum net worth of about £1 million. They are required to buy a property in Gibraltar within six months of achieving residence status. Worldwide income is not taxed and there is no wealth tax.

Selling

There is no capital gains tax or gift tax.

Inheritance tax

This is on a sliding scale from 5 per cent to a maximum of 25 per cent on estates valued at over £100,000. Estate duty for non-residents is levied on Gibraltarian property, although this is waived on properties valued at under £100,000 that are passed to a surviving spouse or children. Property can be owned through an offshore company so that inheritance tax is avoided.

Further information

- **Gibraltar: t** (00 350)
- **Gibraltar Information Bureau,** 710 Madison Offices, 1155 Fifteenth Street, NW, Washington, DC 20905, USA, **t** (202) 542 1108.
- **Gibraltar Tourist Board,** 4 Arundel Great Court, 179 Strand, London WC2R 1EH, UK, **t** (020) 7836 0777.
- **Newcastle Building Society Gibraltar** (Gibraltar), **t** 42136; **www.newcastle.co.uk.**

Estate agents

Both are in Gibraltar.

- **Norwich and Peterborough Estate Agents, t** 48532.
- **RLS Homes, t** 71111.

Greece

Why retire here?

Sun-drenched Greece has sandy beaches, azure seas, olive groves, white-washed villages, the friendliest of people, carpets of beautiful spring wild flowers and sleepy tavernas. It is becoming increasingly popular with buyers searching for a bargain. Fortunately, much of the country remains unspoilt and it is considerably less built up than Spain.

While many parts of the Med sport ill-conceived developments that destroy past paradises, Greek planning regulations preserve archaeological sites and limit building density and the use of agricultural and forestry land, which continues to deter mass development.

You're also assured far more hot days each year than in France, over 3,000 hours per year. Many people have been inspired to visit and live in Greece by the success of films like *Shirley Valentine* and *Captain Corelli's Mandolin*.

Downsides

But before you book that flight over the Med with cheque book in hand, be sure you know what costs may be involved to make the property habitable. Greek property is certainly usually a fraction of British prices, but if the 'bargain' home to renovate you're buying has no water, electricity or drainage, hasn't been lived in since the Beatles first hit the charts, and is situated at the top of a steep hill with no road in sight, you may live to regret it. Local skilled labour is in short supply and illegal workers from Albania and other Balkan states are common.

Being in the northern hemisphere, Greece does not escape cold winters, especially the further north you go, and in many parts it is too cold for swimming or sunbathing at Easter. Central heating is essential.

To the non-linguist, the Greek language and alphabet can be a formidable challenge to conquer, although English is quite widely spoken. Politically, Greece has been rather volatile in recent decades, with weak governments, scandals and tensions with Turkey over Cyprus among other things. Lastly, if you are considering buying an Athens apartment, bear in mind that you'll probably require an aqualung, as Athens suffers the highest pollution levels in Europe.

Property types

A great variety of properties including seaside villas, old village properties and old stone houses ripe for renovation are all available. New developments are sprouting up in many areas, with off-plan, new-build apartments and villas aplenty.

Where to retire

Islands

Many Britons who buy in Greece flock to the romantic islands, where picturesque wrecks in need of complete renovation start at just £5,000. With more than 2,500 islands sprinkled around its coastline, Greece has an isle for everyone. Whether you want sophisticated restaurants and wild nightlife or a quiet, sleepy spot to laze away the days, you can buy a property on a Greek island for a fraction of its British equivalent. Yet the rebuilding and renovation costs can be astronomical and, especially in remote areas, are unlikely to be a good investment. Bear in mind that in winter it may be wet and windy, the tavernas may be closed and flights and ferries reduced to skeleton services. A long ferry trip after a long flight from Britain to Athens can make weekend visits impractical.

The most popular islands, such as Crete, the Cyclades (including Paros, Ios, Naxos and Mykonos), the Ionian islands (e.g. Corfu, Zakynthos and Paxos) and the Dodecanese (for example Kos and Rhodes), are the most well known and loved by Brits. Skopelos boasts a picturesque harbour and pine forests.

Think again before buying on one of the smaller islands. Although many are easily accessible during the summer months, during the winter when the tourists have disappeared and the tavernas may be closed, the direct flights may have stopped and the ferry may call just once a week – if it hasn't been suspended during bad weather.

Crete

If you want a sizeable home in good condition with a generous slice of land, £50,000 would easily cover it on Greece's largest island, **Crete**.

Crete is the most southerly Greek island and the fifth largest island in the Mediterranean. Winter is generally mild, with snowfall only on the high mountain range that crosses the island from west to east. Being large, it can offer both wilderness and wildness, with deserted beaches as well as vibrant nightlife. There are traditional holiday resorts full of shops and restaurants with water sports, other entertainments and glorious beaches as well as its typical sleepy villages. Many overseas property regions that can boast a warm climate the whole year round tend to be pricey but in terms of variety, beauty and climate, as well as value for money, Crete is hard to beat. You tend to get more for your money in Crete than on the mainland and islands of Spain, France and Italy, and in Portugal. And because it is at the crossroads of Europe, Asia and Africa, it tends to be hotter, too.

Surprisingly large properties ready for renovation are often available for under £20,000. If major building works seem too much of a headache, fully furnished one-bed apartments only metres from the sea with terraces and lovely views typically start at around £35,000. £40,000 could easily get you a two- or three-bedroom refurbished home quite near the sea. At a village like Koutsounari, southeast of the island, you could get a small villa ready to move into under a kilometre from the beach with a terrace and sea views for under £45,000. At the old traditional village of Pano Elounda, spacious homes (five rooms or more) near the sea needing restoration are commonly available for under £60,000.

One reason prices are low is because there is a lot of old stock available. Planning laws are strict so there's little new build compared with, say, Spain and Portugal. Crete appeals to people wanting a quiet unspoilt village rather than an apartment complex with a pool.

Saronic Gulf

The Methana peninsula in the **Saronic Gulf** is an excellent choice for a holiday home abroad, as here you will still find the tranquillity, scenery and relaxed way of life of the Greek islands but within easy distance of Athens by car, ferry and hydrofoil. The peninsula, untouched by mass tourism, is dominated by spectacular mountains dotted with little villages. At Vromolimni, for example, on the edge of Methana town and a kilometre from the port, beach and marina, old stone houses requiring renovation, with good-sized gardens and lovely views, regularly sell for under £30,000.

The region is typified by whitewashed buildings, narrow alleys and a backdrop of magnificent mountain scenery, fertile plains and rocky coves. A two-bedroom house with a swimming pool located in a former fishing hamlet laden with pine trees, clear sea waters and golden sands recently sold for £110,000.

Only a narrow strip of water separates the dramatic hills of mainland Greece from the tiny island of **Poros** in the Saronic Gulf. A one-bedroom traditional town house on the waterfront in Poros town will cost around £120,000. Here you can watch the yachts sail by between swimming and enrolling in the water-ski school. The town is clustered with traditional whitewashed houses and boasts a good market and some of the best restaurants in the Gulf.

The Peloponnese

The mainland may not sound as romantic as the islands, but access can be far easier. The Peloponnese peninsulas south of Athens have plenty of fine old properties to restore. The mountainous Pelion Peninsula is rich in forests and skiing is possible in the winter.

The Peloponnese provides the best the country can offer: empty beaches, beautiful mountainous scenery, fewer crowds and easy access to Athens. Increasingly, wealthy Athenians, foreign ambassadors and diplomats are buying summer retreats to escape the summer heat at the exclusive resort of Porto Heli on the island of Argolis in the east Peloponnese. Because of this, the town does not become saturated with tourists and for sailors its lovely sandy bay offers calm waters in which to drop anchor. One-bed apartments here start at around £60,000.

Currency and exchange rate

Euro (€); £1 = €1.50.

Property prices

Two- and three-bedroom homes in seaside locations and old village properties for less than £50,000 are still widely available. A remote old stone house in need of renovation may be under £10,000, and inland properties are generally far cheaper than on the coast. A three-bedroom apartment on an island will typically cost from around £80,000, with an extra £12,000 or so for a swimming pool.

Local mortgages

Mortgages are generally only available to Greek residents and therefore a loan abroad is usually the best option.

Access to and from the UK

There are plenty of flights each week to Athens to choose from, and the flight time from London is around 3.5hrs. Luckily, more and more islands now have year-round direct flights from the UK, including Corfu, Kos, Rhodes and Zakynthos. From May to October, there are numerous charter flights from Cardiff, Gatwick, Luton, Manchester, Newcastle, Glasgow, Cardiff and Belfast to many islands.

Legal restrictions

None.

The buying process

The system is similar to that in numerous countries like Spain, Portugal and Malta, with a notary public appointed to ensure that there are no encumbrances. You will need to open a Greek bank account, which must remain in credit and will require a Greek tax code number from the local tax office to demonstrate that you do not owe any Greek income tax. You may require clearance to buy from the Frontier Territory Committee.

A lawyer experienced in Greek conveyancing is required to establish exactly who owns the property, whether it is one owner or several family members, all of whom will have to grant permission to sell. The lawyer has to ensure that the property is free of debts. If the property is newly built or being bought off-plan (before construction), the lawyer should ensure that the required planning permission has been obtained. Government permission is sometimes required by foreign persons wishing to buy in some areas. Your lawyer should ideally be both fluent in Greek and English.

Once the buyer's offer has been accepted, a deposit of 10 per cent is usually paid (sometimes as much as 30 per cent) after the agreement to buy has been signed. This agreement is usually made in the presence of a notary public, who will check that formalities are in order and that the property has a clear title. Another requirement is that the origin of funds used to buy the property must be declared to the Bank of Greece using an official importation document.

The agreement should include full details of the purchase price as well as the completion date. The agreed price should be fixed for a minimum of three months as, under Greek law. If the vendor reneges on the agreement, or attempts to raise the price, they must return twice the value of the deposit. If the sale collapses because there are problems out of your control such as over title or resulting from the search, the vendor is required to return your deposit. If you, as the buyer, do not go ahead with the purchase, you lose your deposit.

Your lawyer will organise payment of any local taxes and register the property deeds with the registry of mortgages (the land registry) as freehold. After signing the contract, you should allow at least three weeks for an ownership certificate to be issued by the land registry.

Costs of buying

The cost of buying is higher than in the UK and can add as much as a fifth to the cost of the transaction.

Fees include a transfer or purchase tax based on 9–13 per cent of the officially estimated price of the property. Land registry fees are 0.3 per cent of the assessed value of the property and there are extra small stamp duty fees. The notary's fees are usually around 1–2 per cent of the value of the property. The lawyer's fees average about 1.5 per cent of the property's value.

Annual property taxes are also payable at around 0.25 per cent of the declared value of the property, which cover the cost of local services.

Is property a good investment?

The Greek property market has tended to be on a bit of a rollercoaster of late – in 2002, prices rose by an average of 15 per cent, while in 2003 the figure was just 3.5 per cent – but there are still plenty of properties available that are very keenly priced, in need of realistic renovation and suitable for healthy rentals.

Living in Greece

Greece enjoys a low cost of living compared to most EU states, although Athens is exorbitantly expensive. Income tax ranges from 5 to 45 per cent and an annual tax return has to be filled out by property owners even if they are resident and paying tax in the UK. There is an annual property tax of 0.3–0.8 per cent on properties officially valued at €205,000 or more.

Crime is fairly low and Greece has reciprocal health agreements with many countries, including the UK, although the national health service is variable in different regions (almost non-existent on some islands) and under stress, so private health insurance is recommended.

Selling

Capital gains tax should not be an issue as property gains by individuals are generally not taxable.

Inheritance tax

Inheritance tax is based on the value of the bequest and the relationship of the donor and recipient. Rates vary from 25 to 60 per cent.

Further information

- **Greece**: **t** (00 30)

- **Greek Embassy**, 1a Holland Park, London W11 3TP, UK, **t** (020) 7229 3850; **www.greekembassy.org.uk**.

- **Greek Embassy**, 2221 Massachusetts Avenue, NW Washington, DC 20008, USA, **t** (202) 939 5800; **www.greekembassy.org**.

- **Greek Tourist Office**, 4 Regent Street, London W1R 0DJ, UK, **t** (020) 7734 5997.

- **National Greek Tourist Office**, 645 Fifth Avenue, Olympic Tower, New York, NY 10022, USA, **t** (212) 421 5777.

- **www.greekshop.com**: Information on living in Greece

- **www.vacation.net.gr** and **www.gogreece.com**: tourism information.

Estate agents

- **Crete Homes** (Greece), **t** 28410 28804; **www.crete-homes.com**. Established agents with a good choice of stone-built properties, villas and apartments.

- **Crete Property Consultants** (UK), **t** (020) 7328 1829; **www.fopdac.com**. Well-established British-based agency specialising in period homes often in need of renovation.

- **Doma** (Greece), **t** 241 72619; **www.doma.gr**. Based at Symi.

- **Euroland Crete** (Greece), **t** 28250 32557; **www.euroland-crete.com**.

- **Greek Realtors**; **www.greekrealtors.com**.

- **Halcyon Properties** (UK), **t** (01323) 891639; **www.halcyon-properties.co.uk**. Greek and Cypriot specialist property consultants.

- **Ktimatoemporiki Real Estate** (Greece), **t** 2821 052981; **www.ktimatoemporiki.gr**.

- **O'Connor Properties** (Greece), **t** 27210 96614; **www.oconnorproperties.gr**.

- **Pelion Properties** (Greece), **t** 24210 87610; **www.pelionproperties.com**. Specialises in the booming Pelion region north of Athens.

Hungary

Why retire here?

Until 2002 there was a government ban on overseas ownership, but the relaxation of this rule has opened up a spectacularly low-priced property market for foreign buyers in this central European hub between Vienna and the Balkans.

Hungary has a fast-growing economy coupled with a long history of pre-Communist private ownership. Its capital, Budapest, straddles the River Danube and with its wealth of culture, grand Habsburg-era boulevards and elegant cafés is an increasingly popular city destination.

Downsides

The language in this country takes a considerable effort to master.

Hungary's history has left a legacy of inferior infrastructure in places although this is improving all the time.

There is not the choice of low-cost airlines that neighbouring countries enjoy, though this may improve.

As with most eastern European countries, there are possible pitfalls in the buying process and it is vital that your lawyer ensures that the vendor is registered at the land registry as the legal owner.

Property types

These vary from city apartments and villas in new-build developments to larger, older run-down rural properties.

Where to retire

Compact, vibrant Budapest is, unsurprisingly, seeing the largest growth in prices. The best areas to buy are in the inner-city areas that still await full gentrification, such as districts VI, VII and XI, the latter being Hungary's answer to Soho. Around Lake Balaton, south of the capital, prices are rising rapidly. Spa towns like Sarvar, Balf, Gyula and Zalakaros are particularly good places to buy.

Currency and exchange rate

Hungarian forint (HUF); £1 = 365 HUF.

Property prices

Now that Hungary has joined the European Union, a full-scale property boom is not envisaged, but prices in Budapest have been rising rapidly recently. In 2004 on the Pest side, a central two-bed apartment may be £140,000 or so, although properties can still be bought for less than £50,000. On the hilly Buda side, properties are mainly houses and a luxury four-bedroom house with pool costs over £400,000.

Outside Budapest, prices are generally spectacularly low. For example, a two-bedroom villa with a 300ft garden was sold in early 2004 to a British buyer in the large town of Nagykanizsa, a big town about 10 miles from the Croatian border, for £10,000, nearby stream included.

Properties on the shores of Lake Balaton range from around £20,000–70,000 for a small house, and for the same amount you could get a three- or four-bedroom home in outlying villages.

Local mortgages

At present, loan interest rates are very high in Hungary, at 10–14 per cent, and are given for a maximum of 50 per cent of the value of the property, so it is better to raise finance in the UK.

Access to and from the UK

There are daily 2½ hour flights from London to Ferihegy Airport, Budapest. Malev Hungarian Airlines and British Airways have flights from under £130 return; bargain carriers such as easyJet have cheaper deals.

Legal restrictions

You need to set up a local company to buy property here, and this can usually be arranged by the estate agent or property consultant. The company is subject to tax in Hungary but also corporation tax has to be paid in the UK on any company profits – when you sell or from rental income. Currently UK corporation tax is 23.75 per cent on profits between £10,001 and £50,000. However, tax paid on the property overseas can be offset against your British tax bill.

There are no residency requirements for foreign purchasers.

The buying process

After the offer to buy has been accepted and the contract signed, the buyer, if foreign, puts down a 10 to 20 per cent deposit and applies for a buying permit from the local council. If the permit is refused, the deposit is forfeited. Alternatively, foreign buyers are required to form a property company, or they can pay a local agent to carry out the process on their behalf.

Unlike in Britain, the same lawyer will act for both buyer and seller. It is recommended that the property is surveyed, as many Hungarian homes have numerous defects.

Costs of buying

Stamp duty, legal costs and estate agency fees average around 10 per cent of the purchase price.

Is property a good investment?

Hungary enjoys low inflation and low unemployment. Joining the European Union in 2004 will almost certainly result in an even more stable economy and currency, although the euro is unlikely to be adopted before 2007.

Living in Hungary

Most foreign residents of Hungary supplement the state healthcare system with private medical insurance.

Selling

There is currently no capital gains tax payable but there is increasing likelihood that this will be re-introduced.

Inheritance tax

This is dependent on the size of the estate and the relationship between donor and recipient.

Further information

- **Hungary: t** (00 36)
- **British Consulate** (Hungary), **t** 1266 2888. Can provide a list of reliable English-speaking lawyers.
- **Hungarian Tourist Board**, 46 Eaton Place, London SW1X 8AL, UK, **t** (020) 7823 1032; **www.hungarywelcomes-britain.com**.

Estate agents

- **Avatar International** (UK), **t** 08707 282827; **www.avatar-international.com**.
- **Hungary Property** (UK), **t** (01293) 541667; **www.hungaryproperty.net**.
- **www.casaro-hungary.com** and **www.viviun.com**: Hungarian property for sale.

Ireland (Republic of)

Why retire here?

The Republic of Ireland boasts a largely unspoilt landscape of rolling hills, windswept moors, lush green farmland and lakes, and is heaven for the pub-goer or outdoor sports enthusiast, while the people are very hospitable. The easygoing lifestyle and low population make for a real contrast to the hectic ways of much of the UK.

Downsides

You don't come to Ireland for the weather: its climate is similar to that of Britain – generally cool and changeable with plenty of rain. Winters are cold and summers warm.

Property types

These vary from expensive estates and period homes to pretty, rural cottages and farmhouses, as well as many less attractive modern bungalows and houses.

Where to retire

Anywhere close to an airport is popular because of the frequency and price of budget flights. West Cork, Dublin and Donegal are the principal areas where Britons buy, according to local estate agents. Actor Jeremy Irons, Carol Vorderman and film producer Lord Puttnam have homes in west Cork.

Dublin is a friendly, lively, unforbidding city and the cultural centre of the country. Right in the centre is the Temple Bar area, packed with restaurants, hotels, bars and shops. It is more restful in the upmarket residential area of Ballsbridge just south of the centre. And although the nightlife is great, in 15 minutes you can be in some of Ireland's most beautiful countryside.

Kerry and Waterford are enduringly popular, as are the southern and western coasts, which are always near an airport. Galway is a good base; Galway city has a thriving arts scene, nightlife and plenty of restaurants and bars, and a short drive takes you to the stunningly beautiful landscapes of Connemara. Athlone is another area worth considering; pockets of Athlone city, midway between Dublin and Connemara, have lively bistros, restaurants and bars.

Currency and exchange rate

Euro (€); £1 = €1.50.

Property prices

The geography and property types in the Republic of Ireland share many similarities with Scotland, but price is not one of them. While you can pick up neglected cottages in Scotland surprisingly easily for less than £50,000, Ireland has in recent years been experiencing a property boom that has led to hefty price hikes. Property prices overall doubled from a rise of 7.5 per cent in 2002 to 15 per cent in 2003.

In the late 1990s, prices in Dublin rose by 165 per cent in five years, but since then things have cooled. In the Killiney Bay area of Dalkey, just south of Dublin, prices topped £5 million for the best properties in 2000. A number of stars have homes there, including Bono, Van Morrison, Elvis Costello, Enya, Jack Nicholson, Chris de Burgh and Damon Hill.

Newly built homes are relatively cheap compared with British prices, but period homes are generally substantially more expensive. For example, a six-bedroom Georgian home set in a few acres of land in west Cork costs in the region of £2 million, which is considerably more than a similar house in a desirable southern English coastal area.

Properties built on the seafront and on coastal hills are rising in cost more rapidly as these are often sought-after locations, and there are more building restrictions than before.

Dublin is expensive and one-bedroom apartments typically start at over £100,000. You get much more for your money in rural areas and, of course, away from the fashionable areas, detached houses are available for less than £70,000, with cottages to renovate from half that.

At picturesque Clonmacnoise, Athlone, older-style cottages set in large gardens were still available for less than £80,000 in early 2004, but this is certainly a rarity. A five-bedroom rural property in the popular area of Curramore would be around £250,000.

Local mortgages

Fifteen-year mortgages of up to 90 per cent are widely available from Irish banks. A duty of 0.1 per cent is payable on loans over €25,316.

Access to and from the UK

There are scheduled services from the UK operated by British Airways, Aer Lingus and British Midland. Two budget airlines run frequent flights from UK airports to Ireland. Ryanair flies to Derry, Cork, Dublin, Kerry, Shannon and Knock, while easyJet flies to Belfast – a one-hour drive to the border with the Republic of Ireland. Stena Line's HSS ferry service goes from Holyhead to Dun Laoghaire in 99 minutes.

Legal restrictions

None.

The buying process

This is similar to the process in England and Wales, with exchange and completion typically taking place two months after both parties have signed the preliminary contract.

Initially the buyer pays a 5 per cent returnable booking deposit to take the property off the market. Then the buyer pays a 10 per cent non-returnable deposit, with the balance paid on completion. Gazumping is rare.

One difference from the British market is that estate agents have lists of property that are for private sale and where the vendor does not want the transaction to become public. It is also common to buy properties at auction.

Costs of buying

Costs include: stamp duty on second-hand homes on a scale from zero per cent on properties up to €127,001 to 9 per cent on properties over €632,911, legal fees from 1 to 1.5 per cent of the purchase price, survey costs and a nominal sum for deed registration. Land registration costs between about £90 and £450. Stamp duty is not payable by first-time buyers or buyers of new homes.

Is property a good investment?

There is still much scope for Ireland's developing property market.

Recent buyers of property in Dublin have reported 35 per cent price increases in three years.

Living in Ireland

Despite the problems that have occurred in Northern Ireland, the Republic of Ireland is politically very stable and fairly unaffected. The crime rate is comparatively low and medical facilities are good, with a national health scheme for residents paying social security and the retired.

The cost of living is relatively high, although pensioners receive a comparatively high number of benefits including free healthcare, public transport and telephone rental and various allowances for clothing and fuel.

Householders are charged for refuse collection, which varies from a nominal charge to over £450 per year depending on location.

Non-residents are taxed on income earned in the Republic. Income tax is quite high, ranging from 20 to 46 per cent, but writers, artists and sports people are exempt from paying tax on some earnings. Legal residents of Ireland pay a social insurance tax.

Visitors to Ireland can stay for 90 days without formalities. Residence permits for EU nationals, obtainable from the Department of Justice, are generally easy to obtain. If you legally reside in Ireland for four years out of eight, you can apply for citizenship.

Selling

Capital gains tax is 20 per cent, but any gains made from the sale of a principal residence are exempt.

Inheritance tax

There is an inheritance tax, known as Capital Acquisition Tax, at 20 per cent.

Further information

- **Ireland: t** (00 353)
- **Department of Justice**, 72–76 St Stephen's Green, Dublin 2, Ireland, **t** 1 602 8202.
- **Irish Auctioneers' and Valuers' Institute**, 138 Merrion Square, Dublin 2, Ireland, **t** 1 661 1794; **www.ipav.ie**.
- **Irish Embassy**, 17 Grosvenor Place, London SW1X 7HR, UK, **t** (020) 7235 2171.
- **Irish Embassy**, 2234 Massachusetts Avenue, NW, Washington, DC 20008, USA, **t** (202) 462 3939; **www.irelandemb.org**.
- **Irish Tourist Board**, 150 New Bond Street, London W1Y 0AQ, UK, **t** (020) 7493 3201; **www.tourismireland.com**, **www.ireland.travel.ie**. The tourist board has various free publications.
- **Irish Tourist Board**, 345 Park Avenue, New York, NY 10154, USA, **t** (212) 418 0800.
- **Corporate Care; www.corporatecare.ie**: offers a relocation service.
- **Government of Ireland Department of Foreign Affairs; www.irlgov.ie/iveagh**.
- *Irish Guide*; www.theirishguide.com.
- *Irish Emigrant News*; www.emigrant.ie.

Estate agents

All are based in Ireland.

General

- **www.ascotfirst.com**: over 6,000 properties.
- **Michael H. Daniels and Co, t** 253 9145; **www.michaelhdaniels.com**: nationwide listings.

- **www.iavi.ie**: nationwide listings.

Athlone

- **Re/Max, t** 9064 93135; **www.remax.ie**.

Cork

- **Celtic Properties, t** 275 2290; **www.celticproperties.com**.
- **Charles McCarthy Estate Agents, t** 282 1533; **www.charlesmccarthy.com**.
- **Ganly Walters, t** 1 662 3255; **www.ganlywalters.ie**.
- **Hamilton Osborne King, t** 2142 71371; **www.hok.ie**.
- **Henry O'Leary Auctioneers, t** 233 5959; **www.hol.ie**.
- **Jackson Stops, t** 1633 3777; **www.jacksonstops.ie**.
- **Leonard Estates, t** 9156 5853.
- **Sheehy Brothers, t** 2147 72338; **www.sheehybrothers.com**.

Galway

- **Colleran Auctioneers, t** 91 562293.
- **Spencer, O'Toole, t** 91 552999; **www.spentool.com**.

Waterford

- **Jack Flanagan, t** 58 41496; **www.flanaganauctioneers.com**.

Wexford

- **Re/Max Southeast, t** 53 21977.

Wicklow

- **Dooley Poynton, t** 404 62292; **www.wicklowproperty.com**.

Italy

Why retire here?

Romantic Italy, with its rich heritage, attracts arty, literary types and lovers of beautiful countryside and wonderful food and wine. It has some stunning cities, lively towns and very pretty villages, as well as a varied coastline.

The lower cost of living means that a pension goes further than in the UK, and the lower property prices mean that you may be able to move out to Italy with a sizeable amount of capital after selling your UK home.

Downsides

As in France, the weather can be uncertain and winters freezing in many areas. Some parts of the country are prone to earthquakes and flooding. The UK is generally costlier and harder to reach than from Spain and France, and it suffers from over-complex bureaucracy and higher levels of inefficiency in daily life.

Property types

Unlike in Spain, where comfortable new villas are the norm, in Italy retirees invariably search out characterful older properties. New-build developments are a rarity. Much of the coastline has been marred by overdevelopment, although some areas, such as Tuscany, have been somewhat protected by controls on new development and strict guidelines concerning the restoration of existing properties. Inland, however, many towns and villages remain unspoilt and the best buys are old village and country properties in need of restoration. All properties in Italy are freehold.

Where to retire

Most foreign buyers opt for areas north of Rome, such as Tuscany, Umbria, Lombardy, Veneto, Liguria and Le Marche. The Italian lakes and Riviera and northern Adriatic coast are other especially popular regions.

The less-prosperous south of the country has yet to be discovered by British buyers and, although the property market infrastructure is less developed here, adventurous purchasers are likely to be well rewarded with comparative property bargains.

Tuscany

This remains the top choice for many in Italy, being close to beautiful country-side, mountains and sea and within a manageable distance of Pisa and Florence airports. On most people's wish list is the typical Tuscan farmhouse with plenty of land known as a *colonica*. They don't come cheap, and a typical small rural house here costs around £250,000. Celebrities who have bought in Tuscany include Sting, Bryan Ferry and Paul Smith. John Mortimer rents here every summer. This is not the place to look if you want value for money, but the north is cheaper than the south.

Umbria

Many aspirants to Tuscany without wallets to match have instead focused on this charming region, to such an extent that good choice that is value for money is something of a rarity now. Perugia is its capital city, with an international airport.

Le Marche

What everyone tends to want, the bargain traditional farmhouse in need of restoration in an acre of land, has practically dried up now in Tuscany and Umbria. It is better to look at the quieter, cheaper area of Le Marche, east of

Umbria, as there are many more available there. You could buy a four-bed house with an acre of land to do up here for £80,000 – and the improving road network and expansion of nearby Perugia airport makes the UK less daunting to reach.

Bounded by the Apennine mountains on one side and the Adriatic Sea on the other, its property market is more like that of Tuscany a couple of decades ago, with plenty of properties still available to restore and therefore being sold at a low price. Particularly unspoilt, it boasts an admirable coastline. It is culture-rich, too, with ancient historic cities like Urbino, the Florence of the Marches region, and attractive towns like Ascoli Piceno. Buyers are especially looking at properties within easy reach of the Sibillini mountains (for winter skiing), which are also convenient for the coast.

What the region does not have, which Tuscany does, is access to major cities, such as Rome, Siena and Florence, but this can be a blessing in disguise, as the area is likely to stay unspoilt for longer than regions with better connections.

Liguria

Many foreign buyers priced out of Tuscany look to this pretty region on the Mediterranean. Liguria, the Italian Riviera, is rich in property bargains and far less commercialised than next-door France's Côte d'Azur.

Property on the coast itself tends to be expensive, although better value than its French counterpart. There are some gorgeous towns, such as San Remo and Portofino (which some people find almost *too* pretty and geared to the tourist).

Inland it has lots of olive groves and hills going back from the sea, and it is an easy driving distance from Monaco and Milan. Villas requiring full renovation are currently under £50,000; those needing no more than redecoration and updating are selling for around £100,000; while recently renovated ones are fetching more than £200,000.

Lombardy and the Lakes

The northern parts of Italy around the Lombardy lakes are another good source of inexpensive Italian property. A two-bedroom house is easily obtainable for less than £75,000 in villages near the lakes. The area has the added advantage of beautiful summer weather and mild winters, and is close to the ski slopes for lovers of winter sports.

The Veneto and the Dolomites

The northeastern region around the beautiful Dolomite mountains, which form the southeastern part of the Alps, around Trentino and Lake Garda in northern Italy, offers both winter skiing and summer sun-lounging. Well away from the package holiday hotspots, this region boasts fashionable ski resorts such as Madonna di Campiglio (favoured by celebs like Michael Schumacher), numerous gorgeous lakes, and its residents enjoy the longest average lifespans in Europe. Prices are comparatively low, but have been rising quite rapidly of late. At the top end of the market, a lakeside villa will cost over £1 million, but terraced houses with a view of Lake Garda can be bought for a third of that. Apartments in complexes with a communal swimming pool in a lakeside town like Riva del Garda start at around £100,000.

The region boasts numerous culture-rich towns and cities, including Trento, with a very attractive piazza, fabulous Venice and historic, stylish yet laid-back Verona. Access is easy, with good air, road and rail connections including Ryanair flights to Brescia and Treviso and British Airways and Alitalia routings to Verona and Venice.

The South: Calabria and Puglia

Prices generally plunge even further in southern Italy. Calabria, for example, is becoming increasingly popular with holidaymakers, yet few British buyers consider buying in this gloriously unspoilt corner. For this reason, the infra-structure for buying a property is less developed here for overseas purchasers. Bear in mind that access is not as good as in more northern regions, although the wonderful homes on offer – with price tags to match – can amply compensate for this. You could also investigate Puglia.

Islands: Sardinia and Sicily

Despite almost 40 years of the world's glitterati jetting and cruising into the Costa Smeralda in Sardinia, this beautiful Italian island has not kept pace with the Côte d'Azur, the Algarve and the Costa del Sol in terms of exposure and numbers of visitors. Sardinia is rather exclusive and beautiful with wonderful beaches, and the coastline hasn't been spoilt. Many people would buy there in preference to the overdeveloped areas of the Mediterranean mentioned above, if only they knew about it. The Costa Smeralda boasts excellent golf courses and for sailors there are many beautiful islands to visit and beaches to discover, accessible only from the sea and away from other people. But it doesn't come cheap. A three-bedroom villa with a swimming pool overlooking the sea at Costa Smeralda typically costs in excess of £500,000.

Leave Sardinia and the price of island property plunges. The small island of Isola Piana off Sardinia, for example, has properties for less than £50,000. Isola Piana is ideal for anyone wanting to get away from it all. It has a doctor's surgery, church, restaurant, bar, pizzeria, two tennis courts, two swimming pools and a small marina. For main shopping, you would need to take a boat to Sardinia.

Beach-house hunters should also consider **Sicily** – its architectural wealth gives it added value, and prices are still very low. Many foreigners own homes near Taormina and Syracuse.

Currency and exchange rate

Euro (€); £1 = €1.50.

Property prices

In most parts of London, £100,000 does not even buy a studio flat, but focus on Italy and you can take your pick from a fabulous range of villas, rustic farmhouses, village houses and beachside apartments.

Prices may have shot through the roof in many parts of Umbria and Tuscany (although around Lucca you can still obtain picturesque small village houses requiring restoration from about £60,000), but look eastwards to Le Marche (the Marches) and property is much better value.

It is still possible to buy a four-bedroom house with an acre of land to renovate in Le Marche for less than £80,000. Properties recently available in Le Marche include a £70,000 watermill with 11 rooms to restore plus large old outbuildings with exposed beams, and for £90,000 a two-bedroom habitable farmhouse near the sea. Four-bedroom farmhouses to do up with an acre of land in Le Marche are sometimes available for as little as £60,000, a fraction of the typical £250,000 or so you would pay in Tuscany. Inland, in the Macerata area, ruins start at around £15,000 with habitable homes from under £50,000.

Small rustic houses in the Veneto and Dolomites region are available from about £40,000. Prices plunge in southern Italy generally. For example, you could pick up an apartment here for less than £15,000.

Sardinia is not cheap. For around £250,000, you would get something like a three-bedroom, semi-detached house away from the sea in the typical Sardinian style in the exclusive Porto Cervo district of the Costa Smeralda.

Local mortgages

Loans are generally repayment mortgages in euros of between 5 and 25 years and up to 80 per cent of the purchase price. Loans must be paid off by the applicant's 70th birthday. Proof of income and outgoings are required and assumed rental income is not taken into account. Funds imported to buy property in Italy should be officially registered by your Italian bank.

Access to and from the UK

The expansion of Perugia airport and Ryanair's cheap service to Ancona have opened up the unspoilt, beautiful, mountainous Marches on the Adriatic coast, where property prices are significantly lower than in Tuscany and Umbria. Charter flights to nearby Rimini also run in summer. Italian cities are also well served by the bargain air carriers, including Rome, Pisa, Genoa, Turin, Naples, Venice, Brescia, Treviso, Bologna and Milan. Parma airport will also become a budget destination in 2005.

Access to the Lake Como area is easy and there are two airports in Milan as well as ones at Linate and Malpensa. Many cheap flights are available.

Legal restrictions

Planning restrictions on old properties can be very strict, so check the extent of these thoroughly before committing to buy.

The buying process

When you have found a suitable property, the first thing to do is employ a surveyor (*geometra*) to survey the property. For added protection, it is advisable to only use estate agents registered with their local chambers of commerce.

A notary (*notaio*), an independent public official, presides over the sale of property in Italy. Although they are independent, buyers should instruct their own independent, English-speaking lawyer (*avvocato*) familiar with the Italian conveyancing process. She or he will carry out searches to ensure that the property is unencumbered – i.e. that there are no outstanding financial liabilities, which in Italy would become the new buyer's responsibility. In rural areas, a property can be owned by several family members and all must agree to the sale. The vendor may then require a 'buying proposal', legally committing the purchaser to buy but leaving the vendor free to consider other offers.

When both parties have agreed on the purchase price, a preliminary contract, legally binding for both parties, is drawn up by either the estate agent, vendor or a lawyer and signed by both parties. This contract, known as a *compromesso di vendita*, *contratto preliminare di vendita* or *promessa di vendita*, usually discourages gazumping and sets down the terms and conditions of the sale, including the price, completion date, financial details, a description of the property, a guarantee from the vendor and possibly other clauses.

Before signing, the surveyor should have assured the buyer that the property is sound and conforms with local planning laws and building regulations.

The sale must be completed within the time limit stated, which is typically anything from a couple of weeks to more than four months, and averages around two months. A deposit (*deposito di garanzia* or *caparra penitenziale*) of between 10 and 30 per cent of the purchase price is in most cases paid to the notary by the buyer. The buyer loses this if he or she doesn't go through with the purchase, while the vendor loses twice the deposit if he or she drops out. The buyer's lawyer should ensure that the deposit is not described as a *caparra confirmatoria* as this gives the seller the right to take legal action against the buyer should he pull out.

A declaration of value of the property is required to ascertain the rate of registration tax (*imposta di registro*) to pay, which is set at 4 per cent for new properties, 11 per cent for other residential properties and 17 per cent for agricultural land. Your lawyer should be involved in checking the value set. Properties are often undervalued to avoid capital gains tax. Although this is generally not a great problem in Italy – indeed, under-declaring a property's value is not an offence in the country – a British lawyer, if you are using one for your conveyancing, would not be able to ignore the real price because this would breach the UK money-laundering rules.

Buyers are required to obtain an Italian tax code number (*codice fiscale*) before completion. When the final contract, the *rogito*, is ready, completion is made before the notary. The deed or conveyance of transfer (*scritta privata* or *atto di compravendita*) is signed by both parties or their legal representatives. The notary registers the deed of sale with the land registry (*registro immobiliare*) and issues a certified copy to the buyer. At the time of completion, the balance owing as well as any relevant fees and taxes are paid to the notary.

About two weeks later, the buyer should obtain a copy of the deeds from the notary's office and a form to give to the local police to notify them of the purchase.

Costs of buying

Property taxes depend on the assessed value, which is open to negotiation. These consist of a purchase/registration tax of 3 to 4 per cent for Italian residents and 10 per cent for buyers of second homes. Notary fees (fixed according to purchase price) are about 3 per cent of the purchase price and payable by the buyer. There is a stamp duty of between 4 and 17 per cent. In addition, there are valuation, survey, document and search fees. Usually both vendor and purchaser share the agent's fee, which can vary widely.

Is property a good investment?

Despite high prices in many regions, property is on the whole a very good investment, especially in the major cities and resort areas. Overall, Italian property prices have been rising steadily if not dramatically in recent years, and there's no reason why this should not continue. Properties near mountains and lakes, such as in the Dolomites, have year-round appeal, from skiing in winter to sun in the summer.

Living in Italy

Italy enjoys a temperate climate characterised by hot summers and cold winters, although the climate is milder on the Italian Riviera and the islands.

The cost of living is about a third lower than that of the UK, except in cities, where there is little difference. Italy has a quite good health service, although it is as overstretched as in many European countries. Any person eligible for a state pension in any other EU country will receive free healthcare in Italy. Recipients of company or private pensions may also receive free healthcare; pension funds are paid wherever the particular scheme allows, usually either into an Italian bank or otherwise into a UK account and then transferred into an Italian one.

People who have worked in Italy in the past may be entitled to an Italian pension on retirement, and contributions that have been made in another EU country prior to taking up residence are generally taken into account.

Politically, Italy is relatively unstable compared with much of Europe; the crime rate varies considerably but overall is not exceptional for Europe.

There is an annual community tax payable on the notional value of your property, whether rented out or not. Visitors may stay for 90 days while residence permits are valid for a year and renewable annually. Non-EU nationals require a work permit, which can be difficult to obtain.

Selling

There is no capital gains tax payable on properties.

Inheritance tax

Inheritance tax for Italians is much more restrictive than that in the UK and certain groups of people have almost automatic rights of inheritance. The tax rate varies between 3 and 33 per cent but has been abolished on legacies to family members. If you are not Italian, however, you can dispose of your property according to your national law, which for British people is generally as they want – but you must make a will. It is wise to make an Italian will as the alternative, as using your UK will can cause sizeable costs and tax disadvantages. Having no will at all is obviously even costlier still.

Further information

- **Italy: t** (00 39)
- **Italian Consulate General,** 38 Eaton Place, London SW1X 8AN, UK, **t** (020) 7235 9371.
- **Italian Embassy,** 14 Three Kings Yard, Davies Street, London W1Y 2EH, UK, **t** (020) 7312 2200; **www.embitaly.org.uk**.
- **Italian Embassy,** 1601 Fuller Street, NW, Washington, DC 20009, USA, **t** (202) 328 5500.
- **Italian State Tourist Board,** 1 Princes Street, London W1B 2AY, UK, **t** (020) 7408 1254; **www.enit.it**.
- **Italian Tourist Board,** Suite 1565, 630 Fifth Avenue, New York, NY 10111, USA, **t** (212) 245 4822.
- **Tourism Information Service** (UK), **t** 0900 160 0280.
- **Visa Information Service** (UK), **t** 0900 160 0340.

Estate agents

- **Brian A. French and Associates** (UK), **t** 0870 730 1910; **www.brianfrench.com**.
- **Casa Travella** (UK), **t** (01322) 660988; **www.casatravella.com**.
- **Green Umbria** (Italy), **t** 0759 426 500; **www.greenumbria.com**.
- **Knight Frank International** (UK), **t** (020) 7629 8171; **www.knightfrank.co.uk**.
- **Piedmont Properties** (UK), **t** (01344) 624096.
- **Tuscan Enterprises** (Italy), **t** 057 7740 623; **www.tuscanenterprise.it**.
- **www.marchepropertysales.com** and **www.informer.it**: living in Italy.

Lithuania

Why retire here?

Like Estonia, this is a lovely, if at times chilly, little Baltic state that joined the EU in May 2004. It is one of the least costly and least spoilt countries in Europe. It boasts superb empty beaches, fine architecture and unspoilt countryside.

Property prices are exceptionally low due to low owner occupation and years of a problematic, sluggish economy and a very troubled history including years of Russian occupation. Yet EU membership will change this rapidly with large-scale EU investment improving infrastructure and mortgage finance becoming increasingly available to locals causing prices to shoot up. Early investors will be able to rent or sell at a good profit.

Downsides

As with the other Baltic states, Estonia and Latvia, investment here is more of a risk than in more familiar Eastern European countries like Poland, Hungary and Croatia. Also, from October to March Lithuania tends to be very cold and dark. The language is another barrier to most people.

Property types

Despite the country's small size, there is a wide variety of property types, from city apartment blocks to tall merchants houses, rickety, rambling, rural manor houses, wooden homes in the forests and chalets by the sea.

Where to retire

The capital, Vilnius, is very attractive and boasts a stately centre with plenty of vibrant cafés, restaurants and elegant buildings. The second city, Kaunas, is equally pleasant, with a vibrant main drag full of trendy bars and cafés charging 1970s prices.

Currency and exchange rate

Lita (LTL); £1 = LTL 5.26.

Property prices

Since the end of Communism, most council houses have been sold off and now 85 per cent of property is privately owned. Foreign property speculators have been pushing up prices in recent years, but in the capital you can still buy a two-bedroom flat for less than £15,000, although it is likely to be in a rather grim 1970s Soviet apartment block. A two-bedroom house in Vilnius starts at around £20,000, with prices plummeting away from the capital.

Local mortgages

The local mortgage market is way behind that of western Europe and therefore using lenders in your home country is recommended.

Access to and from the UK

There are regular direct flights to the capital, Vilnius, from the UK.

Legal restrictions

None.

Is property a good investment?

All indications are that it is. *The Economist* noted in July 2003 that Lithuania enjoyed the highest growth rate (6.7 per cent) in Europe the year before with booming exports, zero inflation, a rock-steady currency, shrinking (though high) unemployment and a budget surplus. Couple this with its joining the EU, and early investors in property in the country are likely to cash in.

Living in Lithuania

This small country, with a population of 3.6 million, has had an economy lagging way behind most European countries owing to its history as a Soviet republic. The average earnings in 2004 were £2,712 and unemployment officially 10 per cent but unofficially as high as 25 per cent. The cost of living is correspondingly low, with a beer around £1 a pint and an opera ticket under £10. EU nationals are entitled to Lithuanian benefits such as invalidity healthcare although these are low: unemployment benefit ranges from £30 to £60 per month, for example. There are no housing benefits to speak of.

Selling
There is currently no capital gains tax payable.

Inheritance tax
This is dependent on the size of the estate.

Further information
- **Lithuania: t** (00 370)

Estate agents
- **Bristol and Stone; www.bristolandstone.com**.
- **Ober Haus** (Lithuania), **t** 5210 9700; **www.ober-haus.ee**.

Malta

Why retire here?
Just a three-hour flight from London, the central Mediterranean island of Malta (95 square miles) and its smaller sister islands, Gozo (26 sq miles) and Comino (one square mile) have it all. Sandwiched between North Africa and Sicily just 90km (60 miles) away, this haven is half the size of the Isle of Wight boasts long, hot summers of 25–34°C (77–92°F), mild winters of 10–20°C (50–70°F), and has an average 5 or 6hrs of sunshine daily; the country has warm and friendly people, political stability, a low cost of living and very little crime.

Everywhere on the island is less than a 20-minute drive away, which is particularly attractive to Britons used to long journeys and heavy traffic. About 15,000 Britons own properties here.

Because it was a British colony for 150 years (Malta gained its independence in 1969), almost everyone speaks English, although there is also an official Maltese language that retains traces of Arabic. Its culture is an enticing mix of Moorish, British, Spanish, Islamic and French. Malta joined the EU in May 2004.

Downsides
With no natural resources to speak of, Malta's main industry is tourism and there is overdevelopment in many coastal areas. The beaches, dotted with

limestone coves, can't really compare with those in Spain, though the sea is clean, warm and clear and therefore excellent for diving, yachting and water sports. It has no rivers or lakes and few green spaces.

Property types

For such a small island, a wide range of properties is available, from new apartments in holiday complexes to waterside villas and old sprawling farmhouses. Unfortunately, many apartment buildings are not particularly attractively designed.

Where to retire

Properties with a sea view or near the coast are expensive, and the cheapest apartments are generally in touristic areas. Qawra, Buġibba, also Mellieħa and St Paul's Bay in the north, and Marsaskala in the south, have properties that are comparatively cheap. The property market has been boosted of late by a succession of bold development projects, including the huge Portomaso marina development in the parish of St Julian's. Prices at such developments are not cheap, but nevertheless tend to sell quickly.

Gozo, a 25-minute ferry ride from Malta, is in high demand from foreigners, being relatively untouched and smaller, quieter and greener than Malta, which is more commercial, although there are still quiet, untouched villages. There is a far smaller choice of property at even smaller Comino. Two further, tiny islands, Cominotto and Filfla, are uninhabited.

Currency and exchange rate

Maltese liri (Lm); £1 = Lm0.60.

Property prices

At the time of going to press about £50,000 buys a one-bedroom apartment in a holiday complex with a communal pool, while two-bedroom pretty, period town houses start at around £100,000. Houses and villas can easily exceed £700,000, however, and a converted four-bedroom farmhouse with a sizeable garden and pool may cost over £1.5m. Prices in Gozo are generally lower.

Now that Malta has joined the European Union there will almost certainly be an increase in demand for property. Stamp duty was recently slashed from 17 per cent to 5 per cent. Maltese prices are flexible, so its best to bargain hard.

Local mortgages

These are available but terms tend to be lower (over 10–20 years, commonly), rates are higher and the loan to value ratio is lower than with foreign lenders.

Access to and from the UK

Air Malta, British Airways and other major international airlines operate regular scheduled flights between Malta and most major European cities. There are several flights daily from London alone. Cheap charter flights start at about £60 return.

Legal restrictions

It is relatively easy for foreign national to buy in Malta. Even so, there are some restrictions. The Maltese government has set minimum values that foreign buyers can spend on a property. The requirement that overseas buyers obtain permission from the Finance Ministry to buy was waived after EU membership in May 2004 but foreign buyers must still spend a minimum of Lm30,000 (£47,500) on a flat or maisonette (including renovation costs) and Lm50,000 for a house or villa. Properties in need of renovation or in shell form can be purchased for lower amounts as long as the addition of the estimated cost of completion works plus the purchase price reach the Lm30,000/Lm50,000 thresholds. There are plenty of homes available at these prices, and properties in Malta tend to be spacious compared with other Mediterranean destinations.

The buying process

On acceptance of the buyer's offer, both vendor and purchaser sign a binding agreement (*convenium*) and the purchaser pays a non-refundable 10 per cent deposit, lodged with the agent or notary public. The agreement is usually valid for around three months. The notary public makes the various legal checks, and, once these are satisfactory, a deed of sale is drawn up and the balance for the property is paid to the vendor.

A property bought by a foreign national should in theory be sold only to a Maltese, although this law is usually relaxed. Non-Maltese buyers can usually only own one property in Malta, although there are exceptions in special designated areas.

Costs of buying

Fees incurred on buying include registration and search fees (£160 approximately), Ministry of Finance fees (£160 approximately), 1 per cent notary fees and a 5 per cent duty on documents. All property is sold freehold.

Is property a good investment?

Property has proved to be a good investment, and there has been a steady 8–12 per cent increase in value each year since 1969. But in 2002 and 2003 average property values have increased by around 20 per cent, and annual increases of half that in the next couple of years are not unreasonable to expect. Increased interest from Brits looking for an alternative to southern Spain and anticipation of Malta joining the EU in 2004 have contributed to this rise.

Living in Malta

The cost of living is low and health and education standards are particularly high. There are reciprocal health agreements with the UK. There are no annual rates or property taxes. The roads need updating and there are occasional water shortages.

Taxation for residents is low (currently a flat rate of 15 per cent) and there are tax agreements with most western European countries plus Canada and Australia, enabling Maltese residents to either obtain exemptions from tax on certain income originating abroad, or obtain tax relief in Malta. There is no tax on worldwide income or assets.

Malta offers non-Maltese persons of any nationality who can demonstrate an income in excess of US$25,000 per annum the possibility of acquiring permanent residence status. A permanent residence permit entitles the holder to reside permanently in Malta, but there is no requirement to spend any particular time actually residing there.

Selling

When you come to resell, there's always a strong a local market. The population is only around 375,000 but there are over 12,000 property transactions per year, which is very healthy.

Capital gains tax of 7 per cent is charged on the sale of property that has not been the owner's place of residence for the previous three years.

Inheritance tax

Malta abolished inheritance tax in 1992 but there is a 5 per cent transfer tax on property inherited in Malta. Note that if a spouse is the recipient, the transfer tax is levied on half of the value of the property.

Further information

- **Malta: t (00 356)**
- **Air Malta**, 36–8 Piccadilly, London W1V 0PQ, UK, **t** (020) 7292 4949.
- **Association of Estate Agents in Malta**, PO Box 18, Sliema, Malta, **t** 21 343370; **www.maltaestateagents.com**.
- **Bank of Valletta**, BOV Centre, High Street, Sliema SLM 16, Malta, **t** 21 333084. Malta's leading bank.

- **HSBC Bank Malta,** Hexagon House, Spencer Gardens, Blata l-Bajda, HMR 12, Malta; **www.hsbcmalta.com**.
- **Malta Tourist Office,** 36–38 Piccadilly, London W1V 0PP, UK, t (020) 7292 4900; **www.visitmalta.com**.
- **Maltese Consulate,** 2017 Connecticut Avenue, NW, Washington DC 20008, USA, t (202) 462 3611.
- **Maltese High Commission,** 36–38 Piccadilly, London W1V 0PP, UK, t (020) 7292 4800.
- **Ministry of Finance,** St Calcedonius Square, Floriana CMR 02, Malta, t 21 236306.

Estate agents

All are based in Malta.

- **Dhalia Group,** t 21 490681; **www.dhalia.com**. Malta's largest estate agency.
- **Formosa Real Estate Agency,** t 21 323926; **www.mol.net.mt/formosa**.
- **Frank Salt Real Estate,** t 21 353696; **www.franksalt.com.mt**. Perhaps Malta's most established estate agent, with eight branches and guides to buying on the islands.
- **Sara Grech,** t 21 331354; **www.saragrech.com.mt**. Specialises in classic rural houses throughout the island.
- **www.maltarealestateindex.com**: the website of the Malta and Gozo Real Estate Index, with a list of property for sale and to let direct from owners.

Mexico

Why retire here?

As well as the low cost of living, low cost of property prices and easy access to the USA, the climate is very attractive for a UK resident. Winter on Mexico's Pacific coast is like the Mediterranean in the height of summer and there is year-round sunshine. There is an active expatriate community in Mexico, and some will appreciate the Mayan and traditional Spanish culture. Beach enthusiasts can choose between the Pacific and the Caribbean coasts.

Downsides

Apart from the distance from the UK for retirees wishing to keep up strong links, coastal Mexico can be very, very hot and humid during the summer. Mexico City suffers from major pollution problems.

Property types

A great range is available, whether you want the Old World style of a colonial village or a property at one of the new developments of apartments and villas along the coast. Rural inland period properties in need of renovation and going for a song are relatively easy to pick up.

Where to retire

Retirees would be well advised to avoid Mexico City, considering its congestion and pollution problems. There are lots of pleasant, small towns along the Pacific coast, such as San Blas and Boco de Tomatlan, although there are also areas overrun with tourism.

The Yucatan Peninsula – the Mexican Caribbean – is pricier and is overdeveloped in many places, but there are good beaches, Mayan ruins and plenty of leisure distractions. If touristy resorts like Cancun don't appeal, opt for a quieter town like Valladolid or Mérida.

Among the rainforest-covered mountains of the west Pacific coast is Puerto Vallarta, a resort in Bandaras Bay being busily developed and attracting the interest of European buyers especially. There are several good golf courses here. Particularly towards the northern part of the Bay, the Punta de Mita area is attracting a great amount of interest.

There are substantial expatriate communities in the colonial heartland, which contains numerous historic colonial towns and enjoys a pleasant climate. Guadalajara is one city in this area that is very popular with retirees, being more tranquil than Mexico and boasting historic buildings, pleasant parks and, outside the centre, affordable properties. To the south is Ajijic and Lake Chapala, cheaper and quieter and very popular with American retirees.

The colonial heartland also includes the very pleasant historically protected town of San Miguel de Allende, which is much favoured by artists, having lots of galleries. Housing is cheaper still at the pleasant university town of Guanajuato.

Currency and exchange rate

Mexican pesos; £1 = 20.85 Mexican pesos.

Property prices

Prices are gradually rising but are still cheaper than in Europe and the USA. The cheapest properties are in the undeveloped inland towns and villages.

At Puerto Vallarta, a one-bed waterside apartment with shared pool costs about £50,000 while a three-bedroom house with pool is around £90,000. The gated Punta Mita resort here has villas costing £1 million plus.

Local mortgages

Devaluation of the currency in 1994 has resulted in very expensive local mortgages, so obtaining a loan in the UK is likely to be preferable.

Access to and from the UK

British Airways flies to Mexico City and Air 2000 runs a charter service to Puerto Vallarta. Domestic carriers Mexicana and Aeromexico connect all major cities in the country itself.

Legal restrictions

Foreigners buying property in the restricted zone, which is generally coastal and border areas (the area 100km from the border and 50km from the coast), are required to apply for a permit from the Department of Foreign Relations. This permits them to own property via a bank trust (*fideicomiso*). The trust is administered and held by a bank and costs around £300 to set up; there is also a small commission based up on the value of the property and an annual charge, typically around £300. Alternatively, you can buy through a Mexican corporation.

The buying process

No government licence laws regulate estate agents in Mexico. As anybody can offer properties for sale, caution should be taken to choose an established and reputable company. You can do this by checking with local chamber of commerce associations or a prominent law firm.

Most estate agents can sell each others' properties if they are members of the *Asociación Mexicana de Profesionales Inmobiliarios* (AMPI, the Mexican Board of Estate Agents), the only national professional real estate organisation in Mexico. A public notary, a government-appointed lawyer, oversees the buying process, executing searches, preparing the deed, carrying out the property transfer and recording the deed with the public property registry.

Especially in the areas more popular with expatriates, contracts with estate agents are usually provided in both Spanish and English and many agents are bilingual. However, all documents signed before the notary are in Spanish.

The buying process starts with the buyer offering a written purchase offer. When this is accepted by the seller, a purchase–sale agreement (promissory contract) is signed by both parties. Usually a deposit is paid at this time by the buyer. In some areas, it is usual for the buyer to pay an advance payment of 10 to 30 per cent of the total price on signing the purchase–sale agreement. The agreement should contain a penalty clause covering a breach of contract by either of the parties.

When the *escritura* or official deed is signed, which needs to be certified by a public notary, the balance is paid and property ownership is transferred. The whole process should not take more than 45 days.

Costs of buying

Usually the buyer pays the property transfer of acquisition tax and the other closing costs, including the notary's fees and expenses, while the seller pays the capital gains tax and the estate agent's commission. Real estate transfer tax ranges from around 1 to 4 per cent of the tax appraisal value, which is usually less than the sales value. The estate agent's commission is generally in the region of 6 to 8 per cent of the sale value and is often higher in resort areas. Other costs generally work out at around 5 to 7 per cent of the purchase price.

Is property a good investment?

Coastal properties especially have been appreciating well in recent years by as much as 35 per cent in two years in some areas.

Living in Mexico

Most (89 per cent) of the population is Roman Catholic. It is possible to get by without speaking Spanish, especially in the areas popular with expatriates. Away from certain tourist areas like Cancun, the tap water is often unsuitable for drinking and drinking water should be bought bottled or purified.

The crime rate, outside Mexico City and tourist areas, is considerably lower than in the USA. Mexico generally has a pleasant climate with warm seas and temperatures in excess of 26.6°C (80°F) common even in the height of winter.

Retirees who don't intend to work can visit the country for six months on a tourist card, an FMT, which is easily renewable. Britons require an FMT immigration document to live full-time in Mexico. Proof of a monthly income of around $1,000 plus an extra $500 or so per extra family member is required for this visa.

Property taxes of about 0.004 to 0.08 per cent of the value of the property are payable annually. Pensions from abroad are exempt from Mexican income tax and non-residents (those living for more than 183 days per year in another country) pay tax only on income derived in Mexico. Mexican state health insurance is inexpensive but private heath cover to supplement it is advised.

Mexico is very laid-back and relaxed but the downside to this is that something as straightforward as having a telephone installed can involve a very long wait and services like mail delivery can be very inefficient.

Selling

The gain from the sale of a property is treated as income and charged at a tax rate of up to 35 per cent of the rise in value of the property.

The costs and expenses that can be deducted from the amount for which the property is officially sold are the original land cost and the depreciated construction cost, based on the number of years the property was held. This is adjusted for inflation. Any additions, modifications and improvements made to the property are deductible, but not maintenance costs; plus property selling costs. There is no capital gains tax in Mexico if there is conclusive proof that the seller has used the property as a primary residence.

Inheritance tax

There is no inheritance tax in Mexico.

Further information

- **Mexico: t** (00 52)
- **Consulate General of Mexico**, 27 East 39th Street, New York, NY 10016, USA, **t** (212) 217 6400.
- **Mexican Embassy**, 911 Pennsylvania Avenue NW, Washington DC 20006, USA, **t** (202) 728 1600.
- **Mexico Tourist Office**, 60–61 Trafalgar Square, London WC2N 5DS, UK, **t** (020) 7839 3177; **www.mexico-travel.com**.
- **Mexico Tourist Office**, 450 Park Avenue, New York, NY 10022, USA, **t** (212) 755 7261.
- **www.mexconnect.com, www.virtualmex.com** and **www.go2mexico.com** may be of interest and include information on retirement.

Estate agents

All estate agents listed here are based in Mexico.

- **Century 21, t** 322 222 3054; **www.century21vallarta.com**.
- **Coldwell Banker La Costa, t** 322 223 0055; **www.cblacosta.com**.
- **La Punta Realty, t** 329 291 6420; **www.puntarealty.com**.

Montenegro

Why retire here?

Although it was once the playground of superstars like Richard Burton, Elizabeth Taylor, Princess Margaret and Sophia Loren, properties are very afford-able in this small country on the Adriatic coast of the Balkan peninsula. It is situated on the southern border of Croatia and neighboured by Bosnia, Serbia and Albania. Formerly part of Yugoslavia, it offers a wealth of stunning scenery, history and culture. Add the unspoilt beauty and increasing speculation that Montenegro may join the EU (a referendum is planned for 2006), and interest is mushrooming. The adventurous will enjoy diving, white-water rafting, climbing, and paragliding as well as skiing in winter.

Downsides

Montenegro has in the past worked towards acting as one country with Serbia. Now the country is split by those who want it to separate from Serbia and those who don't. If it moves towards independence, there is no guarantee that if, or when, the change happens it will be straightforward or peaceful.

Buying land is a complicated business and not recommended at present. Also, the land registry is not as stringent as in the UK and there is a possibility of issues with title.

Property types

Beautiful old stone houses overlooking freshwater lakes or the dramatic Adriatic coastline and farmsteads in the rolling green hills are still widely available at comparatively low prices. There is also a good choice of properties suitable for businesses such as restaurants, bars and hotels.

Where to retire

Around the northern coast prices are higher and the area more popular than the wilder, more unspoilt south.

Currency and exchange rate

Euro (€); £1 = €1.50. The republic of Montenegro severed its economy from Serbia during the Milosevic era and continues to maintain its own central bank, uses the euro instead of the Yugoslav dinar as official currency, collects customs tariffs, and manages its own budget.

Property prices

Prices are generally a third cheaper than in Croatia, and less than that in some areas inland. Pretty properties abound, especially away from the coast. Prices are likely to rise steadily in the next few years.

Houses start at under £20,000, and a very sizeable house could be obtained for less than £60,000. Examples in 2004 include a five-bedroom renovated stone house with glorious sea views near Sveti Stefan for £125,000 and a 10-room hotel with restaurant near Tivat for £400,000. Properties on the coast are available, unlike in many countries, but are highly valued by the locals and therefore the prices can be quite high.

Local mortgages

The local lending market is restricted and buyers would be better off raising funds in their home country.

Access to and from the UK

Montenegro has two airports, Tivat and Podgorica, but currently direct flights from the UK are limited but available during the summer. British Airways and other airlines have regular flights to Dubrovnik in Croatia, 16km over the border.

Various coach companies offer services from neighbouring countries to Montenegro and these offer a very cheap option; trains operate between Bar and Belgrade.

Legal restrictions

While there is no problem for EU citizens to buy and own a property in Montenegro, land is rather more complicated. It is possible for foreigners to buy land, but it is owned on a lease of 99 years, not sold freehold. Also it is not possible for foreigners to register land in their own name, which could have a number of implications. The position about this is unclear currently, and there are various opinions on the matter, so on the whole at present it is best to steer clear of buying land.

The buying process

This is straightforward and visas, taxes, residency and general bureaucracy issues have been simplified as much as possible by the Montenegran government, eager to encourage foreign investment. But because the land registry system is less stringent than in many countries, it is important to engage a good solicitor listed at the bar to safeguard your interests as much as possible.

The system is rather similar to the notary system in France, where the lawyer initially draws up a legally binding contract for the buyer and seller to sign. Initially a 10 per cent deposit is usually lodged. Properties are often snapped up quickly and long deliberation is likely to result in your losing the property to someone who is prepared to put down an immediate payment.

Usually the same lawyer will act for both parties. At this point, the seller and buyer will sign a pre-contract stipulating the details of the property and the terms under which payment is to be made and the sale completed. Usually this contract will contain a safeguard clause saying that, should the seller pull out, he or she will have to repay the buyer double the deposit, while the buyer will simply lose the deposit if they break the agreement.

Following the terms of the pre-contract, the final contract is then drawn up and final payment made. At this point, the papers are stamped by the court and then the property is re-registered in the new owner's name with the land registry office. The whole process can be quite quick and is usually completed within two months.

Note that properties have often been passed down through families and can have multiple owners. Agreement on a sale is needed from all the owners before it can proceed.

Costs of buying

The cost of buying averages around 10 per cent of the purchase price. More specifically, tax on resales is usually 2 per cent. However, on new builds it is considerably higher and is worked out at a rate of 17 per cent on the difference between the cost of the building and the actual sale price. Lawyer's fees average around 2 per cent of the sale price.

Is property a good investment?

Property is very keenly priced at present, and possible accession to the European Union and an increasingly likely split from neighbouring Serbia will undoubtedly result in prices rising rapidly. Tourism is likely to increase greatly, soon, which would make investment even more sound. Property is a mid- to long-term investment, so may suit retirees better than investors for profit.

Living in Montenegro

Although the Balkan conflict of the early 1990s adversely affected Montenegro's economy a great deal, it was largely unaffected by other aspects of the conflict. The cost of living is comparatively low.

The coast enjoys a Mediterranean climate with warm summers and mild winters. Each year there are around 240 days of sunshine and 180 days when water temperatures reach 21–27°C. Skiing, hunting and fishing are all popular pastimes. Part of Montenegro's charm is its undeveloped nature compared with many of its European neighbours. For example, credit cards are currently generally only accepted in major hotels, shops, restaurants and travel agents.

Access within the country can be difficult. Main roads are acceptable, but smaller ones can be rough and there are many twisting mountain routes. Taxis are often expensive and local buses tend not to be reliable. For quick, easy access from the airport at Tivat to the north of the country, a car ferry service operates from Kamenari to Lepetane across the Strait of Verige.

An unlimited amount of currency can be brought into the country, but there are limits on how many euros may be taken out.

Medical care is of a generally high standard, although foreigners do not have access to the domestic national health system and private health insurance should be taken out.

There is a very minimal annual tax on property of €100–200 per year. There is a double taxation agreement with the UK.

Selling

Capital gains tax is payable at a varying rate.

Inheritance tax

This is dependent on the size of the estate and relationship of the deceased and the beneficiary.

Further information

- **Montenegro: t** (00 381)
- **Montenegro Living** (UK), **t** (020) 8407 0740; **www.montenegro-living.com.**

Morocco

Why retire here?

Morocco has a great climate, a truly exotic location, and value for money. Marrakech is the most sought-after location, where you can buy traditional houses in a beautiful, unspoilt old city.

Downsides

The Moroccan conveyancing system isn't for the faint-hearted, and finding the original title deeds is often a problem. The bureaucracy can take over two years to get through.

Restoration costs can be very high and dealing with builders problematic. If there is no vehicular access to the property, which is often the case in areas such as the Marrakech *medina*, everything will have to be brought in by donkey. Renovated properties may mask a multitude of building flaws and therefore it is actually an advantage to buy a site full of rubble; where the plaster comes away in your hands, you know exactly what you are getting.

Property types

The market that interests foreign retirees generally concerns two types of property, in the case of Marrakech both found in the Old Town, the *medina*. The first is a *riad*, from the Arabic word meaning 'garden', but which here means a traditional home of semi-open rooms built around a central courtyard-cum-garden with a fountain. The most expensive, restored examples have features like chandeliers, marble and ornate tiling. They have an atmosphere that you may find combined in a mosque, Bedouin tent and Roman villa. The size of the courtyard is important: too small and it could be dark and cold. The second type of property is known as a *dar*, a similar house without the central garden.

Where to retire

The exotic *medina* located within the walls of the glamorous city of Marrakech, is where many foreign buyers head, following in the footsteps of such illustrious *riad*-owners as Jean-Paul Gaultier and Yves Saint- Laurent. Outside high summer, the city can get rather cold.

If Marrakech's *medina* is too claustrophobic and chaotic, another option is a neighbourhood of Marrakech's modern section of the city, such as Guéliz or Hivernage, which has a high proportion of French expatriates as well as upmarket restaurants, cafés and shops. The purpose-built resort of La Palmerie outside the city, on the other hand, which covers nearly 50 square miles and has upmarket holiday homes and golf courses, will suit lovers of all mod-cons but has rather less character than the medina.

Tangier's mild, tropical climate (about 28°C in July compared with a typical 37°C in Marrakech) and elegant traditional buildings make it another popular spot for foreign buyers. The town's bohemian spirit in the past attracted artists and writer like Joe Orton and Francis Bacon.

Currency and exchange rate

Dirham; £1 = 16.61 dirhams.

Property prices

Prices have soared in recent years: in 1990, you could buy a good Marrakech *riad* for £1,000. Now those in disrepair start at around £50,000 (count on at least the same again for restoration) and those that have been well-restored, have a good location and large courtyard and are accessible by car can easily fetch over £300,000. A five-bedroom villa with swimming pool at La Palmerie would cost over £750,000.

For a *dar* with two or three bedrooms and a living room in need of restoration, the starting price is around £40,000. This includes two or three bedrooms and a living room. Once renovated, the price typically rises to over £130,000. In Tangier, £160,000 would buy you a six-bed villa near the centre.

Local mortgages

For simplicity, mortgages should be taken out in the UK.

Access to and from the UK

Royal Air Maroc, Air France and British Airways fly to Marrakech.

Legal restrictions

Although in towns there are no restrictions imposed on foreigners buying, in the countryside it can get more complicated, as it may be necessary to obtain a certificate (*vocation non agricole*) allowing the purchaser to convert agricultural land into land for a dwelling, a process that can take many months with no guarantee of success.

The buying process

The buying process can be lengthy, over two years in some cases, not helped by the inheritance laws in Morocco which state that each person with a claim to a property must give the go-ahead for a sale. It is therefore very important to engage a reputable, experienced local legal representative to make all the checks. Some properties do not have title deeds, and getting hold of the paperwork can take many months.

It is vital to ensure that any building works have been carried out to an adequate standard. You need to see photographs of the building works and any bills from builders, architects, engineers and suchlike. As well as your own property, it is important to ensure that any surrounding buildings are secure: you don't want your neighbour's wall crashing down on yours.

A *notaire*, a local authority official, oversees the sale on behalf of both the buyer and seller. He establishes that the deeds are in order, that those with a claim to the property agree to the sale, and that all outstanding accounts are settled. It is a good idea to employ a translator as all dealings are in Arabic.

When the deposit is paid, which is generally 10 per cent but could be as high as 50 per cent, a completion date is agreed. Be prepared for unusual demands, such as a request from the vendor that he stay in the property for several months after the sale while he builds his new home...

Payment for the property is more difficult than normal, too. Moroccan currency cannot be taken out of the country, and all money taken into the country has to be banked and documented. Without this proof that the money has been legitimately imported into the country, you cannot change the money back again when you wish to sell.

Costs of buying

Estate agents typically charge around 3 per cent commission. There is a 5 per cent property tax payable on completion, and conveyancing costs average around 3 per cent.

Is property a good investment?

Yes, as long as there is no question over ownership and steps have been taken to ensure that the restoration has been carried out to an acceptable standard.

Living in Morocco

The average temperature in summer is 35°C and in winter 22°C. The cost of living is low, and you have to allow extra time for most things. Shopping in the tiny shops, for example, can involve a good deal of haggling and couldn't be more unlike a trip to Tesco.

Foreigners will need to take out private health insurance.

Selling

Capital gains tax is payable on profit made from the selling of a property. It is quite common, although illegal, for sellers to under-declare the value of their property to avoid full payment of this tax.

Inheritance tax

This varies according to the size of estate and relationship of the beneficiary to the deceased.

Further information

- **Morocco: t** (00 212)
- **Moroccan Embassy,** 49 Queen's Gate Gardens, London SW7 5NE, UK, **t** (020) 7581 5001; **www.morocco.embassyhomepage.com.**

Estate agents

All estate agents listed here are based in Morocco.

- **Arcade Immo Services, t** 63 03 33 37; **www.arcadeimmoservices.com.**
- **Atlas Immobilier, t** 44 38 62 75; **www.atlasimmobilier.com.**
- **Kantari, t** 44 44 00 22; **www.kantari.com.**
- **Marrakech Riads, t** 44 42 64 63; **www.marrakech-riads.net.**
- **Moroccan Properties, t** 39 33 32 86; **www.moroccan-properties.com.**
- **La Palmeraie Golf Palace and Resort, t** 44 30 19 59; **www.pgp.co.ma.**

New Zealand

Why retire here?

Brits are increasingly being lured by the enviable lifestyle and comparatively low property prices and low cost of living in New Zealand, and currently more than 4,000 are moving there annually.

As well as its great climate, relaxed way of life, charming towns and vibrant cities, friendly people and relaxed lifestyle, New Zealand has a stunningly unspoilt and diverse geography, with mountains, forests, glaciers, geysers, lakes, rivers and volcanoes. In addition to the lack of a language barrier and the glorious beaches, many ideal for surfing, the southern island has an added attraction of an especially established winter skiing industry.

Downsides

Obviously the sheer distance from the UK is a serious disadvantage if you wanted to make frequent visits to the UK, or hope to be visited often by friends and family.

Property types

These vary from city apartments, often called 'units', and town houses, to wooden and brick-built detached houses on generous plots outside the cities.

Where to retire

Wellington, the compact capital, is surrounded by wooded hills and a harbour. Around an hour's drive away is the Kapati coast to the north, a popular beach and mountain location for retirees.

Auckland, the biggest city, is full of restaurants, galleries and museums, and has coastline both north and south of the city, with good beaches. Properties generally cost most here, but are reasonable when compared with many other cities. Christchurch, on the east coast of the South Island, is another pleasant city that retains a peaceful atmosphere and contains attractive 19th-century buildings. Other popular areas for retirement homes include the Coromandel Peninsular in the far north of the North Island and the northern Marlborough region in the South Island.

Currency and exchange rate

New Zealand dollar (NZ$); £1 = NZ$2.90.

Property prices

Property prices have been rising steadily for over five years and generally rose by 10 per cent in 2002. But in some areas, such as Auckland, Christchurch, Nelson, Queenstown, Wanaka and Wellington, prices have surged upwards in the last couple of years. The average home in 2003 cost £71,000 compared with £59,000 in 1998. For twice that you can get a very high-quality property here.

Two- and three-bedroom houses in the suburbs and rural areas generally range from about £35,000 to £85,000, with central city apartments typically starting at the higher end of this scale. A good-sized house in Auckland costs £200,000 or more, while a 100-year-old four-bedroom villa in Wellington near the centre is about £250,000. Away from the cities, you can get amazing properties for the money. For example, one British buyer recently bought a large country house with 10 acres of orchards at Gisborne, a small seaside town in a wine region, for just £90,000.

Local mortgages

A wide range of mortgages are available, usually for up to 80 per cent of value and for 25 years duration. On the downside, there is a set-up fee charged by banks of 1 per cent of the amount borrowed and rates are high compared with the UK, currently over 7.5 per cent. Some local banks, such as Westpac, have recently introduced mortgages geared to foreigners.

Access to and from the UK

Several airlines offer good-value flights to the three international airports, Auckland, Christchurch and Wellington, with a choice of stopovers.

Legal restrictions

Unless permanent residence has been obtained, foreign buyers are required to get permission to buy from the land value tribunal or district land registrar if the land being purchased exceeds one acre. Foreign buyers may be restricted from buying if the property costs more than NZ$10 million (£3.5 million) or is in a sensitive area such as on the beach or on conservation land.

The buying process

Buying is generally straightforward and quick, and deals are often completed within one month. Gazumping is illegal. On the signing of an initial contract to buy, which is legally binding, a deposit (typically 10 per cent) is payable. It is a good idea to include a clause stating that the deposit is refundable if there is any question of the title to the property or if the land is found to be liable to compulsory purchase by the government.

It is prudent for buyers to commission an engineer or builder's report to check the condition of the property. Before completion, the buyer's lawyer checks the title of the property before obtaining a land information memorandum.

Costs of buying

There is a land transfer registration fee of NZ$150 (around £50) and conveyancing costs average £350–700.

Is property a good investment?

As New Zealand is a stable country, the property market is generally reliable and safe.

Living in New Zealand

Made up of two main islands (North and South islands) and numerous outlying ones, three-quarters of the country is hilly or mountainous and half forested. Bigger in area than the UK, yet with just one-fifteenth of the UK's population, the country is green, warm and friendly. New Zealand has one of the lowest crime rates in the world.

The temperate oceanic climate (and subtropical climate in the extreme north) offer hot summers and cold winters. The west coast can receive very heavy rainfall, while the east coasts escape with very little. The main cities, Wellington especially, are affected by strong winds at times.

About three-quarters of the country is of European descent and most migrants today are still from Europe. Indigenous Maoris account for 10 per cent of the four million population. Culturally, though, New Zealand increasingly leans towards its Polynesian roots and is less and less like a bygone Britain, as many people assume. English and Maori are the two official languages.

New Zealand enjoys political stability, a comparatively low cost of living, a very high standard of living – higher than neighbouring Australia. It has a good national health system and reciprocal health agreements covering visitors of other countries including the UK. Note that your UK state pension will be frozen on the day you leave the UK if you go to live in New Zealand, and will not rise with inflation (*see* pp.22–3).

British subjects can stay for three months with a valid passport, and six months on a visitor's visa, with an option to extend this to nine months. To stay for longer can be difficult unless you fulfil certain conditions. You can apply for a family visa if you marry or live with an existing New Zealand citizen or have immediate family members with citizenship or residency. If your partner is a New Zealander, you must prove that your relationship is genuine and has lasted for at least a year, demonstrating this through such things as a joint bank account and other examples of shared commitments.

Income tax ranges from 15 per cent to 33 per cent, and there are residential rates and extra charges for such things as water and refuse collection that average around £350 to £700 for most homes.

Selling

There is no capital gains tax, not even on second homes.

Inheritance tax

There is no inheritance tax.

Further information

- **New Zealand: t** (00 64)

- **Department of Land Information**, PO Box 5501, 160 Lambton Quay, Wellington, New Zealand, **t** 4 473 5022; **www.linz.govt.nz**.

- **New Zealand Consulate General** (USA), **t** (310) 207 1605.

- **New Zealand Embassy**, 37 Observatory Circle, NW, Washington, DC 20008, USA, **t** (202) 328 4800; **www.nzemb.org**.

- **New Zealand High Commission**, New Zealand House, Haymarket, London SW1Y 4TQ, UK, **t** (020) 7930 8422; **www.nzembassy.com**.

- **New Zealand Immigration Service; www.immigration.govt.nz**: government website with details about immigration.

- **New Zealand Tourist Board**, New Zealand House, Haymarket, London SW1Y 4TQ, UK, **t** (020) 7930 0360; **www.newzealandtourism.com**.

- **Real Estate Agents Licensing Board**, PO Box 1247, Wellington, New Zealand, **t** 4 520 6949.

- **Retirement Villages Association; www.retirementvillages.org.nz**: lists retirement accommodation in the country.

- **Westpac Bank; www.westpac.co.nz**.

Emigration advisers

- **Amber Collins** (UK), **t** (020) 7371 0213; **www.ambercollins.com**

- **Emigration Group** (UK), **t** (01244) 321414; **www.emigration.uk.com**.

- **Four Corners** (UK), **t** 0845 841 9453; **www.4-corners.com**.

- **Global Visas** (UK), **t** (020) 7009 3800; **www.globalvisas.com**.

- **Migration Bureau** (UK), **t** (020) 8874 2844.

- **Migration Expert; www.migrationexpert.com**.

- **Overseas Emigration Visas; www.overseas-emigration.co.uk**.
- **Workpermit.com** (UK), **t** (020) 7842 0800; **www.workpermit.com**.

Estate agents

Are all based in New Zealand.

- **Bayleys, t** 9 309 6020; **www.bayleys.co.nz**.
- **Harcourts Real Estate, t** 3 441 0777; **www.harcourts.co.nz**. Estate agency group with branches nationwide.
- **Premium Real Estate, t** 9 486 1727; **www.premium-realestate.co.nz**.

Poland

Why retire here?

Poland boasts large tracts of beautiful, unspoilt countryside and property prices that are exceptionally low because of low owner-occupation and years of a problematic economy. Yet EU membership will change this rapidly, with large-scale EU investment improving infrastructure and mortgage finance becoming increasingly available to locals, causing prices to shoot up. Early investors will be able to rent or sell at a good profit.

Downsides

Although EU membership has made things more secure for investors, the necessary legal frameworks and lending services are not as stringent as they could be. Furthermore, the World Bank recently rated real estate as one of the most corrupt areas of Poland's economy. On top of that, reliable estate agents are few and far between.

Property types

These range from anything between city apartments to sprawling rural detached villas.

Where to retire

Although property in the capital, Warsaw, is very good value by western European standards, the city is regarded as ugly and overpriced; instead buyers should consider Krakow in the south, which is a significantly more attractive city. Property in Krakow is around half to three-quarters of the price of property in Warsaw. As soon as you leave the cities, beautiful properties in need of reno-vation are available in spellbinding countryside for unbelievably low prices.

Currency and exchange rate

Zlotych; £1 = 6.94 Zlotych.

Property prices

A large detached mansion in Warsaw would set you back £600,000 or so, while a two-bed apartment in the centre would typically be under £100,000, and studio flats in the centre are still available for less than £25,000. Annual capital growth in the city is currently running at about 25 per cent. Rural houses are widely available for less than £60,000 and on the outskirts of Warsaw for around £100,000. In Krakow, prices are highest in the Old Town centre averaging around £35,000 for a small flat, rising to over £120,000 for a more spacious, well-preserved historic apartment. To give an idea of the low level of prices, land in the lakeside northern Suwalki region currently costs around £12 a square metre compared with over £100 a square metre across the border in Germany.

Local mortgages

Bear in mind that, like most eastern European countries, there is no mortgage code of conduct or consumer credit act, and it is usually preferable to use a lender in your home country.

Access to and from the UK

There are regular direct scheduled and budget flights to Krakow and Warsaw from the UK.

Legal restrictions

Foreigners who are not EU citizens are required to obtain a permit from the Ministry for Internal Affairs in order to purchase a property in Poland. EU citizens must obtain a permit if the property is to be a second home.

The buying process

The buying process is overseen by a notary representing both parties. After the buyers' legal representative has checked that the deeds are in order and there are no encumbrances affecting the property, the notary oversees the signing of the contract by buyer and seller.

Costs of buying

Costs include stamp duty at 2 per cent and a nominal permit fee. Notarial fees are determined by the Ministry of Justice and vary from 0.25 per cent plus PLN (Zlotych) 5,800 for properties with a value of over PLN 1 million to 3 per cent plus

PLN 200 for properties up to PLN 15,000. The above fees are subject to 22 per cent VAT. The cost of land registration varies depending on the transaction, and the estate agent's fee is typically 1 to 2 per cent, usually paid by the seller.

Is property a good investment?

Poland's accession to the European Union, coupled with its exceptionally low property prices, mean that early investors are set to make substantial capital gains as prices are likely to rise significantly in the next few years.

Living in Poland

Most foreign residents of Poland supplement the state healthcare system with private medical insurance.

Selling

Capital gains are usually added to the regular income of an individual and based on their income tax rate. If a property is sold at least five years after it has been bought, capital gain is exempt from tax.

Inheritance tax

The rate is progressive, based on the relationship between donor and recipient.

Further information

- **Poland: t** (00 48)
- **Polish Real Estate Federation** (Poland), **t** 22 825 39 56; **www.pref.org.pl**.
- **Polish Tourist Office**, 310–312 Regent Street, London W1, UK, **t** (020) 7580 6688; **www.visitpoland.org**.

Estate agents

- **Ober Haus** (Poland), **t** 22 829 12 12; **www.ober-haus.ee**.
- **www.viviun.com** and **www.immobel.com**: Polish property listings.

Portugal

Why retire here?

Portugal has a splendid temperate climate with plenty of sun similar to Spain, but without the overdevelopment seen so much on the Spanish coast. It boasts a relaxed pace of life, lots of championship-standard golf courses, rich Moorish and Roman history and more than 800km (500 miles) of Atlantic coastline. As well as superb sandy beaches, Portugal has vast forests, charming mountain villages, vast hilly areas and much grassland.

Downsides

Property prices are generally notably higher than in Spain, while some areas, such as parts of the Algarve, are overdeveloped and the standard of driving leaves much to be desired. Non-linguists may baulk at the language.

Property types

Property types vary from well-constructed but pricey new-builds along the coast to crumbling cottages and farmhouses in the rural areas inland.

Where to retire

The Algarve, with its great climate and dramatic coastline, is where the majority of foreign buyers head. Stretching from the south Spanish coast to Cape St Vincent, it has one of the best all-round climates in Europe, with mild winters and hot summers cooled by Atlantic breezes, although April often brings lots of rain. The most popular area extends from Faro to Lagos.

For many years, wealthy foreign buyers have flocked to the neatly manicured luxury golfing estates here. Celebrity home owners here include Cliff Richard, Michael Owen, Alan Shearer, David Seaman, Chris Evans, Judith Chalmers and Annie Lennox.

With the Atlantic to the south and west, the Guadiana River to the east and Caldeirão and Monchique mountain ranges to the north, the Algarve has a character distinct from elsewhere in the country. Luxury leisure resorts are booming and the most popular new developments are within a 45-minute drive west of Faro Airport on the new motorway that opened in 2003. The region east of Faro boasts numerous unspoilt fishing villages.

Although the Algarve is the traditional area targeted by retirement home owners in Portugal, its location in the south of the country makes it a long, uncomfortable journey if anyone wishes to visit you by car. Parts of it are marred by overdevelopment (for example, around Albufeira, Vilamoura and Quarteira), although a 1993 planning law has put a stop to this.

Focus your sights northwards for a host of possibilities. The Portsmouth or Plymouth ferries to the Spanish ports of Bilbao and Santander make it a manageable drive to northern Portugal. The Portuguese consider the Minho, the province north of Porto, to be one of the country's most attractive regions, and it boasts unspoilt coastline, wooded hills, river valleys and pretty villages untouched by modernity. Pressing on a bit further, the Beira Litoral in the centre of the country, dominated by the historic city of Coimbra, is little more than half a day's drive from the north Spanish ports. Rich in relatively inexpensive old farmhouses and cottages, again the area is peaceful and unspoilt.

On the coast west of the cosmopolitan capital city, Lisbon, are Cascais, Sintra and Estoril, which are popular with foreign buyers. Not only are new homes popular, but cheaper, older properties with character are increasingly being sought in this area. The Silver Coast, the Obidos area, is also popular.

Rural inland areas are the best place to look for good-value older properties suitable for renovation.

The Portuguese islands of Madeira and Porto Santo (also known as the Funchal Islands) off the Moroccan coast, with their mild year-round climate, and the Azores in the Atlantic northwest of Madeira, are more exotic options for the property-buyer.

Currency and exchange rate

Euro (€); £1 = €1.50.

Property prices

Oddly, properties here are generally considerably more expensive than many other European sun spots. Even so, prices are cheap when compared with the UK. Portugal has a far higher population density than neighbouring Spain and the country's low interest rates may be encouraging many nationals to buy second homes here, in stark contrast with, say, France. A small Algarve apartment typically costs at least £150,000. At an upmarket resort with a low-density building policy, like Quinta do Lago in the Algarve, resale apartments typically start at over £225,000, while a new villa is more than £1.3 million.

For the cheapest properties on the mainland, head into the rural areas. Village properties for sale in the Beira Litoral area, for example, typically include large houses for restoration with mountain views for less than £35,000, three-bedroom renovated cottages for less than £120,000 and 18th-century spacious manor houses for £275,000 or so.

Property on Madeira is around a third cheaper than the Algarve.

Local mortgages

Portuguese mortgages require proof of income and outgoings and normally a maximum of 80 per cent of the purchase price can be raised. Life cover is required, and repayment mortgages are the most common type of loan.

Access to and from the UK

There is a wide choice of flights to the Algarve and flights between London and Faro take just under 3hrs. Flights to Lisbon are cheaper and more frequent, and Lisbon to Faro takes about 4hrs by car and 5hrs by train.

Legal restrictions

Those hoping to buy a property through setting up an offshore company to avoid local taxes and inheritance laws should read on. In January 2004, a law came into effect stating that any offshore company owning a property in Portugal is liable to an annual charge of 5 per cent of the value of the property unless it is registered in Delaware, Malta or New Zealand. This means that anyone owning a Portuguese property of £300,000 through an offshore company would have to pay £15,000 annually, which means that owning property through offshore companies is no longer an attractive option.

The buying process

Before buying, confirm with the land registry office (*conservatorio do registo predial*) that the property is registered in the vendor's name.

The buying process is regulated by a notary (*notario*), a neutral official chosen by the government, who is responsible for making various checks on the property and for witnessing and registering the transfer of ownership from the vendor to the purchaser. It is possible to sell a property without the use of a notary, but the contract would not be binding on a third party wishing to make a claim on the property or a lender wishing to grant a mortgage on it.

Buyers need to engage an experienced, independent, English-speaking lawyer (*advogado*) to protect their interests and safeguard against possible problems such as restrictive clauses or debts relating to the property. Buyers should also only approach government-registered estate agents (*mediator autoizado*).

When buyer and seller have agreed the purchase price, a preliminary contract (*contrato de promessa de compra e venda*) is drawn up by the vendor's representative and is signed by both parties, which is legally binding to both buyer and seller. This contains such details as the purchase price and completion date, a description of the property, confirmation of the identities of both buyer and seller, the deposit agreement and the 'clear title' of ownership.

Before signing, the vendor should provide various documents for checking by your solicitor, such as the *cardetta*, confirming that there are no debts on the property, and if the property was built after 1951, a habitation licence.

The buyer pays a deposit, commonly 10 per cent but often more, which is normally non-refundable should the buyer later pull out of the deal. If the vendor backs out, normally he or she is required to pay the buyer double the value of the deposit.

If funds are being imported to buy a property, a licence must be obtained from the Bank of Portugal (*Boletim de Autorizacao de Capitals Privados*).

When buyer and seller are ready to complete, they both (or their legal representatives) sign the final contract in front of the notary, which represents the sale and conveyance deed (*escritura de compra e venda*). The notary will read out the contract aloud to both parties, and request to see such documents as the promissory contract, the buyer's habitation licence and property transfer tax receipt. The balance owing is then paid by the purchaser and the sale registered at the local land registry office. This last action takes several months. The buyer is responsible for registering the property with the Inland Revenue (*Reparticao Financas*) in relation to payment of taxes and rates on the property.

Costs of buying

This usually translates as around 10 and 12 per cent of the purchase price. A property transfer tax (SISA) of between 0.5 and 15 per cent of the purchase price of the property is applicable, and there are legal (1 to 2 per cent) and notary and registration (3 per cent) fees payable. Estate agency fees average 6 per cent of the purchase price, as do land registry fees.

Is property a good investment?

The Portuguese property market is buoyant.

Living in Portugal

Portugal's mainland climate largely consists of mild winters and warm summers, although the northeast has longer, colder winters and hot summers. The islands are subtropical.

The official language is Portuguese, but English is widely spoken in the resort areas. The standard of living is quite high, and since the country joined the EU in 1986, the cost of living has risen steadily. The crime rate is comparatively low and healthcare is of a good standard; there are reciprocal agreements in place. To obtain healthcare using the state health service (CAIXA) you should contact your local Centro de Saude, although the refund received from the state is generally small and therefore private medical insurance is likely to be advisable.

Income tax ranges from 12 to 40 per cent. Foreign property owners are required to have a tax card and a fiscal number. Tax is payable by non-residents on income received in Portugal, for example from letting.

An annual property tax (*contribuicao predial*) of between 0.7 and 2 per cent is payable, based on the assessed value of the property. There are exemptions for some principal homes in urban areas. Local rates (*contribucion autarquica*) are also payable.

Residence permits are no more than a formality for EU nationals and work permits unnecessary. Visitors may remain in the country for 90 days. If you spend less than 183 days per year in Portugal, you are generally classed as a non-resident and are required to appoint a fiscal representative (a friend or lawyer, for example) resident in Portugal to receive correspondence relating to your affairs in the country.

Selling

Capital gains tax is payable at the same rates as income tax but only for 50 per cent of any gain made from property.

Inheritance tax

This is levied at between 3 and 50 per cent.

Further information

- **Portugal: t** (00 351)
- **American Club of Lisbon**, Rua Castilho 38, Lisbon, Portugal.
- **Anglo-Portuguese Society**, 2 Belgrave Square, London SW1X 8PJ, UK, **t** (020) 7245 9738; **www.portembassy.gla.ac.uk**.
- **Barclays Bank Portugal** (Portugal), **t** 214 848632.
- **Caixa Geral de Depositos, t** (UK) (020) 7623 4477, (Portugal) 21 795 3000; **www.lardocelar.pt/uk/**. Portuguese bank with over 800 branches offering a full local banking service for UK owners of property in Portugal.
- **Portuguese Consulate General**, 62 Brompton Road, London SW3 1BJ, UK. **Portuguese Embassy**, 11 Belgrave Square, London SW1X 8PP, UK, **t** (020) 7235 5331; **www.portembassy.gla.ac.uk**.
- **Portuguese Embassy**, 2125 Kalorama Road, NW, Washington, DC 20008, USA, **t** (202) 328 8610; **www.portugal.org**.
- **Portuguese National Tourist Office**, 590 Fifth Avenue, New York, NY 10036, **t** (212) 354 4403, **t** (UK) (020) 7581 8722.
- **Portuguese tourism information request service, t** 0900 160 0370.
- **Portuguese Tourist Office**, 22–25a Sackville Street, London W1S 3LY, UK, **t** 0906 364 0610; **www.portugalinsite.com**.
- **Portuguese Visa Information Service** (UK), **t** 0900 160 0202.
- **www.portugal-info.com** has English website links.
- **www.portugalvirtual.pt** and **www.portugal.org** have lots of Portugal-related links and information.

Estate agents

- **Canadian Association of Retired Persons; www.50plus.com**: information about retirement homes and developments in Portugal.
- **Caroline Thomas** (Portugal), **t** 917 735917 .
- **Christopher Garveigh** (Portugal), **t** 282 769341; **www.garveigh.com**.
- **Country Homes Portugal** (Netherlands), **t** 035 691 8418; **www.rusticportugal.com**.

- **David Headland Associates** (UK), **t** (01933) 353333; **www.headlands.co.uk**.
- **Jones Homes Portugal** (UK), **t** (01625) 548405; **www.joneshomesportugal.com**. New-build properties.
- **Lacey Property Brokers** (UK), **t** (01702) 603210; **www.laceypropertybrokers.com**.
- **Lapis Lazuli** (Portugal), **t** 239 455773; **www.lapis-lazuli.co.uk**.
- **Premier Properties International** (UK), **t** (01935) 881199; **www.premierpropertiesonline.net**. Specialises in rural properties in central and western Portugal.
- **Quadrant Overseas Property** (UK), **t** (01276) 507513.
- **World Class Homes** (UK), **t** (01582) 832001; **www.worldclasshomes.co.uk**.

Republic of Cyprus (Greek)

Why retire here?

If you're looking for a place to retire, Cyprus, the third-largest island in the eastern Mediterranean, is hard to beat. Not only does it have one of the most agreeable climates in the world – around 330 days of bright sunshine and the warmest seas in the Med – but also inexpensive property, a low cost of living, low taxation, very little crime, a disarmingly friendly, widely English-speaking population and plenty of cheap flight connections from the UK. On top of that, its joining of the European Union in 2004 will no doubt cause property prices to rise significantly in the next few years.

As well as some great beaches and tranquil pine forests on the Greek section of the island – 62 per cent of it – you can ski on Mount Olympus from December to April. Water sports are very popular and widespread. Cyprus also has a fascinating history that has left a host of prehistoric settlements, temples, Roman and Venetian fortifications, amphitheatres, Crusader castles, Byzantine churches and monasteries to explore.

Although Cyprus gained its independence in 1960, its history since 1925 as a British Crown Colony is still very influential today. Cyprus is now the fifth most popular destination for British property-buyers, behind only Spain, France, Portugal and Florida. About three-fifths of buyers today are British and the British community totals over 60,000 in a total island population of 750,000.

Downsides

Although inland areas are generally unspoilt, overdevelopment, coastal tower blocks and a large tourist industry have resulted in many spoilt coastal areas, although the town of Paphos has been protected to an extent by strict building regulations.

The bitter history of troubles on the island and division into a Greek side and Turkish side since 1974 has caused Cyprus to be politically unstable at times in recent years. Well over 100,000 Greek refugees fled the now Turkish side in 1974. There have been numerous attempts to unify the island, most recently in April 2004 when the United Nations drew up a unification plan in advance of the Greek side's joining the European Union. The plan was rejected by 75.8 per cent of Greek Cypriots, even though 64.9 per cent of the Turkish Cypriot minority were in favour of the plan.

Property types

A wide choice, from period properties both in need of renovation and fully restored, and newly built apartments in holiday developments and luxury seaside villas.

Where to retire

Buyers of retirement properties tend to focus on established, popular coastal areas such as Paphos, Larnaca, Protaras, Ayia Napa and Limassol, while the Troodos Mountains are also popular. If you are seeking peace and quiet, the northwest of the island is the least developed.

Currency and exchange rate

Cyprus pound; £1 = C£0.88.

Property prices

A 2004 survey found property prices to be substantially cheaper than Spain (around 30 per cent cheaper than southern Spain), Italy and Portugal. The wide choice of locations and property types means that budgets from around £40,000 to over £500,000 are accommodated. One-bedroom apartments typically start at around £35,000, with villas starting at just over double that. But a four-bed villa in a good location on the beach could easily exceed £300,000. A three-bed villa at Paphos, the most popular resort, now costs around £400,000. Prices will almost certainly rise now that Cyprus is a member of the EU.

Local mortgages

Repayment loans are available, commonly for 5–10 years and for less than 70 per cent of value of the property, but better terms are likely to be available in the UK.

Self-certification and non-status mortgages are not available on the island.

Access to and from the UK

Cyprus has two international airports handling numerous daily 4hr 30min chartered and scheduled flights from London and other European cities. Flights start at under £100 return but these are rare, at the last minute or at awkward times. Typical returns between London and Larnaca hover around £200, rising to £300 or so at peak periods. EU membership could mean lower prices, with low-cost carriers launching routes.

Legal restrictions

If Cyprus manages to find some kind of unity, which has seemed far more likely since 2003 when border controls were more relaxed than they have ever been since 1974, potential problems over property ownership resulting from the partition in 1974 are likely to be far less serious in the south of the island when compared with the north.

Turkish Cypriot properties in the south have been held in trust by the Greek Cypriot government and rented to people who came from the north. Turkish Cypriots can do what they like with these properties and can dispose of them whenever they want.

Non-Cypriots are only permitted to own one property on the island, and there are restrictions on the amount of land that can be owned, usually 3 *donums* – 4,012 sq m (43,200 sq ft) – or around two-thirds of an acre. This rule may be relaxed as a result of joining the EU.

Incomers are not permitted to earn money in Cyprus and therefore retirees are required to satisfy the authorities that they have adequate funds to buy the property and support themselves. The country's minimum income requirement is a joint income of £8,500 per annum for a couple. Foreign currency must be imported to purchase property, and the land registry office requires a foreign currency certificate documenting this.

The buying process

The house-buying process is based on the British model. A local lawyer familiar with the system should be used. After the purchaser and vendor have signed an agreement or contract to go ahead with the sale and the purchaser has paid a deposit, searches are made to ascertain that the title is unencumbered. It is important that the buyer's lawyer verifies that the seller is the owner of the property and that it has an unbroken chain of legitimate ownership.

Signing the agreement and paying the deposit cause the buyer to be legally committed and therefore there is no gazumping – but the purchaser remains legally bound even if problems with the contract or title are later found.

As a formality, the purchaser applies for permission to buy from the Council of Ministers. This is simple, requiring bank and character references, criminal records checks, and affirmation that only one home will be owned in Cyprus, that the maximum land size is not being exceeded and that minimum required funds to live on the island are available. This process can take up to a year, but in the meantime, the buyer can take possession of the property.

Ownership of the property is transferred from the vendor to the buyer through the Cypriot land registry via a solicitor.

Costs of buying

Stamp duty is C£1.50 (about £1.70) per C£1,000 (£1,135) of the property price up to C£75,000 (£85,000) and C£2 (£2.30) per C£1,000 over C£75,000. Transfer fees of 3 per cent are payable on the first C£50,000 (£57,000) of the value of the property, with 5 per cent payable on the value from C£50,000 to C£100,000, and 8 per cent on the value over C£100,000. A property bought by a couple has a generous allowance. Lawyer's fees average around 1 per cent of the purchase price and the application to the Council of Ministers costs approximately £230.

Is property a good investment?

In recent years, property prices have risen steadily (at over 20 per cent per annum in the last couple of years and one British agent is claiming rises of up to 48 per cent in 2003 alone) and EU membership will accelerate this rise.

Living in Cyprus

Cyprus can seem very familiar to a British visitor. Cars drive on the left side of the road and road signs are in English and Greek. The legal system is based on the English one.

The cost of living is generally very low (around 30 per cent lower than the UK) and it is possible to live comfortably for less than £8,000 per year. This has been just as well in the past, as it is usually not possible for incomers to gain employment on the island, although an increased number of work permits have been issued as Cyprus got nearer to EU membership. The crime rate is low and medical facilities are generally excellent. Buying a property allows purchasers to become resident, subject to approval by the Council of Ministers.

One great advantage is that pensions and investment income is subject to only 5 per cent income tax for tax residents, and a double taxation agreement with the UK means that residents do not have to pay tax in both countries.

An annual property ownership tax is payable: 2 per cent on properties valued at C£101,000–250,000 (about £115,000 to £285,000); 3 per cent on properties valued at C£250,001–500,000; and 3.5 per cent on properties valued more than that. There is also a municipal tax of under £120 per year levied locally, based on the value of the property. Officially, foreigners are not permitted to let their properties, although this rule is generally not strictly observed and therefore many owners do so unofficially.

There are reciprocal health agreements with the UK but many foreign residents supplement the state provisions with private medical cover.

Selling

Capital gains tax of 20 per cent may be applicable when the property is sold, although there are exemptions.

Inheritance tax

Inheritance tax is 10–30 per cent, payable on estates of over C£20,000 (about £22,700) by non-residents on property owned on the island.

Further information

- **Cyprus: t** (00 357)
- **Conti Financial Services**, 204 Church Road, Hove, East Sussex, BN3 2DJ, UK, **t** (01273) 772811; **www.overseasandukfinance.com**. Offers loans in Cyprus secured on Cypriot property.
- **Cyprus Embassy**, 2210 R Street, NW, Washington, DC 20008, USA, **t** (202) 462 5772.
- **Cyprus High Commission**, 93 Park Street, London W1Y 4ET, UK, **t** (020) 7499 8272.
- **Cyprus Tourism Organization**, PO Box 24535, 1390 Nicosia, Cyprus, **t** 23 37715; **www.cyprustourism.org**.

Estate agents

- **Antony Loizou and Associates** (Cyprus), **t** 25 871552; **www.aloizou.com.cy**. Cyprus's largest estate agents and chartered surveyors with branches in Limassol, Larnaca, Paphos and Paralimni. The company can assist with government permits for permanent residency and property acquisition, and provide ongoing maintenance assistance and property management.
- **Aristo Developers** (Cyprus), **t** 26 841841; **www.aristodevelopers.com**. Various new developments on the island.
- **Cybarco, t** (Cyprus) 22 741300, **t** (UK) (020) 8371 9700; **www.cybarco.com**. For new properties in Larnaca, Limassol and Paphos.
- **Halcyon Properties** (UK), **t** (01323) 891639; **www.halcyon-properties. co.uk**. Greek and Cypriot specialist property consultant and UK associate company for Antony Loizou and Associates.
- **Pafilia Property Developers** (Cyprus), **t** 26 848800; **www.pafilia.com**.

Romania

Why retire here?

This exotic little-known land has gorgeous properties with tiny price tags, as well as great beaches and a sunny climate. Parts of the Black Sea coast are very beautiful. Its troubled Communist history is very much a thing of the past and now the country is developing rapidly. The fact that Romania is set to join the European Union in 2007 means that the country's economic condition is likely to improve greatly.

Downsides

Bitterly cold winters will cause you to look on the climate of northern Britain fondly. Although the country's infrastructure is rapidly improving, there are still many shortcomings, including bad roads and drab concrete buildings. In addition, some of the countryside is quite tatty compared with many European countries.

Property types

These vary from newly built city apartments to seaside villas and older, large detached rural houses.

Where to retire

Romania has lots to offer, with a very varied and beautiful landscape, including the dramatic forested mountains of Dracula country, the Transylvanian Alps, and vast fertile plains. The Alps, ideal for skiing in the winter and walking in the summer, boast alpine meadows, unspoilt medieval towns, Gothic castles and untouched monasteries. Transylvania is home to many unspoilt medieval villages, including Sibiu, Prejmer, Nasaud, Bistrita, Harman and Sighisoara, which has a UNESCO-protected historical centre. Winter sports centres in the region include Poiana Brasov, Predeal, Sinaia and Busteni.

The beautiful 'Romanian Riviera' on the Black Sea is hard to beat. The city of Constanta has an easygoing atmosphere and lively cultural life, with numerous restaurants and bars, an opera house and theatre. North of here is the popular Black Sea resort of Mamaia, and others include Cosinesti, Mangalia, Eforie Nord, and Olimp and Neptun by the Comorova forest.

For tranquillity and value for money, head for the unspoilt rural villages, and for vibrant, exotic city life choose Bucharest, although during the oppressive Ceaușescu area much of the historic centre was destroyed. The picturesque town of Brasov, founded in the 12th century, has numerous houses available in need of renovation.

Currency and exchange rate

Lei (ROL); £1 = ROL 62,000.

Property prices

You could buy a Swiss-style chalet on the Romanian Riviera for less than £30,000. Rural farms with land have been sold recently for less than £10,000. Houses in rural villages, such as Agigea, start at around £5,000.

In Eforie Nord, a three-bed villa near the beach would typically cost £30,000. In Constanta, a new-build two-bedroom apartment with sea views costs around £25,000, while for £35,000 or so you could get a four-bedroom town house with a large garden.

Local mortgages

Local borrowing opportunities are scarce and it is advisable to use a UK lender.

Access to and from the UK

British Airways and Tarom offer daily direct flights from the UK.

Legal restrictions

Although overseas purchasers may buy anywhere in the country, they are not allowed to own the land except in the following circumstances:

- **If they buy the property and take over the exclusive use of the land for the lifetime of the house, paying a small tax for the land annually.**

- **If they form a limited company established in Romania to own the land.**

- **If the property is purchased by a foreign person and the land that is part of the property is bought by a Romanian subject who gives exclusive right of use of the land to the owner of the building for the lifetime of the building.**

In the third case, the Romanian subject is not permitted to sell the land to another party without the express agreement of the owner of the building.

The buying process

It is advisable only to use an estate agent who is a member of the National Union of Estate Agents (UNAI). It is also advisable to appoint a surveyor to establish the local worth of the property, as it is common for Romanian vendors to inflate asking prices if they know that a foreign buyer is interested. Although it is possible to buy without engaging a lawyer, this would open you to possible pitfalls in the system.

Once the purchase price has been agreed, a pre-purchase agreement is drawn up by the estate agent and signed by both parties and then the buyer typically pays a 10 per cent deposit, which they lose if they renege on the sale. If the vendor backs out of the deal, he or she is liable to pay the purchaser double the value of the deposit. The agent is responsible for the local searches and the transfer of title and registration is handled on behalf of both parties by an independent notary. Both parties attend to sign the final contract in front of the notary and then the sale is registered with the land registry.

Costs of buying

Estate agency fees vary greatly in different parts of the country, for example they are typically around 2 per cent in Brasov and 6 per cent in Bucharest. In some instances, buyers and sellers may both pay a commission charge to the estate agent. Other costs typically add around 10 per cent to the purchase price. Notary fees and transfer taxes are in accordance with charges set by the government relating to the value of the property concerned.

Is property a good investment?

Property prices are still in the bargain-basement category, but once Romania joins the European Union in 2007, prices are likely to shoot up.

Living in Romania

Romania has a Mediterranean climate and although the standard of living is lower than much of Europe, the cost of living is very low also. A meal in a good restaurant with wine is unlikely to cost more than £5.

The healthcare system in Romania is significantly underfunded and patients regularly experience long delays for treatment, therefore private medical insurance is essential.

Selling

Capital gains tax is payable according to the size of the estate and relationship of the beneficiary to the deceased.

Inheritance tax

The rate is progressive, and dependent on the relationship between donor and recipient.

Further information

- **Romania: t** (00 40)

• **Romanian Embassy**, Arundel House, 4 Palace Green, London W8 4QD, UK, **t** (020) 7937 9666; **www.roemb.co.uk**.

Estate agents

• **Elion** (Romania), **t** 241 508 217; **www.elion.ro**.

• **www.viviun.com**: a selection of Romanian properties for sale.

Slovenia

Why retire here?

Little-known Slovenia, once part of the former Yugoslavia, is tipped for a tourist boom following EU accession in May 2004. The small country, with a population of just two million, boasts a pleasant small coastline on the Adriatic Sea, an alpine interior ideal for skiing, as well as a lovely capital, Ljubljana.

Downsides

Language is a real barrier here and not being fluent can cause endless frustration to a home owner.

Property types

City apartments, seaside villas and older, large detached rural houses.

Where to retire

Ljubljana offers both old-world flair and modern entertainment. The pretty Old Town sits along the Ljubljanica River. Ljubljana boasts a beautiful blend of architectural styles as well as many pavement cafés, restaurants and cultural events. Bled, 35km from Ljubljana airport, has a lake with an idyllic island and is surrounded by stunning unspoilt countryside. Portoroz is a bustling seaside resort. As well as the beach, there are thermal pools, waterfront bistros, restaurants and discos.

The Goricko National Park has lots of cheap property in a beautiful rural setting. It is currently being developed for tourism and will soon be linked to Ljubljana by a direct motorway.

Currency and exchange rate

Tolar; £1 = 362 Tolars. The Tolar is expected to be replaced by the euro in a few years.

Property prices

In the best areas of Ljubljana, a two-bed apartment would typically be over £125,000, but in the countryside you can get a three-bedroom country house still for less than £50,000 or a cottage for half that. Some rural houses are priced at under £15,000.

Local mortgages

Mortgages for foreigners are still a real rarity and the base rate is high anyway, therefore it is better either to buy with cash or raise the finance in the UK with an equity release scheme.

Access to and from the UK

Access is improving and easyJet has in 2004 launched flights to the capital, Ljubljana.

The buying process

Foreigners cannot buy property in Slovenia without a tax registration number, obtainable from the local authority. Local banks will also require this number before they will open an account. A government-appointed notary acts for both buyer and seller, but it is vital for buyers to appoint an independent English-speaking lawyer.

The buying process is quick and straightforward and greatly helped by a computerised land registry that can complete searches within 24hrs, as well as an efficient legal system and high-tech banking. The sales contract is signed in front of the notary and the law in Slovenia requires that an official court translator to be present when the contract is signed to ensure that the purchaser fully understands the contract.

Costs of buying

Estate agents generally charge 3 per cent. The vendor pays stamp duty of 2 per cent of the purchase price. If the property is bought and then resold within two years, the tax becomes 10 per cent. The translator of the sales contract receives a small sum, around £25, and the notary receives about £200, sometimes paid by the buyer and sometimes by the seller.

Is property a good investment?

Until EU accession, it was very difficult for foreigners to buy here and early exploiters of the change are likely to benefit handsomely financially.

Living in Slovenia

The Slovenian language is very difficult, and few if any words are recognisable in more common languages like English, French or German. However, English is widely taught in schools and many people speak German because many German tourists visit the country.

Although the country is still developing in many respects, this is at a rapid pace and in many areas standards are very modern. For example, the banking system is modern with cashpoints commonplace.

Most foreign residents of Slovenia supplement the state healthcare system with private medical insurance.

Selling

Capital gains tax is 25 per cent.

Inheritance tax

Heirs of first succession do not pay tax. In the second succession of inheritance, the tax varies 5–14 per cent, while in the third succession the tax is 8–11 per cent. All other individuals pay tax of between 11 and 30 per cent.

Further information

- **Slovenia: t** (00 386)
- **Slovenian Tourist Board, t** 0870 225 5305.

Estate agents

- **Euroburo** (Austria), **t** 6137 20099; **www.euroburolimited.co.uk**.
- **Nepremianine** (Slovenia), **t** 3 567 9110; **www.nepremianine.net**.
- **www.viviun.co.uk**: features properties in Slovenia.

South Africa

Why retire here?

Most people looking for a retirement home abroad want sun, sea, tranquillity and an inexpensive home in a beautiful setting, as well as a low cost of living. South Africa certainly meets such criteria and has in recent years become an increasingly popular second home and retirement location for British buyers.

Although it has crime hotspots, it is essentially a safe and friendly destination. English is widely spoken, and the country is never more than 2hrs in advance of the time in the UK. The climate is consistently good and generally healthy, averaging 26.5°C in January on the Cape.

As well as 2,900km (1,800 miles) of coastline, the very varied geography encompasses mountains, vast plains, forest, lakes and rivers. There are also numerous game reserves to discover.

Downsides

Before buying in South Africa, there are a number of factors to consider. The country has long had a history of political instability, widespread social and economic problems and civil discontent. On the international money markets this has been reflected in the performance of the currency, the rand. The rand has fluctuated greatly in recent years, by as much as 40 per cent against the pound sterling.

As with many other African countries, the possibility of a coup resulting in a change of regime and causing the loss of your home can never totally be discounted, although it is very unlikely. Apartheid officially ended in 1991 and South Africa is one of Africa's most stable countries; the current democracy appears to be relatively stable, too.

British buyers may also be concerned about crime and violence in the country. In 2000, for example, there were 20,000 murders in South Africa. The majority of crime is in the cities, especially Durban and Johannesburg. Cape Town is considerably more relaxed, with a slight old English feel. The crime rate in the Western Cape remains lower than New York or Los Angeles, but electrified fences, residents employing armed response units and guards are a common occurrence. Police corruption is common.

Even so, many holiday areas are many miles from crime hotspots. There is virtually no crime at Knysna, for example, which is a sleepy market town. If someone's car in broken into, it's almost front page news.

Although flights, at around 11hrs, typically take no longer than a drive from London to northern Scotland, they are expensive and if you want easy access to the UK it is important to ascertain whether the cost and the length of the journey would be an important factor.

Another disadvantage is that the Atlantic Ocean, with currents coming from the Antarctic, is usually too cold to swim in. The stretch of coastline bordering the Indian Ocean is warmer.

Lastly, the huge gulf between owning something like a luxury beachside villa in a country with many sprawling poverty-stricken shanty towns can be unacceptable for many.

Property types

A wide range is available, including new developments of coastal villas and apartments, attractive period Dutch gabled houses, game lodges, thatched cottages and large, older town houses. If your budget stretches to it (£650,000 or so) in the remote countryside are Cape Dutch homesteads with 18th-century thatched whitewashed houses set in landscaped gardens. Building standards overall are generally high.

Where to retire

Foreign buyers tend to focus on the coastal areas of the Western and Eastern Capes, the Garden Route, game farms in the Mpumalanga region and KwaZulu-Natal. The attractive city of Cape Town is particularly popular and near to the Kruger National Park. Knysna in the Western Cape embraces a large lagoon which is an inlet to the warm Indian Ocean, with a backdrop of hills leading to forests and mountains inland. The old market town of Knysna is unspoilt, unhurried and tranquil. It is particularly popular as a retirement location, as are the Franschhoek and Paarl wine regions.

False Bay, to the southeast of Cape Town, is a popular area for seaside homes. Upmarket Cape Town suburb Constantiaberg is very popular and also Camps Bay, where the Twelve Apostles mountain range runs south from Table Mountain into the sea above huge expanses of sand. Here there are fabulous architect-designed houses perched on cliffs overlooking lovely sandy bays and the Atlantic.

The Atlantic seaboard is most popular for apartments because of its position between the sea and Table Mountain. The mountain protects it from the chilling southerly wind.

Currency and exchange rate

Rand; £1 = R11.92. The rand has fluctuated greatly in recent years, by as much as 40 per cent against sterling.

Property prices

Prices have been cheap – especially as a result of spectacular falls in the value of the rand at the end of 2001 – but the property market has experienced something of a boom in recent years, especially in Cape Town, following an increase in political stability and the rand's strengthening considerably. In late 2003, the average house price in South Africa was £38,000, and £41,000 in the Cape Town Metropolitan area.

A number of developments have been springing up, fuelled especially by British, German and other foreign buyers. A good apartment is easily available for less than £20,000 and a villa with a pool for less than £40,000.

In Cape Town, a two-bed flat in the centre starts at around £35,000 but a large villa by the sea with a pool could easily cost £500,000. Move out of the fashionable areas and you get plenty of value. False Bay, West Coast and Walker

Bay are all within a two-hour drive from the airport and have a good choice of property.

The Eastern Cape Coast, South Coast and Natal North Coast are current hotspots with a good choice of property. Natal's coastline is less than an hour's drive from Durban and has seen prices rise 30 per cent from early 2003 to early 2004; a villa here will currently cost £200,000 or so, and one-bed apartments a quarter of that.

For about £25,000, you could buy a two-bed flat in the Knysna area, while a spacious three-bedroom detached house in the hills overlooking the lagoon costs £35,000 plus; £200,000 would net a luxury residence.

In the KwaZulu-Natal region, three-bedroom apartments begin at £65,000 or so, and a three-bed villa with its own pool costs at least £125,000.

Local mortgages

Known as bonds in South Africa, these are usually considerably more expensive than in Europe. They are available to non-residents for up to 50 per cent of the purchase price, who are required to bring at least 50 per cent of the funds to buy into the country. Residents can obtain 100 per cent loans.

Access to and from the UK

Flights from the UK typically start from over £600 but have become increasingly economical and frequent off-season and overnight flights are now available directly into Cape Town, Johannesburg and Durban. Transfers for non-direct flights are usually frequent and cheap. Flights are of around 12hrs' duration. As well as international airports at Cape Town, Durban and Johannesburg, there are six other major airports. Because South Africa is in the same longitude as the UK, rather than in a different time zone, jet lag isn't a problem.

Legal restrictions

All funds brought into the country must go through the South African Reserve Bank via a registered banker. This can add another 10 days or so to the buying process.

The buying process

Most property is owned with a freehold title. Conveyancing and land registration are relatively straightforward, especially as transactions are in English. The process takes around 10 weeks, but can be as quick as 14 days. Agents are required to register with the Estate Agents Board and often handle much of the paperwork on a buyer's behalf.

Offers to purchase are made in writing, and, once signed by both parties, a contract comes into existence, therefore legal advice should be taken before signing an offer to purchase. The same lawyer acts for both parties, with the vendor selecting one and the buyer paying the fees, on a predetermined scale based on the purchase price.

The buyer then pays 10 per cent deposit to the vendor's estate agent. A contract is drawn up, stating the legal obligations of both parties.

Non-residents are entitled to hold title to land via a company or trust, which can be beneficial to tax planning.

Costs of buying

Conveyancing costs average 1–2 per cent of the purchase price and legal and other fees are another 1 per cent or so. Notary fees for preparing and registering the title deed range from £230 to £660. Stamp duty is 0.5 per cent of the purchase price.

A transfer duty is payable by the buyer on resale properties. This varies from 1 per cent on the first R60,000 (£5,000 or so), 5 per cent from R60,001 to R250,000, and 8 per cent on the remainder. Where the purchaser is a trust or company, the duty is payable at a flat rate of 10 per cent of the purchase price. Transfer duty is not payable on new properties, which attract 14 per cent value added tax, and stamp duty of 0.2 per cent is payable on a mortgage.

Is property a good investment?

If you buy when the rand has fallen and prices are amazingly low, and prices then rise, clearly property here is a good investment. Unfortunately, life is seldom so simple. Those who bought in 2001 saw the value of their properties plunge the next year, as the rand shot up from 11 to 16 to the pound.

Property values are likely to increase as more South Africans relocate from the cities like Johannesburg and Pretoria, which provide a solid investment for overseas buyers. Cape Town saw increases of 20 per cent in prices in each of the three years up to 2004.

Living in South Africa

As well as its great beauty, one major attraction of South Africa is its particularly low daily cost of living. A good bottle of white wine is about £1.20 and petrol is just 30p per litre, for example. Eating out is extremely good value – two people can eat out very well for less than 10 pounds.

Around 65 per cent of the population speaks English. Africaans is also widely spoken along with nine other official languages.

Europeans will feel at home: there are around six million residents of European origin including over 500,000 Britons. Areas popular with foreigners have plenty of Dutch, German, French and British buyers. State medical facilities are generally relatively good, but private health insurance is necessary.

The climate is excellent, with summer peaking in December and January with temperatures ranging between 20°C and 40°C. The east coast is semi-tropical and can be humid in summer, while around Cape Town it is more like that of the Mediterranean. Being warm and sunny much of the year (the rainy season and mild winter is from June to September), South Africa ideal for those considering retirement. On the coast the sea breezes mean it does not get humid and the air quality is superb.

Annual community fees average from around £150–£1,000 and rates are approximately £100 –£500, depending on property size and location.

Income tax of 19–45 per cent is payable on any income gained in the country, such as from renting out a property. A fiscal representative to make your annual tax returns costs less than £400. Property taxes are payable, varying by region and size of property.

Without a residence permit, EU citizens may stay for up to six months each year, as long as they can demonstrate that they can support themselves and can produce a return ticket. Applying for a residence permit involves a hefty fee, currently over £1,000, which is non-refundable.

To qualify for a retired person's residence permit, which is valid for four years (after which you qualify for citizenship), you must have a monthly pension worth R20,000 (£1,700) or a net worth of at least R12 million (£1,040,000) coupled with a monthly income of at least R15,000 (£1,300).

Note that your UK state pension will be frozen on the day you leave the UK if you go to live in South Africa, and will not rise with inflation (*see* pp.22–3).

Selling

Any money gained from selling can be taken out of the country, although capital gains tax is levied on gains from the sale of a non-primary residence.

Inheritance tax

This is applicable at 25 per cent on estates valued in excess of R1 million (about £85,000).

Further information

- **South Africa: t (00 27)**
- **Institute of Realtors of South Africa** (South Africa), **t** 21 531 3180.
- **South African Embassy,** 3051 Massachusetts Avenue, NW, Washington, DC 20008, USA, **t** (202) 232 4400; **www.southafrica.net**.
- **South African High Commission,** Trafalgar Square, London WC2N 5DP, UK, **t** (020) 7451 7299; **www.southafricahouse.com**.

- **South African Property Overseas Marketing Association** (South Africa), t 31 573 1966; **www.sapoma.co.za**.

Estate agents

- **Bren Gleeson** (South Africa), t 21 782 7692; **www.gleesonprop.co.za**.
- **Capsol** (South Africa), t 21 461 1083; **www.capsolsales.com**. Specialises in the Cape Town area.
- **Cluttons, t** (UK) (020) 7403 3669, t (South Africa) 021 425 8989.
- **Elan International, t** (UK) (01935) 881762, t (South Africa) 31 573 1966; **www.elanpark.co.za**.
- **FPD Savills** (UK), t (020) 7824 9077; **www.fpdsavills.co.uk**.
- **Pam Golding International** (South Africa), t 28 284 9384; **www.pamgolding.co.za**. Largest international estate agent working in conjunction with FPD Savills.
- **Private Property Listings** (South Africa), t 83 913 1000; **www.privateproperty.co.za**.
- **Seeff Residential Properties** (South Africa), t 23 344 3291; **www.seeff.com**.
- **Sotheby's International Realty** (UK), t (020) 7598 1600; **www.sothebysrealty.com**.

Spain

Why retire here?

After a relaxing few days of sun, sea and sangria, it's easy to be seduced into retiring in Spain in a gorgeous villa or farmhouse sporting a price tag that is small when compared with property in the UK. On top of that, the cost of living is significantly lower than that of the UK, and EU subjects can use the health-care system just as a Spanish pensioner can.

Retiring to Spain has been popular with UK residents for many years, not least because of the splendid climate in many areas. Indeed, it is estimated that more than three-quarters of expatriates in Spain are retired.

Unlike in France, sunshine is guaranteed in many parts of the country for much of the year. Many people claim that it has the best climate in Europe. The healthier the climate, lifestyle and cuisine, the more likely it is that a retired person will lead an active, fit and healthy retirement. Outdoor pursuits, like swimming, golf, tennis and sailing, are widely available almost all year.

The generally significantly lower cost of properties in Spain means that there may be funds to invest after selling a UK home, and the lower cost of living allows pensions to stretch further than they would in the UK.

Spain has magnificent beaches, spectacular countryside, culture for art-lovers and fine wines and cuisine. It also boasts good transport links with the UK, with a good road network and plenty of cheap flights. The north of the country is convenient for ferry ports so visits to and from the UK can be made by car.

Many buyers appreciate English being widely spoken and the strong British presence long established in many of the beach resorts. The country has great contrasts: parts of the north can resemble Scotland while the south can have a Moroccan feel.

All this contributes to the fact that an estimated 750,000 Britons have now bought retirement houses in Spain.

Downsides

The climate in the north is very different from that of the south and can suffer freezing winters. The south of the country may enjoy the most sun but at popular times, such as the summer, flights can be expensive and could deter a retiree from visiting the UK or friends and family from visiting. Also, many sections of the coast suffer from overdevelopment and therefore it can take time and persistence to find the right property.

Property types

Unlike the French market, where British buyers almost all buy period homes, many Brits in Spain opt for new-build villas and apartments, and this is the section of the market in which many of the companies geared to British buyers operate.

Where to retire

There are a number of sizeable British and German retirement communities along the coast, most notably around the northern Costa Blanca and the central Costa del Sol. These have the best accessibility by air and a good selection of properties for all budgets, although some areas are so overdeveloped, especially on the Costa del Sol, that people have taken to describing certain pockets as almost 'slums in the sun'. Popular areas boast lots of associations and clubs geared to almost every interest, such as amateur dramatics, tennis and bridge, and the Costa del Sol has more than 100 alone.

Yet if your intention is instead to *avoid* the British or foreign contingent and settle in Spain with local people it is not difficult to do so, as Spain is the second-largest country in western Europe after France, and has a coastline of 2,125km (1,320 miles).

Beware of buying in a remote area away from essential facilities, however. Rural living can be very attractive when you are in good health, but when elderly and frail, long, gruelling drives on bumpy tracks to shop, socialise or visit the dentist can be no joke. An *urbanizacion* near a town may be far more practical.

As well as the Costa Blanca and the Costa del Sol, other *costas* have been rapidly rising in popularity in recent years, including the Costa Brava, Costa Daurada and Costa de la Luz. The Balearics (Menorca, Mallorca and Ibiza) and the Canary Islands (Tenerife, Gran Canaria and Lanzarote) are eternally popular, and city-lovers are focusing on Barcelona, Madrid, Seville and Granada.

The most popular and built-up areas include the areas that first saw mass tourism several decades ago, such as Marbella, Puerto Banus, Benidorm and Estepona. The infrastructure is generally good in the popular resort areas, being geared to tourism and expat residents alike.

Spain is one of the countries in Europe targeted by skiers. Bear in mind that if you choose a detached home in a ski resort, heavy snowfall may greatly impede access, and winters can be hard and long. If you are buying a property in a ski resort, view it also when the snow has melted, as this can cover up ugly features like rubbish tips.

Balearic Islands: Mallorca, Menorca, Ibiza

As well as a fabulous climate, the Balearics boast excellent access due to the large range of cheap flights.

Mallorca, Britain's favourite holiday destination, welcomed 2.5 million British holidaymakers in 2003. Topographically it offers a great deal, with the coastline ranging from sandy beaches to cliffs, and mountains, river valleys and rich farmlands in the central plain. The island has something for everyone, including lively towns, unspoilt tranquil inland villages and family resorts. The mountain region between Soller and Valldemossa is popular with celebrities, including Richard Branson, Michael Douglas and Andrew Lloyd Webber. Claudia Schiffer and Boris Becker also have homes on the island.

Environmental controls have restricted the availability of building plots. The capital, Palma, is very attractive, and the property market here is dominated by upmarket apartments and villas. To escape the mass tourism on the island, you need to head away from the large resorts in the south, which are most likely to suffer from overdevelopment. Many people aspire to an old farmhouse (*finca*) to restore, but these are increasingly less easy to source.

Menorca boasts a good range of unspoilt beaches and its coastal resorts are quieter and dominated by family-friendly rented apartments and villas rather than hotels, as on Mallorca. Its two main towns, Ciutadella and Mahón, are pretty, old ports with good cafés, restaurants, shops and architecture.

For retirees, the Balearic islands of Menorca and Mallorca are the most popular choice. Ibiza is not likely to be top of the list as a location for many retirees because of its reputation for attracting huge numbers of young, hedonistic clubbers, although in fact away from the beaches it is easy to discover quiet, unspoilt villages.

Costa del Sol

Andalucía, in the south, is one of Spain's most varied regions, with the beaches on the Costa del Sol, skiing in the Sierra Nevada and sherry production in Jeréz. Access is excellent and you can fly into Málaga on the Costa del Sol from at least half a dozen UK airports. The temperature nudges 13–27°C (55–80°F) the whole year round and rainfall averages no more than three days per month from June to September.

The coastline is fringed by high mountain ranges and there is extensive woodland. The heart of the Costa del Sol, which has a population of 1.3 million, is the province of Málaga, between Estepona and Nerja. This area is considerably built up and includes Marbella, Fuengirola and Torremolinos. The least developed area is the far western side, which still has large stretches of countryside.

The Costa del Sol is ideal for sports enthusiasts, especially golfers. It is often called the 'Costa del Golf' as there are over 50 golf courses there now. Robert Kilroy-Silk, Kevin Keegan and Terry Venables all have homes here.

But, for all its attractions, increasingly the Costa del Sol is being shunned by British buyers due to overdevelopment, bad roads, rapidly increasing costs of living and overpriced properties.

Costa de la Luz

Far quieter than the Costa del Sol and in contrast hardly untouched, is the coast in the far southwest of Andalucía, the Costa de la Luz (Coast of Light), which stretches from windsurf capital Tarifa to the border with Portugal. Here, you'll find beaches fringed with pines and eucalyptus groves, sleepy villages and wildlife parks like the Coto de Doñana, protected national parkland stretching from Tarifa to Conil. The coast is famous for its magnificent sand dunes and windswept marshes.

Property is significantly cheaper than on the Costa del Sol, and in character the region is like Marbella was three decades ago, before the lager louts and fish and chip shops appeared. It has a pleasant climate, although there are strong winds much of the year.

An up-and-coming hotspot is Chiclana, a seaside town busy with tourists in July and August yet quieter at other times. It has good beaches and lots of restaurants and bars. A three- or four-bedroom villa here, near the beach and with a pool, costs around £140,000 to £200,000.

Costa de Almería

The Costa de Almería, sandwiched between the Costa del Sol and Costa Cálida, boasts almost as high annual temperatures as the Costa del Sol and less rainfall. It is characterised by busy tourist resorts contrasting with beautiful, unspoilt land. Far less densely populated than the most well-known *costas*, the area contains the national park of Cabo de Gata, a beautiful marine reserve.

Costa Cálida

Along the southeastern coast slightly to the north of the Costa del Almería lies the cheaper, less developed Costa Cálida, the coast of Murcia, with the Mar Menor and La Manga resort, popular with the Spanish but still relatively untouched by Brits. It has an even climate throughout the year and is flat rather than mountainous, and therefore ideal for those thinking of retiring. Prices are steadily rising and the best properties have seen a threefold increase in price since 1999. The Costa Cálida is not for people wanting English-style pubs, but will suit the more adventurous. The expansion of Murcia airport and upgraded motorway network mean access is fast improving. Alicante and San Javier airports are other options.

Costa Blanca

The Costa Blanca has a population of about 750,000 and extends 100km (63 miles) along the east coast, principally in Alicante province. More rural northern Costa Blanca, boasting a dramatic backdrop of high mountains, is more renowned for its unspoilt beauty, and prices are substantially higher than in the south generally. Prices in the select areas have doubled between 2001 and 2004. More and more British buyers have in recent years been favouring the Costa Blanca over the more overdeveloped Costa del Sol. The Costa Blanca boasts 80 blue flag beaches as well as 12 marinas.

The coast features cliffs and sandy coves while inland there are pretty villages, including Orbeta, Orba and Tormos. There are numerous golf courses, although not as many as on the Costa del Sol.

Although the temperature in the region is very similar to the Costa del Sol throughout the year, the rainfall is notably higher.

Costa Daurada

The Costa Daurada south of Barcelona is favoured by the Spanish and boasts fine, sandy beaches with forested mountains and valleys in the interior. The coast has well-developed resorts but also tiny villages and ports. Apartments, semi-detached and terraced properties are plentiful, but detached houses rarer and therefore pricey.

Costa Brava

People are attracted to the Costa Brava, the wild coast between France and Barcelona, for the quality of life and striking beauty of the surroundings rather than the promise of constant hot weather. While summers are hot (with temperatures over the year almost as high as the Costa del Sol), winters can be bracing and rainfall is substantially higher. However, the climate is ideal for many sports, and facilities ranging from sailing to golf are numerous. Mountain-walking and winter skiing are options.

The travel revolution is putting this area on the property map at long last, with the A7 motorway linking France with Barcelona and giving much easier access to historic towns like Girona. The Eurostar–TGV extension of services to Barcelona will make the region even more popular. Ryanair, easyJet, BA and Iberia all fly locally, while P&O and Brittany Ferries sail from Portsmouth and Plymouth to Bilbao and Santander.

Catalonia enjoys strict building regulations and therefore is nothing like as spoilt as many other areas of the country. Still, the region has its fair share of places to avoid, such as the package tour resorts of Estartit at the northern and Lloret de Mar at the southern end of the *costa*. Sa Tuna, near the medieval hilltop village of Begur, on the other hand, is delightful.

Canary Islands

Their geographical position, and proximity to Africa, gives these islands of volcanic origin a fabulous climate, with a dry heat that is ideal for a number of health conditions. For winter sun you can't beat the Canary Islands. Here, you can swim in an outdoor pool in winter (although sea bathing in midwinter can be only for the hardiest) and wear shirt sleeves in the evening. Even so, the Canaries get their fair share of windy, overcast periods. And apart from wind-surfing, there isn't a great deal to do.

The islands include Gran Canaria, La Gomera, Lanzarote, Fuerteventura, La Palma, Tenerife, Hierro and numerous other smaller isles.

They suffer from the effects of mass tourism, namely ugly apartment blocks, rowdy British pub-style bars and concrete shorelines, but also have some excellent beaches and many opportunities to get off the tourist track. They offer plentiful apartment complexes with communal pools to choose from. Tenerife and Gran Canaria have the most Spanish flavour and the quieter, more upmarket islands include La Gomera and Lanzarote. Fuerteventura has dramatic mountains and moonscapes and pretty inland villages and is one of the cheaper, quieter islands.

Costa Verde

Although the daunting distance causes few motorists to contemplate regular drives to the hot, sunny south of Spain, buying a property within comfortable distance of the northern Spanish ports of Santander and Bilbao is an increasingly popular option.

Inland: Catalonia

Greatly improved travel options such as extended Eurostar–TGV train services and fast motorways are opening whole new areas of Spain to those seeking a retirement home. The Catalonia region of northern Spain, away from the madding crowds, is easily accessible using the A7 motorway linking France with Barcelona and giving much easier access to historic towns, and by air via Barcelona airport or the airport at the small town of Reus on the Costa Daurada. The area has had comparatively little real development.

The wine regions of southern Catalonia, south of Barcelona, have largely been overlooked by British buyers (and the Barcelonese) searching for a retirement home. As ever, they prefer colonising the coast.

Dubbed by some as 'the new Provence', village and town houses and farm-houses in need of restoration in many villages and towns range from under £60,000 in a village such as Albarca or market towns like Villafranca de Penedes, to over £200,000 in a rustic mountain village like Siurana, 20 miles inland from Reus Airport.

Inland: rural Andalucía

Turn your back on the sea and head for the hills and you find the real, undeveloped Andalucía, with plunging property prices to boot. Access is good, with regular Ryanair and British Airways flights to Jeréz and Monarch flights to neighbouring Gibraltar.

Inland, just over an hour's drive down twisting roads from the overdeveloped Costa del Sol, the region around the town of Ronda can be a very welcome escape to tranquillity and tradition. A Moorish stronghold for seven centuries, Ronda attracts the bohemian set, such as writers and artists. Properties are scarce and you could expect to pay £70,000 or so for a cottage in a village around here, maybe £375,000 for a new four-bed home with a swimming pool.

Antequera is one of a series of quaint red-roofed and white-walled villages, and boasts Baroque churches, a bullring, streets shaded by almond and orange trees and wide marble pavements. Nearby are extensive olive groves as well as the impressive lake of Iznajar. Around here, you are likely to find old houses ripe for renovation and very little new development. In a nearby village, for example, terraced houses with courtyard gardens go for around £50,000 to £60,000.

Bear in mind that isolated properties located in the countryside in rural areas like these often lack utilities, and electricity and telephone coverage may be absent, and water only obtainable from a well. English is seldom spoken in such areas.

Cities: Barcelona, Madrid and Valencia

Barcelona is Spain's most popular city for foreign buyers, thanks to its exquisite waterside setting. Interest has also boomed in vibrant Madrid.

Valencia, until now almost always overlooked, is likely to become more popular, not least because of its substantially lower property prices. Indeed it is tipped by analysts as being the next Iberian hotspot, helped by being host to the 2007 America's Cup yacht race and the airport being extended. However, see 'Legal restrictions', below.

Currency and exchange rate

Euro (€); £1 = €1.50.

Property prices

Most property bought by foreigners is newly built, and tends to be considerably higher in price than period options; most properties under £50,000 tend to be apartments. Even so, little stone cottages in unspoilt inland villages can still sometimes be picked up for less than £35,000 or so all around the country.

The Costa del Sol has a wide price range, with four-bedroom villas with pools averaging £425,000 and two-bed apartments costing on average £200,000. Inland prices are around 20 per cent lower. Prices on the Costa Blanca north are generally 20 per cent cheaper than the Costa del Sol and another 20 per cent cheaper at Costa Blanca south.

Prices on the Costa Cálida and Costa de Almeíra are on average almost half those of the Costa del Sol. A two-bedroom apartment on the Costa del Almeíra currently averages £110,000, while a four-bed villa is commonly around £225,000. A three-bedroom apartment with sea view in a touristy area, like the coastal town of Rosas on the Costa Brava is around £250,000 and more than double that around a desirable village like Begur or Llafranc.

A large proportion of new-build homes sell off-plan (before they are built) and in a number of areas there is seldom enough resale property to satisfy demand.

It is not unusual for properties on the islands to be 25 per cent more than on the Costa del Sol. Good property has become expensive in Menorca, and has more than doubled in the last five years. A good house will typically cost between £800,000 and £1m, and therefore the days of selling an average house in the UK to fund an above-average home in the Balearics and still have half your capital left are long gone.

Interest in buying property in Spanish cities has soared recently, and in 2003 prices rose by 20 per cent in Madrid and Barcelona, even to the extent of catching up with Paris in some neighbourhoods – an unthinkable notion a few years ago. Expect to pay around £200,000–250,000 for a two- or three-bed flat in the Gracia district (*barrio*) of Barcelona, popular with artists and intellectuals and around half a mile north of the central Placa de Catalunya. A one-bed apartment on the harbour front costs much the same.

In Madrid, prices are similar to Barcelona and a central two-bedroom apartment is in the region of £400,000. For cheaper Spanish city living (around 30 per cent lower than Madrid and Barcelona) opt for Valencia, which is imminently set to rise considerably in popularity.

Local mortgages

Spanish mortgages require full proof of income and outgoings and do not take into account any potential income from lettings. A deposit of 25 per cent of the purchase price is generally the minimum required, and most mortgages are on a repayment basis.

Access to and from the UK

Spain enjoys a large choice of scheduled, chartered and budget flights easing access to the *costas* and beyond. In recent years, having a weekend retreat in a vibrant Spanish city is an affordable possibility, with bargain flights available to destinations such as Barcelona, Bilbao, Jeréz, Valencia and Madrid.

The greater variety of routes and the expansion of regional airports such as Murcia, serving the Costa Cálida and the southern part of the Costa Blanca, means the busiest airports, like Alicante, can be avoided. Smaller UK regional airports like Glasgow, Bristol and Manchester are increasingly taking traffic away from Heathrow and Gatwick and making a retreat in Spain a far more attractive proposition to British buyers in the west and north of England and in Scotland. Brittany Ferries operates regular services from Plymouth to Santander, while P&O Portsmouth run from Portsmouth to Bilbao. Buying a property near these ports is uncommon because of the lack of sun, but the northeastern *costas* – Brava, Daurada and del Azahar on the Mediterranean – are within easy driving distance because of the fast-improving roads.

Greatly improved travel options such as extended Eurostar–TGV train services and fast motorways are opening whole new areas of Spain to those seeking a holiday or retirement home. The Catalonia region of northern Spain is easily accessible using the A7 motorway linking France with Barcelona and giving much easier access to historic towns like Girona.

Legal restrictions

If you spend less than 183 days a year in Spain, you are usually classed a non-resident and will be required to nominate a fiscal representative (a person the tax authorities can correspond with in Spain), pay local rates, make a Spanish income tax declaration, pay car tax and insurance if you have a car in Spain, make a declaration of your capital assets in Spain and possibly pay a small percentage of wealth tax on them, as well as pay regular utilities bills.

Rules governing land can sometimes be a minefield and make it all the more vital for buyers to engage the services of an experienced, English-speaking lawyer. In Valencia province, for example, which includes the Costa Blanca, there is a possibility that land attached to some properties could later either be compulsorily purchased for development and/or the owner be liable to pay a contribution towards development costs. Agents and developers are not legally required to mention this.

Spain has a law of subrogation, where debts connected with a property, such as mortgages, rates, community charges and local taxes, remain with the property and are the responsibility of the buyer, whether they caused the debt or not. Therefore it is very important your legal adviser clarifies whether there are any outstanding debts on the property.

The buying process

Buying property in Spain can have its problems and therefore it is wise to be aware as possible of the buying process.

As well as using an estate agent (*inmobiliaria*), it is worth checking out locations in person, as many Spaniards sell privately to avoid paying commission. Look out for 'for sale' (*se vende*) signs; in rural areas properties may be advertised in bars. Spanish property transactions are overseen by a notary (*notario*) appointed by the government. This public official is paid by the purchaser and/or vendor. She or he is not required to verify clauses or safeguard against fraud and therefore is no substitute for independent legal advice.

When you have found the property you wish to buy, as property laws vary considerably in Spain it is important to engage an English-speaking lawyer who specialises in overseas legal services. Few people take as much professional advice as they should when buying, and it is common for buyers to sign documents casually and hand over money before realising that there is no title to the property, it has not been built yet, or it was built without planning permission.

Appropriately experienced legal firms can carry out the property acquisition, which involves vetting the contract, providing translations and carrying out local enquiries and searches. These include checking that the seller has legal title to the property and that there are no unpaid debts accrued against the property, ascertaining whether the local authority has imposed any building restrictions and checking the boundaries of the surrounding land. Some specialist firms can also advise about related matters such as commissioning a survey, raising finance, timeshare sales, emigration and retirement, setting up in business in Spain, and dealing with taxation and foreign inheritance laws.

Generally, when you have selected a property, a private sale and purchase contract, completely binding on both parties, is drawn up by the estate agent or your lawyer. If the contract (*contrato privado de compraventa*) is drawn up by the estate agent, your lawyer should vet the contract before signing.

This contract typically states details of the purchaser and vendor, amount of deposit (usually 10 per cent of the agreed sale price), completion date, payment method, extras the buyer has agreed to buy, and any other conditions. The contract fixes the price, eliminating gazumping, and states the date of the final payment and signing of the public deeds to the property. The deposit can only be refunded under certain strict conditions and therefore it is important to be aware of what these are.

If you are offered a deal where the property is officially sold at an artificially low price with the balance as 'cash under the table', avoid it, as apart from being illegal, such deals can create inflated capital gains tax problems if you later sell the property, as the gain appears to be larger on paper than it is in reality.

Before signing, you should be aware of added expenses such as the community fees and annual rates payable as these can be quite high. You need to see a copy of the deeds, stating that the people claiming to be the owners are those named on the deeds. You need to see the *nota simple*, a land registry document stating who owns the property and indicating whether an out-standing mortgage (which would be passed on to you) or other encumbrance affect the property.

If the property is new or was built in the last few years, you require documents from the local town hall proving that a building licence was obtained and, if the property has already been lived in, a licence of first occupation. If buying 'off-plan', that is, before the building has been built, payments are normally made in agreed stages. Ensure that the contract allows you to retain a final payment for 6 or 12 months after completion of building works so that any faults that crop up can be rectified.

Rural properties, such as an old village cottage or a farm, may have been handed down from generation to generation and therefore deeds may not exist. This situation will require specialised legal help and you will probably have to draw up a topographical plan noting such things as boundary lines, rights of way and water rights. Obtaining title deeds for such a property can take considerable time.

The Spanish conveyancing process involves numerous other points that a good legal representative should be able to take you through, such as ensuring that transfer of utilities charges, local taxes and other expenses relating to the property are made on the day of the sale, so that you are not liable for any unpaid previous ones.

The balance of the purchase price and any outstanding fees are payable when the purchaser and vendor sign the definitive contract, which is the same as the title deeds of the property (*escritura de compaventa*) drawn up by the notary. This gives details of all ownership history. All parties involved should attend or otherwise arrange to have a power of attorney attend in their absence.

Rural properties seldom have a straightforward *escritura*, and for this reason, it is imperative that your lawyer checks every aspect of the title deeds before you commit yourself. It is common for the property size and boundaries to change over the years with no documentation. Your legal representative should indicate whether there are any possible adverse clauses in the deeds.

After signing, the notary lodges the deeds with the land registry to register the change in title, as in Spain a property's title deeds are assigned after the contract has been sealed rather than before, as in the UK. This can result in an extra three- or four-month wait before the sale can be completed. Land registry fees are then due.

The notary should provide a copy of the deeds for your lawyer to complete other legal formalities. The notary's fees are due on completion.

Costs of buying

Total costs of buying average at least 10 per cent to the purchase price of the property. Transfer tax (*impuesto de transmisiones patrimoniales*) varies from region to region and in Andalucía is 7 per cent of the sale price of the property. There are registration fees of 0.5 per cent, plus the notary's fee and the lawyer's fee. Other costs include a possible surveying fee and mortgage valuation. The estate agent's fee, typically between 5 and 10 per cent, but sometimes as much as 15 per cent (although rates have been increasingly going down in recent years in response to buyer dissatisfaction), is often included in the purchase price. The buyer is also usually obliged by Spanish law to pay 5 per cent of the value of the property to the tax office on account of the seller's potential tax liabilities.

Is property a good investment?

Prices in Spain have been rising rapidly in recent years overall, at a rate of 15 per cent in 2002 and 2003. Although slowing in 2004, the prices along the coast will continue to grow steadily, helped by the large increase in numbers of northern Europeans retiring to Spain.

For those wishing to own a property in Spain through an offshore company to avoid local taxes and inheritance laws, the Inland Revenue in the UK has in 2004 given notice that homes owned through a company structure may be taxed as a benefit in kind. The charge would be based on an assumed value for the property and therefore the more it is thought to be worth, the higher the amount to pay. The Inland Revenue would assume a rateable value for the first £75,000 and charge what it calls the interest on beneficial loans on any excess amount. The rate is currently 5 per cent.

Living in Spain

Overall Spain enjoys a superb climate (the climate on the Costa Blanca is considered by the World Health Organisation to be among the healthiest in the world), political stability, a high standard of living yet lower cost of living than much of Europe. It has a low crime rate and good standard of healthcare which is free to EU residents.

Once you have financial dealings in Spain, whether a resident or non-resident, you are required to have a fiscal number (*número de identificación de extranjero*). Without this, you cannot register the deeds of a property, pay or claim back tax, open a bank account or take out insurance, among other things. Non-resident property owners are also required to appoint a fiscal representative to deal with their tax dealings.

Banking

Spanish banking differs from that in the UK. The use of personal cheques is rare and most people pay by credit, charge or debit card. Bank charges tend to be higher than in the UK, more than 0.1 per cent interest is rarely offered, and currency transfers out of Spain can attract as much as a 4 per cent charge. For such regions, it is wise for deposit accounts to be held in the UK or in an offshore account. Regular payments like utility bills are usually paid by standing order (*domiciliación de pagos*).

Retirement and Health

At 65, you receive two sizeable benefits of retired residency: tax breaks and free medical care. A 2004 World Health Organization report ranked Spain among the top 10 countries in the world for healthcare, compared with 18th place for the UK. Retired EU citizens (but not those from the USA or other non-EU countries) are entitled to full use of the Spanish health service, which is 80% privately run, just as a Spanish person. Free public healthcare is also available to employees and dependants paying Spanish social security as well as EU citizens visiting the country who are in possession of an E111 form, available from any post office. If a private retirement scheme insuring you covers medical costs, you also have rights to the same medical cover as a Spanish person.

To qualify for the benefits, you are required to notify your change of residence to your pension authorities in the UK before you leave and to obtain a form E121 from the Department of Work and Pensions in the UK and submit it immediately to the health authorities in Spain.

Pensions

Any person eligible for a state pension in any other EU country is free to receive it in Spain. Recipients of company pensions may also do this, and funds are paid wherever the particular scheme allows, usually either into a Spanish bank or otherwise into a UK account and then transferred into a Spanish one. Non-EU pensioners can also do this.

People who have worked in Spain in the past may be entitled to a Spanish pension on retirement, and contributions that have been made in another EU country prior to taking up residence are generally taken into account. To forecast your pension income and state entitlement if you were to retire in Spain, the DSS in the UK can provide a BR19 form so that you will receive an accurate projection.

There are numerous property developments specifically aimed at the retired, which may have medical clinics, nursing care and shopping facilities within the complex.

Tax

If your principal residence is in Spain or you remain in Spain for more than 183 days in any tax year (1 January to 31 December), whether in one block or made up by different visits, you become a tax resident of Spain and liable for Spanish taxation on worldwide income and investments. Non-resident property-owners are liable for income tax if the property is rented out.

Income tax (*impuesto sobre la renta de las personas físicas* or *IRPF*) in Spain is complicated and very different from the UK system. The tax is on a sliding scale from 18 up to 48 per cent although personal allowances are more generous than in the UK. There are also local income taxes, which vary from region to region.

A local property tax (*impuesto sobre bienes inmuebles*) is payable by home-owners and generally varies from 0.3 to 1.7 per cent. It is based on the value of a property as assessed by the local authority (*ayuntamiento*) and is relatively low, perhaps £100 or so for a small cottage and £500 for a large house. The tax is calculated on the basis of the notional rental value (*valor catastral*) of the property multiplied by the tax rate fixed locally. If you do not agree with the notional value put on your property, you are entitled to appeal, although the amount being disputed is likely to be too small to make this worthwhile.

Some localities charge a refuse tax (*basura*), and in addition, the local authority is entitled to raise taxes for projects and to cover shortfalls.

Spanish wealth tax (*patrimonio*) is payable on your worldwide assets, varying from 0.2 per cent for assets up to €167,129 to 2.5 per cent for assets over €10,695,996.

Residence permits

Residence permits are a formality for EU nationals, and non-EU pensioners generally find it easier than non-EU nationals of working age to become legally resident, only being required to prove that they have sufficient income to support themselves in the country. Retired applicants for a EU residency card are required to prove that they have adequate medical insurance and sufficient financial resources that will cover other family members also. They are required to prove that they are entitled to retirement benefits in the place of residence.

Visitors may remain in the country for six months each year without a residence permit.

Selling

People over 65 who sell their main residence pay no capital gains tax. Otherwise, capital gains tax (*impuesto sobre incremento de patrimonio*) is at 18 per cent for residents and 35 per cent for non-residents and there are various exemptions.

Inheritance tax

For Spaniards, inheritance rules apply that are far more restrictive than the rules under English law. Certain groups of people almost have automatic rights to a proportion of a deceased Spanish person's property. Yet if you are not Spanish, you can dispose of your property as your national laws permit, which in the UK is generally as you wish.

Inheritance tax is paid in Spain on the value of any assets in Spain at the date of death. This varies from 7.65 per cent up to €7,993.46 to 34 per cent for values over €797,555.08. There are various exemptions and conditions and those receiving the inheritance pay tax on what they receive.

Spanish succession tax (also called gift tax) is payable if the recipient of the gift or the heir of an estate resides in Spain, or if the asset being passed on the event of death or gifted is a property in Spain. The tax is governed by the autonomous communities, or regions, and these are moving towards abolishing succession tax or offering tax relief between spouses, direct blood descendants and adopted children. As the tax position is currently changing, check with a qualified Spanish tax adviser.

It is wise to make a Spanish will as the alternative; using your UK will, can cause sizeable costs and tax disadvantages. Having no will at all is obviously even costlier still.

Further information

- **Spain: t** (00 34)

- **24-hour visa information service** (UK), **t** 0900 160 0123.

- **Foundation Institute of Foreign Property Owners**, Apartado 418, 03590 Altea, Alicante, Spain, **t** 96 584 2312; **www.fipe.org**.

- **Spanish Consulate General**, 20 Draycott Place, London SW3 2RZ, UK, **t** (020) 7589 8989.

- **Spanish Embassy**, 39 Chesham Place, London SW1X 8SB, UK, **t** (020) 7235 5555; **www.cec-spain.org.uk**.

- **Spanish Embassy**, 2375 Pennsylvania Avenue, NW, Washington DC 20008, USA, **t** (202) 452 0100; **www.spainemb.org**.

- **Spanish Tourist Office**, 22–23 Manchester Square, London W1U 3PX, UK, **t** (020) 7486 8077; **www.tourspain.es**.

- **www.aboutspain.net:** information on different Spanish regions.

- **www.britishexpat.com** and **www.directmoving.com**: advice about Spain, Spanish property, living in Spain and associated matters.

- **www.escapetospain.co.uk**: information on the most popular Spanish *costas*.

- **www.idealspain.com**, **www.spain-info.com** and **www.typicallyspanish.com**: information on different aspects of Spain.

- **www.red2000.com:** tourist information about Spain.

- **www.spainexpat.com**: geared to the Spanish expatriate.

- **www.spanish-living.com:** property listings and lots of advice.

- **www.tuspain.com**: property information on Spain.

Finance

- **Currencies Direct** (Spain), **t** 96 570 7971.
- **Barclays Spain** (Spain), **t** 91 336 1610; **www.barclays.es**.
- **Norwich and Peterborough Spanish Home Loans** (UK), **t** (01733) 372006; **www.norwichandpeterborough.co.uk**.
- **Banco Halifax Hispania** (UK), **t** (01422) 333868; **www.halifax.es**.
- **Siddalls** (UK), **t** (01329) 288641; **www.siddalls.net**. Provides tax, pensions, inheritance and investment planning advice to British nationals in Spain.

Estate agents

General

- **Catalan Country Life** (Spain), **t** 93 467 1523; **www.catalancountrylife.com**.
- **European Villa Solutions** (UK), **t** (01223) 514241; **www.europeanvs.com**.
- **Mercers** (UK), **t** (01491) 574807; **www.spanishproperty.co.uk**.
- **Property Finder** (UK), **t** (01908) 218 753; **www.thepropertyfinder.com**.
- **Your House in Spain** (Spain), **t** 93 306 3541; **www.yhis.com**.
- **www.themovechannel.com** lists websites selling property in Spain.

Balearic Islands

- **Escape2balearics.com** (UK), **t** (0161) 351 2160; **www.escape2balearics.co.uk**.
- **Kuhn and Partner** (Spain), **t** 97 122 80 0; **www.kuhn-partner.com**.
- **Prestige Properties** (Spain), **t** 97 119 0455; **www.ibizaprestige.com**.

Andalucía

- **Flamencoshop** (Spain), **t** 62 798 9543; **www.flamencoshop.com**.
- **Intereality** (Spain), **t** 95 270 6380; **www.intereality.es**.
- **Properties Abroad** (UK), **t** (020) 8441 2078; **www.propertiesabroad.com**.
- **The Property Finders** (UK), **t** (01908) 218753; **www.thepropertyfinders.com**.
- **La Serrania** (Spain), **t** 95 287 7286.
- **Travellers Way** (UK), **t** (01527) 559 000.

Costa Blanca

All agents are based in the UK.

- **Atlas International**, **t** 0800 531 6500; **www.atlasinternational.com**.
- **QSD**, **t** 0800 783 1616; **www.qsdgroup.com**.
- **Ultra Villas**, **t** (01242) 221500; **www.ultravillas.co.uk**.

Canary Islands

- **Amazing Property Services** (Spain), **t** 92 271 7166; **www.amazingproperties.com.**
- **Engels and Volkers** (UK), **t** (020) 7590 3170; **www.engelvolkers.com.**
- **Main's Amis Estates** (UK), **t** (020) 8311 1110; **www.mainsamisestates.co.uk.**

Catalonia

- **World Class Homes** (UK), **t** 0800 731 4713; **www.worldclasshomes.co.uk.**

Ronda

- **Hamptons International** (UK), **t** (020) 7589 8844; **www.hamptonsinternational.co.uk.**

Rural Spain

- **Greenbox Properties** (UK), **t** (01670) 528258; **www.greenbox.co.uk.** Cottages in rural Andalucía and Murcia from £20,000.
- **Inmobiliaria Almanzora** (Spain), **t** 95 012 0406; **www.inmobiliaria.com.** A selection of rustic farmhouses and *fincas* in the Almanzora Valley from £20,000.
- **Real Spain** (UK), **t** 0871 871 6755; **www.real-spain.net.** Resale and period property both on the coast and inland.
- **Siroco Estates** (UK), **t** (01253) 294848/402188; **www.sirocoestates.com.** Country properties half an hour's drive from the coast.

Madrid, Barcelona and Valencia

- **Ambassador** (Spain), **t** 91 577 5642.
- **John Taylor** (Spain), **t** 93 241 3082; **www.johntaylorspain.com.**
- **Knight Frank** (Spain), **t** 91 788 0700; **www.knightfrank.co.uk.**
- **Lonbar** (UK), **t** (0118) 951 9811; **www.lonbar.com.**
- **Proincasa** (UK), **t** (020) 7079 1412; **www.proincasaresidential.com.**
- **Promora** (Spain), **t** 91 650 4242; **www.promora.com.**

Switzerland

Why retire here?

Switzerland, bordered by France, Germany, Italy, Austria and Liechtenstein, is at the crossroads of Europe. It boasts economic stability, almost clinical cleanliness, affluence, neutrality, low taxes and a healthy climate. Not only is Switzerland renowned for its skiing, with the Alps reaching altitudes of over 4,000m (13,000ft), but its breathtaking scenery is also a wonderful backdrop for hot summers. As well as its stunning mountains, it has crystal-clear lakes, vibrant cities and charming little villages.

Many people assume that its property is only for the super-rich, yet there is great opportunity to buy at an affordable price. Switzerland's ultra-efficiency, with such things as trains running on time, is a revelation to many British.

Downsides

There are a number of restrictions concerning property ownership, including not being permitted to buy in some areas or sell within two years of purchase in most circumstances.

The cost of both living and of property is high in Switzerland. The super-efficiency and general neatness might be too much for some. Be sure to view properties not only when the snow has fallen, but once it has melted, too. Snow can cover a multitude of sins, such as ugly roofs and rubbish tips.

Property types

Chalets and chalet apartments in resort areas are of principal interest to retirees, and, to a lesser extent, apartments in the main cities such as Zürich, Berne and Geneva.

Where to retire

A number of *cantons* restrict foreign property ownership and this, combined with the high price of property and a lack of properties for sale, means that there is not a great deal of choice compared to neighbouring countries.

The Bernese Oberland has rustic wooden chalets among pretty hills, while Switzerland's only Italian-speaking *canton*, Ticino, provides lakeside villas and a hotter climate. Villars in the western *canton* of Vaud is near enough for visits to Geneva. Other areas popular with foreign buyers include Montreux and Châteaux d'Oex in the *canton* of Vaud, Klosters in Canton des Grisons and Gstaad in the Bernese Oberland. Internationally famous Verbier is popular, boasting more than 600km of pistes; there are plenty of pubs, clubs, restaurants, excellent shops and a golf course.

Crans-Montana is a chic and elegant resort uniquely situated on a south-facing plateau overlooking the Rhône Valley. It enjoys an unusually sheltered climate and has two good golf courses, four lakes, hotels, restaurants and night-clubs. Nearby, with more family atmosphere, is Anzère, situated just above Sion, which has a relatively high proportion of chalet-style apartment complexes.

Currency and exchange rate

Swiss franc; £1 = Sfr 2.31.

Property prices

Prices have been rising steadily, at around 12 to 16 per cent in 2003 alone. The pretty, sleepy little town of Châteaux d'Oex has one-bed apartments starting at £115,000. In the swish, cosmopolitan town of Montreux, a one-bedroom apartment would typically cost £150,000 or more, with £200,000 the starting price for two bedrooms. In Villars, you would typically pay about 25 per cent more. A five-bed chalet in Chailly, north of Montreux, is around £300,000.

At Verbier, studios start at under £50,000, one-bed apartments from about £100,000, two bedrooms from £145,000 and three beds from about £180,000.

Local mortgages

These tend to enjoy lower rates than those in the UK, although there is significantly less choice as to mortgage types.

Access to and from the UK

There are plenty of flights to Swiss cities from many British airports and carriers include Swissair, British Airways and easyJet.

Legal restrictions

It is difficult to buy homes outside tourist resorts and in some German-speaking areas. Not all of the country's *cantons* allow foreigners to buy property, although recent years have seen restrictions relax slightly. Those *cantons* that do allow sales may have special conditions, such as quota systems, designated regions that foreigners can buy in, or restrictions on the type of property that can be bought or on whom a vendor can sell to.

Foreign owners are required to occupy a Swiss property for at least three weeks per year. Letting can be for a maximum of 11 months per year. In an attempt to discourage property speculation, there is a rule that properties cannot be sold for two years after the purchase date, except for certain reasons, such as family illness or death.

The buying process

Before buying, permission must be obtained from the local *canton* and the government, which takes anything from two months to three years. Sellers usually do not accept offers below the asking price. An official notary is appointed by the selling agent to act for both buyer and seller, who sign a legally binding contract for the sale, written in French, German or Italian, depending on where the sale is taking place in the country. At the same time, the buyer pays a 10 per cent deposit, which is forfeited if the buyer subsequently pulls out of the deal. On completion, the title deed is registered by both the local land registry and the central land registry situated in Berne.

Costs of buying

The notary and land registry fees and transfer tax usually amount to around 5 per cent of the purchase price of the property.

Is property a good investment?

In the long term property represents a good investment, especially as property is generally in short supply in this country, but various restrictions make it difficult to successfully speculate about the short-term prospects.

Living in Switzerland

Switzerland is split into 26 largely autonomous *cantons* that have diverse culture, geography and climates. Indeed, its weather conditions are probably Europe's most varied in such a small area. North of the Alps (which extend from west to east), there is a continental climate with hot summers and cold winters, while the south has a Mediterranean climate of hot summers and mild winters.

Politically, Switzerland is very stable. The standard of living is high, yet the cost of living is not as high as people assume and is lower than 20 years ago. German, French and Italian are the official languages, although English is widely spoken.

The crime rate in Switzerland is low and healthcare facilities are of a very high standard, although expensive so private health insurance is necessary.

Taxation rates vary in each of the 26 *cantons* in the country and non-residents are required to pay Swiss income tax on any income earned in the country. Peculiarly, members of the Catholic, Old Catholic (Protestant) and Reformed churches are required to pay a variable church tax.

Residence permits, except for short-term employment, are difficult to obtain, although it helps if you have a job that is in demand, are over 60 and/or have wealth. Those wishing to retire in Switzerland are required to prove that they have sufficient funds to support themselves and must sign a declaration stating that they will not seek paid employment. Non-residents can spend a total of six months per year in the country, as a maximum of three months each time.

Bear in mind that if you choose a detached home in a ski resort, heavy snow-fall may greatly impede access, winters can be hard and long, and you may require someone to visit your property frequently to clear the snow and check the central heating. Uncleared snow can result, once the temperature has risen and it refreezes, in a glacier around the property.

Selling

Capital gains tax, which is usually only applicable to profits made from property, varies from *canton* to *canton* and are dependent on the amount gained and length of ownership.

Inheritance tax

Rates of inheritance tax vary from *canton* to *canton*, and is not levied by Schwyz *canton*.

Further information

- **Switzerland: t** (00 41)
- **American Citizens Abroad**, 5 Rue Liotard, 1202 Geneva, Switzerland, **t** 22 340 0233; **www.aca.ch**.
- **British Resident's Association of Switzerland**, Chemin de Chenalettaz 105, 1807 Bloney, Switzerland, **t** 21 943 1788.
- **Swiss Embassy**, 16–18 Montagu Place, London W1H 2BQ, UK, **t** (020) 7723 0701; **www.swissembassy.org.uk**.
- **Swiss Embassy**, 2900 Cathedral Avenue, NW, Washington, DC 20008, USA, **t** (202) 745 7900; **www.swissemb.org**.
- **Switzerland Tourism**, Bellariastr 38, 8027 Zürich, Switzerland, **t** 1 288 1111.
- **www.myswitzerland.com**: tourist information about Switzerland.

Estate agents

All estate agents are based in the UK.

- **Alpine Apartments Agency, t** (01544) 388234; **www.alpineapartmentsagency.co.uk**.
- **Engel and Voelkers, t** (020) 7590 3170; **www.engelvoelkers.ch**.
- **Investors in Property, t** (020) 8905 5511; **www.investorsinproperty.com**.
- **Overseas Homesearch, t** 0870 240 3258; **www.overseashomesearch.co.uk**.
- **Sotheby's, t** (020) 7598 1600; **www.sothebysrealty.com**.
- **Villas Abroad, t** (020) 8941 4499.

Turkey

Why retire here?

Although Turkey has a long way to go before it could be considered a popular choice as a retirement home location, the surge in popularity in recent years by tourists for its west coast has caused increasing interest for buying there.

Fantastic weather, coupled with a very low cost of living, the friendliest of people and a truly exotic culture as Europe merges with Asia (95 per cent of it is in Asia) make it a great choice for buying. The majority of the country is unspoilt and it enjoys a rich, fascinating history and culture.

Its popularity has also increased since it was recommended for consideration for EU membershop by the European Commission in October 2004, though this could easily take another 10 years to happen.

Downsides

Turkey's borders, established only in 1923, are with Iraq, Iran, Syria, Georgia, Armenia, Greece and Bulgaria – so it is hardly the most stable region in the world. Still, the areas popular with the vast majority of buyers – the Aegean and Mediterranean coasts – are well away from Middle East trouble spots.

There are internal problems caused by Islamic militants and its Kurdish population demanding their own state, as well as Turkey has had a poor record of democracy and of human rights, and a long-standing poor relationship with Greece. Yet there has recently been greater stability and and in recent years real steps have been taken to resolve the Cyprus problem.

There is also a history of geographical instability, in the form of a tendency for earthquakes, although in fact, Italy suffers more of them than Turkey. The Turkish lira has historically been very unstable and therefore the exchange rate can vary greatly, which plays havoc with proposed budgets when purchasing.

The property market is unregulated, so buyers need to beware of unscrupulous operators, who tend to populate the more popular tourist centres.

Property types

Properties popular with foreign buyers are generally in new developments with purpose-built holiday facilities, such as swimming pools, tennis courts, children's play areas and other sport and leisure features.

Where to retire

The bulk of properties popular with foreign buyers are on the Aegean and Mediterranean coasts, not least because there is good infrastructure, many facilities for holidaymakers, a great stretch of coastline and temperatures averaging around 28°C (82°F) in July and August. The most popular areas are around Antalya, Belek, Bodrum, Fethiye, Izmir, Kalkan and Kaş. Some areas, such as Kalkan, enjoy strict conservation laws.

Currency and exchange rate

Turkish lira; £1 = 2,700,000 TL.

Property prices

Prices are relatively low, not least because the Turkish lira has been unstable and subject to devaluations. A three-bedroom villa in good condition near the sea at Marmaris is typically be around £90,000, while a one-bed apartment at Kalkan, an unspoilt town east of Marmaris, could be picked up for less than £25,000. A spacious four-bedroom villa at Fethiye in southern Turkey on the Mediterranean coast would probably cost about £120,000.

Local mortgages

UK lenders do not as yet lend on Turkish property, so raising cash would have to be by another way, such as remortgaging or selling a UK home. Turkish banks offer loans, but better terms are usually available abroad and the Turkish lira can be extremely volatile.

Access to and from the UK

There is a good choice of scheduled flights to Istanbul. Turkish Airlines has year-round flights from the UK via Istanbul to Bodrum, Izmir and Dalaman, taking around 6hrs. Cheaper charter flights are generally available from May to September, and there is more choice in the summer months, such as direct flights from London to Dalaman taking around 4hrs.

Legal restrictions

Property purchase in military areas or security zones and certain villages and towns or outside the boundaries of a municipality are not permitted. Military permission must be obtained by all foreigners buying property. However, forming a company to purchase the property may get round this problem.

The buying process

Strict rules govern foreigners buying property in Turkey and therefore a bilingual lawyer familiar with Turkish conveyancing is essential. It is important that your lawyer explains Turkish inheritance laws as these vary considerably from British ones.

Non-Turkish buyers are required to gain permission from the Turkish government to buy property. Nationals of certain countries that do not have reciprocity with Turkey are not permitted to buy property in the country, but these countries do not include the UK, USA and most European countries.

Market values for properties in Turkey can be non-existent or vague and therefore a good degree of haggling may be necessary before you agree on a price. When vendor and purchaser have agreed the purchase price, they sign a preliminary contract with the vendor's estate agent and the buyer pays a deposit, typically of 10–25 per cent. This does not bind vendors to sell and buyers can claim only expenses they have incurred if vendors pull out of the deal. On the other hand, buyers lose the deposit should they subsequently not go ahead with buying.

The initial contract contains details of the sale such as the completion date, conditional clauses and details about the property and buyer and seller. Conditional clauses should be included to cover you against the possibility of there being debts on the property, there not being clear title or your failure to secure a loan on it.

To get around the problem of the vendor's not being bound to sell to you, you can obtain an undertaking to sell (*sati vaadi sozle mesi*) from the vendor, prepared by a notary public at a cost of an extra 1.2 per cent of the purchase price. This formal contract will include full details of the sale, vendor and purchaser and any conditions.

The purchaser instructs his or her lawyer to make the necessary checks and searches. The transaction is prepared by the land registrar and a contract for the sale is drawn up. This process can all take six months or so. When the sale is ready for completion, the deeds are signed in the presence of the land registrar and a copy is given to the purchaser. Buying from another overseas owner is considerably quicker than buying from a Turkish national, as the necessary searches and checks will have already been done.

Costs of buying

Funds for purchasing a property must be imported from abroad, backed up by official proof. There is a property transfer tax of 1.5 per cent of the declared value of the property, which is generally lower than the purchase price. Notary fees are 0.8–1.5 per cent. Vendor and purchaser both pay 4.8 per cent of the declared value of the property in stamp duty. As well as conveyancing costs, there is a registration fee for the contract of 0.54 per cent of the contract price. The vendor and purchaser are required to pay estate agency fees of around 3 per cent. The buyer pays 3 per cent of the purchase price to the land registry, although sometimes buyer and seller agree to split the cost.

Is property a good investment?

With more and more foreign buyers, and an increasing possibility of Turkey's joining the EU, means that property here could have good investment potential.

Living in Turkey

Turkey is a huge country with a wide variety of climates and ways of life. Although much of eastern Turkey is very undeveloped and in parts winters can be harsh, the areas popular with buyers, around the Aegean, Mediterranean and Marmara coasts, have a Mediterranean climate with more than 300 days of sunshine each year and mild winters.

The majority of the population speaks Turkish with a minority speaking Kurdish or Arabic, and therefore outside the main cities and tourist areas, English and other major languages are rarely spoken, although many Turks speak German from working in Germany.

The cost of living is a third of that in the UK, but inflation tends to be very high. Income tax varies between 20 and 55 per cent. There is an annual property tax of 0.6 per cent of the estimated market value of land and 0.4 per cent of buildings, although there is a 25 per cent reduction on this on new properties for the first five years. Crime is low and medical facilities are adequate. There is no reciprocal health agreement with the UK, so you will need health insurance.

Selling

There is no capital gains tax as long as a property has been owned for at least five years.

Inheritance tax

This varies between 1 and 30 per cent.

Further information

- **Turkey: t** (00 90)

- **Turkish Consulate General**, Rutland Lodge, Rutland Gardens, London SW7 1BW, UK, **t** (020) 7589 0949.

- **Turkish Economic Counsellor's Office**, 43 Belgrave Square, London SW1X 8PA, UK, **t** (020) 7235 2743. This can provide a list of Turkish estate agents.

- **Turkish Embassy**, 43 Belgrave Square, London SW1X 8PA, UK, **t** (020) 7393 0202; **www.turkishembassy-london.com.**

- **Turkish Embassy,** 1714 Massachusetts Avenue, NW, Washington, DC 20036, USA, **t** (202) 659 8200; **www.turkey.org/turkey**.
- **Turkish Information Office,** 821 United Nations Plaza, New York, NY 10017, USA, **t** (212) 687 2194.
- **Turkish Law Office,** 93 Westway, London W12 0PU, UK, **t** (020) 8740 5581.
- **Turkish Tourist Office,** 170–173 Piccadilly, London W1V 9DD, UK, **t** (020) 7629 7711; **www.gototurkey.co.uk**.
- **Turkish Visa Information** (UK), **t** 0906 834 7348.
- **Yamaner and Yamaner** (USA), **t** (212) 238 1065; **www.yamaner.com**. Bilingual Turkish lawyers specialising in conveyancing for foreign buyers.

Estate agents

- **Kalkan Estates** (UK), **t** 08707 282827; **www.kalkanestates.co.uk**. Specialises in properties around Kalkan and the Kaş Peninsula.
- **Kent Property Services** (Turkey), **t** 252 412 2247; **www.kentestateagency.com**. Anglo-Turkish agency operating around Marmaris.
- **World Class Homes** (UK), **t** (01582) 832 001; **www.worldclasshomes.co.uk**.
- **www.istanbulrealestate.com** and **www.tapu.co.uk:** property listings.

Turkish Republic of Northern Cyprus

Why retire here?

If you're looking to buy a dream retirement or holiday home abroad, the Turkish Republic of North Cyprus (TRNC) has it all. Possibly the last unspoilt corner of the Med, this sleepy idyll boasts almost year-round sun, deserted beaches, spectacular mountain ranges, stunning monuments, disarmingly friendly people, no high-rise developments, amazingly low living costs and beautiful historic buildings going for a song. Unsurprisingly, this tiny republic has been enjoying an unprecedented property boom in recent years, mostly fuelled by Brits. There are now more than 30 estate agencies operating in the Kyrenia area alone, where in 1999 there were less than five. Official records are scant but it is reckoned that more than 2,000 Britons now own a property on the northern section of the island.

Downsides

There is a serious potential catch to owning property here, which could turn a property purchase into a legal and financial nightmare. Cyprus is a volatile island strictly separated into Greek and Turkish sectors after the Turkish military intervention in 1974 led to much bloodshed, disappearance and uprooting of both Turks and Greeks. Turkish Northern Cyprus is officially recognised in the world only by Turkey and is shunned by the UN and most other countries.

Because the bitter division between the Greek and Turkish sides of Cyprus is still unresolved, there's a real question mark over the ownership of many of the properties for sale. Many Greek Cypriots whose homes were occupied by or lost to Turkish invading forces in 1974 want their homes back. To counter this, Turkey recently initiated a compensation system in the north in an attempt to prevent court cases over disputed ownership, although the move has elicited little response.

If such homes are not legally owned by their new British buyers, they could in theory be taken away at a moment's notice. Two test cases in the European Court of Human Rights have already found in favour of Greek owners of land in the north and against buyers who bought post-1974.

If you buy a property here, you receive Turkish, foreign or TRNC title deeds. The first two demonstrate Turkish Cypriot or foreign ownership pre-1974 yet properties with TRNC title deeds, which the majority of properties in Northern Cyprus have, were Greek Cypriot-owned before 1974. According to the Cyprus High Commission in London, 168,000 Greek Cypriots own property and land in the north and therefore the scale of the problem is large. There is a real possibility that if the Cyprus problem is resolved in a way where the Greek who was turfed out of his home in 1974 comes back to reclaim it, the owner with TRNC title deeds to his house will be engulfed in a bitter wrangle over ownership of the home. Anyone considering buying a property in Northern Cyprus, until the political problems are sorted out, should only buy a property where it can be proved that ownership was Turkish or foreign – not Greek – before 1974 unless they are prepared to pay possibly hefty compensation or even lose the property should the owner or descendants of the owner return to claim the property.

A solution to the Cyprus problem has been on the cards for years but has faced many setbacks. As recently as 1998, there were serious fears of war because the Greek Cypriots planned to take delivery of anti-aircraft surface-to-air missiles to counter the huge Turkish army presence in the north of the island. Turkey retaliated by sending F-16 fighter jets.

However, at the time of going to press, the island has a better chance of reunification than ever. During the lead-up to the island's joining the EU in May 2004, there was an even more exhaustive flurry of discussions to solve the problem, including a UN blueprint on the cards, which would involve territory handovers by both sides and large population shifts. Yet a majority of Greek Cypriots rejected the reunification plan even though a majority of Turkish Cypriots voted for it. The willingness to solve the problem by the Turkish side impressed EU officials and there will probably now be noticeably more steps taken to end the economic isolation of the TRNC.

Property types

Small-scale modern holiday developments are increasingly cropping up here, and old properties abound, from glorified piles of rubble to sizeable historic houses.

Where to retire

The most popular village the British have been buying property in is Karaman, which is rather like a twee, well-manicured English village, with well-manicured English villagers, rather than locals, in residence. With homes in Karaman increasingly difficult to come by, the new boom village Brits are flocking to is Lapta, about nine miles west of Kyrenia/Girne.

Lapta, which pre-1974 was the Greek village Lapithos, has cafés full of men lounging over a Turkish coffee and a game of backgammon, shops selling almost nothing and half-built homes begun before the economy crashed. Polly Peck's Asil Nadir has a pad here. Lapta has plenty of gorgeous old buildings. It recently had a magnificent seven-bedroom villa for sale at £40,000, but as this was Greek-owned pre-1974, there is potentially a huge question mark over ownership. In contrast, a couple of years ago, a magnificent old house nearby that was of a similar size with a swimming pool and a small block of six modern apartments was for sale for 10 times that amount, principally because it was English-owned before 1974.

Currency and exchange rate

Turkish lira; £1 = 2,700,000 TL.

Property prices

Property prices have been very low for years, but as the island's planned membership of the EU move nearer (the Greek side of the island joined the EU in 2004) and a boom in British buyers has occurred, they are moving up steadily. Around Kyrenia/Girne, a one-bedroom cottage in need of much renovation would cost less than £20,000 while three- and four-bed houses start at around £60,000. A villa with swimming pool now costs around £90,000.

Local mortgages

With Northern Cyprus at present being recognised only by Turkey, it would be unwise to investigate funding for a property on the island at present.

Access to and from the UK

There are several flights each week from London to the recently upgraded Ercan airport near Nicosia in Northern Cyprus, but these are significantly more expensive than flights to southern Cyprus and are often booked up weeks in advance. Because Northern Cyprus is unrecognised internationally, flights have to land in Turkey first, and the flight from Turkey to the island is therefore treated as a domestic flight. In practice, travel from London to northern Cyprus therefore takes almost twice as long as to southern Cyprus, around 7–8hrs.

However, Northern Cyprus's eagerness to unify with the Greek side as proposed by the United Nations-backed plan in April 2004 is likely to be rewarded with an easing of international embargoes and one of the first of these is likely to be the granting of direct flights, possibly by the end of 2004.

Legal restrictions

According to the Cyprus High Commission in London, selling Greek Cypriot properties in Northern Cyprus is illegal. It says that the legitimate owners can take the new buyers to the European Court of Human Rights and there have been cases where Greek Cypriots have taken the new owners to court and won. Yet the TRNC says that if there is a settlement on the island, there will be compensation for both the Greek and Turkish Cypriots who had to leave their properties in 1974.

The buying process

Buying a property with foreign title deeds is simplest as checks have already been made by the government concerning ownership of title. First, a contract is drawn up by the purchaser's solicitor, setting down the terms of the sale, including the purchase price, timescale and any special conditions. The contract is signed by the vendor and purchaser and the purchaser pays in full unless a delayed completion is agreed; then normally the vendor receives a 10 per cent deposit with the balance paid on completion. The title is then transferred to the purchaser's name.

When buying a property with a Turkish or TRNC title deed (obviously the latter cannot be recommended), the vendor and purchaser sign a contract stating the terms of the sale and the purchaser provides a 10 per cent deposit. The buyer's solicitor applies for a purchase permit from the Ministry of the Interior, which carries out checks as to the title. This typically takes three or four months. When the permit is received, the purchaser pays the balance to the vendor and the title is transferred to the purchaser.

Costs of buying

Typically there is a cost of around £600 for applying for the purchase permit, where applicable. Stamp duty is 6 per cent of the purchase price.

Is property a good investment?

As long as you buy a property that was foreign- or Turkish-owned before 1974, the way prices have risen in recent years there is a very good chance that you have made a good investment. If direct flights are granted, making it as easy and cheap to visit the undeveloped north of the island as the overdeveloped south, property prices should increase significantly.

Living in Northern Cyprus

If you like an easygoing, extremely cheap, sun-drenched way of life, northern Cyprus is hard to beat. Roads are quiet and in good condition, there is very little development and no high-rise buildings. Yet this also means that everything from health facilities to choice in the shops lags behind almost everywhere else in Europe. There are no rates or community taxes but a council tax of under £50 per annum.

You will need health insurance, as Turkey has no reciprocal health agreement with the UK.

Selling

With Cyprus's volatile history, saleability can be adversely affected very rapidly whenever there are tensions. Selling a property with a TRNC deed (Greek-owned, pre-1974) could prove very difficult indeed.

Inheritance tax

No tax is paid by foreign residents; otherwise there is a sliding scale according to the size of estate.

Further information

- **TRNC: t** (00 90 392)
- **North Cyprus Tourism Centre**, 29 Bedford Square, London WC1B 3ED, UK, t (020) 7631 1930; **www.go-northcyprus.com.**

Estate agents

All are situated in Girne, northern Cyprus.

- **Boray Emklak Estate Agency, t** 822 2919; **www.borayestates.com.**
- **Ian Smith Estate Agency, t** 815 7118; **www.iansmithestate.com.**
- **Korinia Real Estate Agency, t** 815 2985; **www.korinia.com.**
- **Stringer Estates, t** 815 8844; **www.stringerestates.com.**
- **Unwin Estates, t** 822 3508; **www.unwinestates.com.**

USA

Why retire here?

USA-bound Brits overwhelmingly flock to Florida, both for the wealth of theme parks and other leisure attractions, and for the good weather: it has a subtropical climate, and is so sunny it is known as the Sunshine State. But there are endless other options available in a land so varied topographically, from superb ski resorts to stunning coastlines, from vibrant cities to sleepy rural backwaters. America's largely English-speaking population is another attraction to non-linguists, and the cost of living is lower than in the UK. Indeed, the *Daily Mail* compared 24 goods bought in Britain and the USA, from cameras to jeans, and found that only two were cheaper in the UK and that UK buyers pay an average 48 per cent more for everyday goods than American ones.

Downsides

America is very strict about the amount of time you can stay in the country, and does not issue visitor residence permits to retirees, although they are entitled to stay for six months at a time as visitors if they successfully obtain a long-stay visa – otherwise visits will be limited to 90 days .

The weather in such a huge country isn't always glorious and in places can be extreme. Even Florida has its fair share of hurricanes and torrential rainstorms.

For retirees from the UK wanting easy access to Europe, the long-haul flights are certainly a disadvantage, both for their length and their cost, which is often high, especially around school holidays and the summer.

The crime rate in America is high, although varies considerably from state to state and neighbourhood to neighbourhood. It is important to check the crime rate in the area you are buying; you may get a surprise. When deciding to move from London to Florida in 2004, journalist John Price found that according to the Home Office and FBI crime reports of reported offences per 1,000 population, Islington in London notched up 31 violent crimes against the person where New York scored 10 and Miami Beach 13.

Property types

This huge country has a vast and varied property market including apartment complexes with facilities like swimming pools and golf courses, waterside homes, homes in ski resorts and large, comfortable detached homes.

Where to retire

Every state has something to offer holiday-home-owners and residents. Florida, California and New York are the most popular destinations for foreigners. For winter sports, buyers opt for mountainous states like New Mexico, Colorado, Arizona and Idaho, while Virginia, Carolina and Georgia are becoming more popular.

Florida

More and more Florida-bound Brits are preferring to buy their own accommodation rather than sink their funds in pricey hotels, as they get far more living space and privacy and often their own pool. Florida has numerous natural attractions including 1,200 miles of coastline and 30,000 lakes, but most buyers head for the town of Orlando, the biggest tourist attraction in the world. It has a wealth of theme parks and other attractions, such as Epcot, Universal Studios and Seaworld; it is the home of Disney World and therefore ideal for families. It is not a place to consider if you like heritage or culture.

When buying in Orlando, it is important to choose the location of the property carefully to benefit from the maximum rental income in the weeks you're not holidaying. More than a 20min drive from Disney World, rental demand can drop dramatically. It is crucial to obtain professional advice and only deal with established companies fully licensed with the State of Florida's Department of Business and Professional Regulation, especially as there can be rental restrictions, and the four counties there have differing rules concerning property. To make sure a property can accommodate short-term lets suitable for holiday-makers, check with City Hall.

Also, homes in Florida, while cheap by UK standards, seldom appreciate significantly in value, both because there is so much building going on and because buyers tend to go for new, more modern properties rather than resales. Developers of such properties usually offer an ongoing management and letting service so that your property can be rented out in the weeks you are not there. They typically offer inspections visits from about £200.

The continued expansion of the Orlando area over the next two decades is assured by Disney World's huge investment in its 'Celebration' residential, shopping and cultural city, as well as a number of new theme parks and other major projects that are being planned. For many, this is welcomed development as it ensures an even greater choice of things to do, but for others such expansion will lead some people to seek a more tranquil setting for their vacation.

Many British buyers are indeed now looking further afield to discover quieter locations. The easygoing but sophisticated town of Naples on the south west Gulf coast is an increasingly popular alternative to Orlando. Known for its abundant fishing, 55 golf courses and variety of shops, Naples has some of the finest beaches on this coastline and is becoming one of the hottest towns on the Gulf. Property in Naples is significantly more expensive than the Orlando area, typically 20 per cent more than what you pay in Orlando. A much older town, it has a higher proportion of retirees, not least because it avoids the hustle and bustle of Orlando.

With an increasingly high number of tourists to the Naples area, the rental demand for homes is also growing. Purchasers of typical pool homes can realistically expect to let the home out for over half the year to holidaymakers, generating a valuable income to offset running costs. But while property near Orlando is easy to let out throughout the year because of the many attractions for holidaymakers, on the coast it is a different story as the rental market is much more seasonal and there is also great competition from hotel special deals.

Buyers who wish to locate further north of Naples, near Fort Myers, will find that the west coast at Port Charlotte, near Venice Beach, has rich wildlife, including dolphins, pelicans, cormorants, egrets and ibis. All the beaches in the area are ideal for swimming, boating, fishing and diving, and there are superb golf courses and lakes and rivers in abundance.

Miami, despite being an attractive city on the ocean with golden beaches and year-round sunshine, is seldom considered by British buyers. It has an enticing mix of the glamorous film-making set, as well as Haitian, Jewish and Cuban contingents. There are architectural gems like the narrow red-brick lanes of Coconut Grove and Art Deco properties at South Beach. Where, at the time of writing, the average price of a London home is £262,000, in Miami it is £76,643. According to the National Association of Realtors, the Miami and Sarasota areas have been enjoying property price rises of over 20 per cent in 2004, compared with 8.5 per cent in the Orlando area.

Recently, British buyers have also been heading for the Pensacola area, north Florida, where a five-bedroom home retails at around £110,000.

California

Although most Britons planning a property purchase in America set their sights on Florida, a country as gigantic as the USA has much more to offer than that. For sheer variety, California is hard to beat. It covers a larger area than any other state except Alaska and Texas. The main attraction is its many environments, with every geographical feature, a very varied climate allowing anything from skiing to sunbathing, a huge coastline, and mountains and lakes. California also boasts beautiful valleys, thick forests, barren deserts and fertile plains as well as natural wonders like redwood groves and volcanic cones. Wide, sandy beaches, golf courses, ski resorts and other facilities are plentiful.

California has four of America's 20 largest cities: San Diego, San Jose, San Francisco and Los Angeles, home of Hollywood and the luxury excesses of glamorous Beverly Hills. Nearby is Santa Barbara, one of the most beautiful areas along the Californian coast, but also one of the most expensive.

While Florida is hot and steamy and flat as a pancake, Santa Barbara has a true Mediterranean climate, with breezes coming off the ocean. It means it's never too hot and never too cold. Many visitors and new residents are attracted by California's outdoor way of life. The warm, dry climate of southern California permits outdoor recreation almost all the year round.

At Lake Tahoe, for example, the deepest of California's 8,000 lakes and about 150 miles inland east of San Francisco, you can enjoy water sports, hiking, fishing and relaxed mountain living in the summer, or skiing and snowboarding at the many local resorts during winter. Year-round the nightlife rivals that of larger urban cities. The south Lake Tahoe area boasts six casinos and excellent restaurants, shops and nightspots.

This is a great holiday location and a very environmentally sensitive area. Most property is situated near the huge national forest and is relatively inexpensive. A two-bedroom mountain chalet typically costs from £125,000. For £90,000 or so, you can get a two-bed furnished apartment in a ski resort.

New England

New England, midway between Boston and New York, has wide, open spaces, warm summers, glorious red autumns, winter skiing and usually a white Christmas, beautiful countryside, pretty villages, lively city life, culture spots and arts festivals as well as affordable properties. You can go mountain-biking, sailing and canoeing in the many lakes and rivers. Unsurprisingly, numbers soar here during the summer as New Yorkers flee the heat and humidity.

The Berkshires, at the western end of Massachusetts, is a particularly delightful spot, and has a high proportion of second home-owners from New York and Boston. Cape Cod is another popular area, with a rocky coastline and sandy coves, and its peninsula is dotted with pretty colonial villages and towns.

Prices are rising by around 10 per cent a year. While a large house with private beach at the offshore island, Martha's Vineyard, as favoured by the rich and famous like Bill Clinton and Carly Simon, is out of reach to most at £6 million plus, three-bed homes away from the sea and harbour come in at around £215,000. The Lake Sunapee region, 90mins from Boston, is a 2004 hotspot, with houses averaging £220,000.

Aspen, Colorado

With average house prices presently running at £3 million, Aspen has the world's most expensive real estate and houses a host of celebs including Cher, Melanie Griffith, George Hamilton, Kevin Costner, Don Johnson, Jack Nicholson and Martina Navratilova. No doubt they are attracted to the summer arts festivals and fabulous winter skiing. Aspen, a four-hour drive from Denver Airport, has a small-town feel, with a permanent population of only around 5,000.

Currency and exchange rate

US dollar ($); £1 = $1.80.

Property prices

In such a huge country (the third-largest country in the world after Canada and China), property prices vary greatly. Overall, they are significantly cheaper than in the UK, although in many areas they do not appreciate in value a great deal. In Florida, coastal properties tend to be very expensive. Affordable properties in the intense building programmes here are all inland. In rural areas and smaller towns, a spacious house in its own grounds is easy to obtain for less than £120,000. The same-sized home would be four or five times the cost in San Francisco and as much as 10 times that amount in New York City.

In Miami, £350,000 will get you a six-bedroom waterfront property with moorings, and in the Bal Harbour district, a three-bed ocean-view apartment.

Prices in Florida are kept down by the intense competition and tend to be cheapest north of Tampa. A standard three-bedroom villa with a swimming pool in the Orlando area is around £100,000; in the Tampa Bay area on the Gulf coast, about £110,000; and in Sarasota, nearer £150,000.

One of the most expensive areas is the select neighbourhood of Palm Beach. A three-bedroom property with pool, 15mins from the beach, is in the region of £300,000.

In east Naples, Florida, a two-bedroom, two-bathroom apartment in a private gated community costs from about £130,000. Three- and four-bedroom villas typically cost from about £180,000, inclusive of a swimming pool. Most homes are located a gentle 10-minute drive from the beaches.

A three-bed chalet or clapboard house in the woods of Connecticut is typically currently around £90,000, while a three-bed period house with land would cost around twice that.

A two-bed apartment in Manhattan, New York, cost around £570,000 in early 2004, £20,000 more than for a similar property in London. Prices rose by 40 per cent in New York in 2003 alone, with no signs of faltering.

Local mortgages

Foreign mortgage applicants must be home-owners in their country of residence. Mortgages of 80 per cent of the purchase price and up to 30 years are widely available from a variety of sources, although it is probably easier and cheaper to obtain a mortgage in the UK. Sterling mortgages for Britons buying properties in America have recently become available. Interest-only, as well as repayment mortgages, are available.

Retirees will no doubt be interested to note that American anti-discrimination laws make it illegal to refuse a mortgage on the grounds of age and therefore a 65-year-old should be able to obtain a 30-year mortgage.

Access to and from the UK

There are many flight options from the UK to New York and all major cities. For Florida, flights to Orlando and Fort Lauderdale are usually cheaper than for Miami.

Legal restrictions

Note that, as a citizen of a number of western countries including Britain, you can only spend 90 days at a time on the visa-waiver programme, and a maximum of six months on a longer-stay visa if you can obtain one. If you have ever been arrested, you do not qualify for the waiver, regardless of how long ago it was or whether it resulted in a criminal conviction.

Longer stays require a visa, which can be hard to obtain unless you have a business in the USA, blood relatives there or a company transfer.

Some counties and communities do not allow short-term lets.

The buying process

The conveyancing process is quite straightforward, which is unsurprising considering that American real estate laws are based on English laws.

Typically, a 1–5 per cent deposit is paid and a legally binding contract is then signed by both buyer and seller. Some states, such as California, require all funds to be paid to a neutral third party, known as the 'escrow agent', responsible for checking the progress of the transaction and paying out all necessary funds.

If you decide to back out from the purchase, you either lose your deposit or can be forced to continue with the sale, unless specified conditions of the contract, such as acceptance of a mortgage or there being a satisfactory survey, have not been met. These conditions can vary in different states.

Before purchase, check that all local taxes have been paid to date, as these charges are often transferred to the new owner. Typically, if you are buying new, you choose your plot (known as a 'lot' in the USA) and house-type and construction begins (taking around 4–5 months) when you have paid the first down-payment of around 25 per cent. You can move in after the last payment has been made.

If you are buying an apartment, expect to be 'vetted' by the building's residents' committee. It is common for other residents of a building to want to ensure newcomers are 'suitable' and that they can pay the ongoing charges.

Land, council and property taxes can be very high, so ensure you know the figure before deciding to purchase. Older homes should have a termite inspection, as wood-boring insects are a common problem.

Costs of buying

Known as completion expenses, these total around 5 per cent of the purchase price and can include a survey and a valuation fee by the lender, conveyancing fees, title search and mortgage tax. Realtor (estate agency) fees, which are higher than in Britain, are usually split between buyer and vendor.

Is property a good investment?

Property in North America is often significantly cheaper than in the UK, but in many areas, it does not appreciate in value much. Popular cities like New York and San Francisco are a notable exception, being pricier but also in constant demand.

Living in America

America's climate cannot really be summed up, as it varies greatly, from subtropical to arctic. It has one of the highest standards and the lowest costs of living. Annual property and council taxes vary greatly from state to state. An average new-build home in Florida will attract real-estate taxes of 1 per cent of the value of the property.

Federal income taxes also greatly vary, from around 15 to 40 per cent of earnings; some states, including Florida, have no state income tax at all. Tax relief on business expenses is more generous than in the UK. Some states and counties also impose further local income taxes, as well as other taxes such as sales tax and tourist development tax on letting income. US residents are subject to tax on their worldwide income.

There are no reciprocal health agreements between the USA and the UK, and, as healthcare in America is prohibitively expensive, private health insurance is vital.

The United States does not offer a visa to the retired, although there are other options available for UK citizens. One is to marry an American citizen, another is family-based residency, where if any members of your immediate family (parents, children or spouse) are citizens or residents, you may be entitled to residency in the country.

Another option is to apply for the B visa (tourism/business). This allows you to stay for six months at a time rather than the normal 90 days. If you do not abuse your visa privileges (for example, staying in America for six months, returning to the UK for a week and then returning to America to spend another six months), it is possible to stay for more than eight months in the country each year, as long as each visit is broken up into shorter periods, such as three or four months each.

Visas for a greater length of time can take several months to process and usually require the help of an experienced immigration lawyer. As permanent residence can be difficult to obtain, many retirees have to be rich enough to keep up another home in the UK and allocate funds for flights back and forth. Further information is available on the US Embassy websites.

Selling

Non-residents usually pay capital gains tax at 15 per cent up to US$23,350 (around £13,000) and at 28 per cent over this amount.

Inheritance tax

There are federal estate and gift tax rates from 18 to 55 per cent and some states also impose estate tax on estates left to a spouse or child.

Further information

- **USA: t** (00 1)
- **American Citizens Abroad**, 5 Rue Liotard, 1202, Geneva, Switzerland, **t** (00 41) 22 340 0233; **www.aca.ch**.
- **Department of Housing and Urban Development**, 451 7th Street SW, Washington DC 20410, USA, **t** (202) 708 1112; **www.hud.gov**.
- **Immigration and Naturalization Service**; **www.ins.usdoj.gov**.
- **United National Real Estate**, 4700 Belleview, PO Box 11400, Kansas City, Missouri 64112, USA, **t** 800 999 1020; **www.unitedcountry.com**.
- **United States Embassy**, 24 Grosvenor Square, London W1A 1AE, UK, **t** (020) 7499 9000; **www.usembassy.org.uk**.
- **www.flausa.com**: Florida's official tourism website.
- **www.sunnysarasota.com**: a website for Sarasota, Florida.
- **American Association of Retired Persons**, 601 East Street NW, Washington DC 20049, USA, **t** 800 424 3410; **www.aarp.org**.
- **British Home Loans** (UK), **t** 0800 096 5989; **www.britishhomeloansflorida.com**. A mortgage brokerage based in Orlando, Florida.
- **Canadian Association of Retired Persons**; **www.50plus.com**. Information about retirement homes and developments in Florida.
- **Continuing Care Accreditation Commission**; **www.ccaconline.org**. Lists retirement communities and sheltered accommodation.
- **Florida Brits Group** (UK), **t** (01904) 471800; **www.floridabritsgroup.com**. A property advisory service and support group for more than 1,200 British home owners in Florida.
- **www.worldlawdirect.com**: free advice on American property law.

Emigration advisers

- **Four Corners** (UK), **t** 0845 841 9453; **www.4-corners.com**.

- **Global Visas** (UK), **t** (020) 7009 3800; **www.globalvisas.com.**
- **Overseas Emigration Visas, www.overseas-emigration.co.uk.**
- **Workpermit.com** (UK), **t** (020) 7842 0800; **www.workpermit.com.**

Estate agents (realtors)

Florida

- **Florida Countryside** (UK), **t** (01702) 481600; **www.floridacountryside.com.**
- **Florida Homes International** (UK), **t** (01703) 262888; **www.floridahomesint.com.**
- **Overseas Homes and Investments** (USA); **www.oshomes.co.uk.**
- **Sotheby's Realty** (USA), **t** (561) 659 3555; **www.sothebysrealty.com.**
- **Waterfront Brevard** (USA), **t** (321) 268 3640; **www.waterfrontbrevard.com.**

Lake Tahoe
All are in the USA.

- **McCall Realty, t** (530) 544 1881; **www.mccallrealty.com.**
- **Village Properties, t** (805) 969 8900; **www.villagesite.com.**

Miami, Florida
All are in the USA.

- **Buy Beach, t** (305) 531 6929; **www.buybeach.com.**
- **Exquisite Properties, t** (305) 538 7123; **www.exquisiteproperties.com.**
- **Joe Warren, t** (305) 531 5803; **www.jwrealtor.com.**
- **Yolande Citro, t** (305) 535 4162; **www.yolandecitro.com.**

San Francisco
All are in the USA.

- **Betty Brachman, t** (415) 345 3125; **www.bettybrachman.com.**
- **McGuire, t** (415) 351 4663; **www.mcguire.com.**
- **Realtor.com, t** (415) 229 1393; **www.realtor.com.**

New England
All are in the USA.

- **Brockman Real Estate, t** (413) 528 4859; **berkshirerealty.com.**
- **Elyse Harney Real Estate, t** (860) 435 2200; **www.harneyre.com.**
- **Harding Realty Corp, t** (508) 563 9777; **www.hardingrealtycorp.com.**
- **Newcastle Square Rentals, t** (207) 563 6500; **www.mainecoastproperties.**

- **Sotheby's International Realty, t** (561) 659 3555; **www.sothebysrealty.com.**

New York
All are in the USA.

- **Cobble Heights Realty, t** (718) 596 3333; **www.cobbleheights.com.**
- **Coldwell Banker, Hunter Kennedy, t** (212) 255 4000; **www.cbhk.com.**
- **Sotheby's International Realty, t** (212) 431 2440; **www.sothebysrealty.com.**
- **Stribling, t** (212) 570 2440; **www.striblingny.com.**
- **Timothy Scott, t** (212) 813 3573; **www.tscottre.com.**

Aspen
All are in the USA.

- **BJ Adams, t** (970) 923 2111; **www.bjadamsandcompany.com.**
- **Brian L Hazen, t** (970) 920 0563; **www.realestateaspen.com.**
- **Frias Properties, t** (970) 920 2000; **www.friasproperties.com.**
- **Rich Wagar Associates, t** (970) 920 3131; **www.wagarrealestate.com.**
- **Whitman Fine Properties, t** (970) 544 3771; **www.whitmanfineproperties.com.**

Finding a Property

Location

Location is obviously of paramount importance, especially if you are planning to make the property your permanent residence. The local leisure facilities, amenities, health services, public transport and shops all need to be carefully assessed before you even start viewing properties.

Do you want sunshine all-year-round? If you wish to ski, what is the local snowfall record? Do you wish to integrate into the local community (and are your language skills up to this?) or would you be happier in an area very popular with expatriates from your home country?

Is the area susceptible to such things as hurricanes, tornadoes, floods, fires and earthquakes? Does the area become overrun by tourists in the summer season yet all but closes down in winter? This may not be an important factor if you are buying a holiday home, but is something to consider seriously if you are retiring full-time.

City versus country

Many retirees who have been city-dwellers all their lives at some point consider leaving the urban big smoke for some rural tranquillity. The natural beauty of the countryside is relaxing, even invigorating, and you are usually able to obtain a significantly larger property for your money. Yet beware of the disadvantages. In the country, public transport diminishes and you are likely to be far more reliant on a car, although driving will probably be more pleasant, with few traffic jams and parking problems.

There are likely to be very reduced leisure facilities, cultural opportunities and general services and amenities outside the cities, and maintenance and domestic fuel costs usually increase in country homes. Small, terraced town houses sheltered in a built-up area are usually substantially cheaper to light, heat and maintain than large, detached buildings on a hill.

There are other factors to consider before taking the plunge into the rural lifestyle. For example, does the property have mains drainage, a telephone or electricity supply? Installing such things, or a septic tank, and a generator or solar panels for the electricity supply if these are not possible, can be very expensive and troublesome. Could you cope with the upkeep of the garden, now and in 10 years' time?

What are the neighbours like? Even if they are some distance away, they could spell trouble. A local farm could cause considerable disruption. Those used to the high density of population in a hectic big town may feel isolated living down a lonely country lane. Many country areas become inhospitable in winter, because of fog, cold and snow. Doctors, hospitals, chemists and dentists may be a significant distance away and local shops non-existent or badly stocked.

Socially there can be a lack of choice in the country and it often can take time to become accepted in a community, especially if you are from abroad and your grasp of the local language and foreign ways leave something to be desired. Yet the slower pace of living can encourage contact with neighbours and a friendlier atmosphere.

Pollution comes in different guises in the country – from chemical sprays used in farming, from spending more time in the car because the shops are 30 miles away instead of three, or from ozone, a pollutant most prevalent in the country-side. Think twice if the dream cottage you wish to buy is near a coal-fired power station, which emits sulphur dioxide and causes respiratory problems. Asthma sufferers should seek medical advice before moving from the city in an attempt to improve their condition: the disease can worsen in many rural areas rather than improve on leaving the city because of the different triggers there.

And then there's noise pollution. Some confirmed townies, used to next door's ghetto blaster pounding away on a Saturday afternoon, can't abide an inconsiderate cockerel crowing at some godforsaken hour. Prospective country buyers should also ask whether there is an airport nearby. The grounds of that idyllic pile, peaceful when you viewed it, won't be so attractive if it turns out to be near a fast-growing airport.

The city generally has more housing choices, public transport, recreation, entertainment and shopping facilities, as well as closer healthcare, although housing is likely to be costlier and healthcare overstretched. There may be less privacy, more noise and pressure in the city.

The secret to a successful move out of the city to supposed rural bliss is not to attempt too much too soon. Going from a maze of busy streets to the back of beyond can be a costly, time-consuming mistake. It may be safer to consider moving to the edge of suburbia, where you have a combination of rural peace and urban facilities nearby, or renting in the country for a year to see whether it really is for you.

Property types

Once you have decided where to retire, work out exactly the kind of property you are looking for. Many prospective buyers waste untold time and money because their search is too vague. Draw up a checklist of requirements. You could start with a wish list of the things you would be looking for in a perfect home. This list could include things like having at least four bedrooms, being built before 1900, having a garage and a large garden, and being situated in a quiet village but near a train station and shops.

Because few people have the budget to buy their ideal home, you could translate your dream list into a checklist of minimum specifications. This list could change to maybe including any property built before 1930, having two bedrooms and a small garden, and a regular bus that gives access to both shops and the railway station.

Whatever you choose, don't allow a property's charm to cause you to disregard the practical disadvantages. A chocolate-box exterior is all very well but if the property is riddled with dry rot and renovation works that will see you through to the next century, and excursions to buy a pint of milk take the best part of a day, maybe you should think again.

Old properties

Many old properties boast lots of character and are not necessarily more difficult to maintain than newly built homes. Many older properties – though not in all countries – were built to extremely high standards using superior materials and have thick, solid walls that are in complete contrast with the paper-thin walls that many new properties have today. Although building regulations in many countries today are more strict than ever, many housebuilders are more interested in saving money during the building process than in creating long-lasting, maintenance-free homes.

Restoration and refurbishment

Buying and restoring a dilapidated property can net you great savings when you buy and big profits when you sell – if it goes well and there is a strong local property market. Yet often the cost of restoration is far higher than first envisaged and is often not recovered when you come to sell. Many foreign buyers take on too large a project, seduced by a very low asking price, underestimating both the cost of restoration and maintenance.

Such a project is not for the faint-hearted – especially abroad – and you need huge reserves of patience and commitment. Many things can go wrong, including language mix-ups, bureaucratic mayhem, expanding budget difficulties, unforeseen extra building works, baffling local building regulations and mammoth planning hold-ups.

Many people get into difficulties with restoring and renovating because they underestimate budget and timescales through not taking the time and effort to prepare detailed costings. Don't forget any local taxes that may be added to any quotations for work to be done.

If you are buying an older property, the cost of maintenance and renovation or conversion should never be underestimated, especially as larger properties tend to be far more affordable in many countries, compared with the UK. Properties ripe for renovation typically need a damp-proof course, new windows and doors, a new roof, walls replaced or repaired, timber treatment, a new kitchen and bathroom, replumbing, rewiring, installation of central heating, a garden makeover and complete decoration. The cost of rectifying such things can be immense. Be aware that properties for renovation can harbour lots of hidden problems – seek plenty of professional advice, from experts like a surveyor, an architect and builder with experience of similar projects. Bear in mind that the cost of renovation may be very different abroad compared with the UK. For example, DIY items like plywood and plumbing parts can be three or four times more expensive in France than in the UK and many British renovators who live in France hop on to a ferry and have a spending spree at B&Q, Homebase or other DIY superstores in Britain for items they need for their French homes.

When you find a suitable property, ask yourself whether it is right for you. A charming little dark cottage with low ceilings and small windows can't be transformed into an oasis of light without wrecking it, and a high-ceilinged barn won't be cosy and snug. Restoration may need planning or other local permissions so check with the planners at the local council. Don't be seduced by a low asking price for a property. Restoration costs regularly exceed the market price for the property had it been restored. Installing services like electricity and water to rural properties can be very costly indeed.

Often it is better to employ local builders – if your grasp of the language is sufficient – rather than foreign workers, not least because they are likely to understand both the local building techniques, planning laws and building regulations better than outsiders. Using them will ease you into the local community more readily. They are likely to be cheaper, and in some countries, such as France, work by registered builders is guaranteed.

The work is likely to require being overseen to ensure that instructions and plans are correctly carried out. An architect would charge around 10 per cent of the cost of the job to do this in most cases. If you plan to renovate, accept that the incessant arrival of huge lorries and a noisy building site disrupting every-thing for weeks may incur the wrath of your neighbours.

Keep all receipts. If you do everything by the book – which is strongly advised as you can fall foul of some serious laws attracting large fines in some countries – you can in many cases claim back your expenses against capital gains tax when you come to sell. If you pay cash in hand, you have no protection or proof of payment should problems later arise. Also, doing things by the book means you receive certificates for works done which act as a guarantee if problems crop up later.

Resale properties

Properties that are neither brand-new nor charming wrecks, but instead are relatively recently built second-hand properties, can be a good bet because they are often good value, any teething problems have probably been resolved, and they are bought as seen, unlike properties bought off-plan.

New properties

Buying a newly built home can avoid many of the stresses of homebuying. You may sidestep the uncertainties, costs and considerable time of buying a house in a 'sale chain', although some buyers inevitably experience postponed completion dates and other problems. You may avoid an estate agent's fee; you don't have to worry about problems that can beset older properties like rotting timbers, leaking roofs, subsidence and rising damp; and you may be able to take advantage of special offers from the developer.

As well as being brand-new and spotless, new homes should conform to the latest building standards and advancements, which could include sophisticated security systems and the latest high-tech computer, heating, lighting and audiovisual systems. There may be carpeting, bathroom fittings, a fitted kitchen, new appliances and energy-efficient features.

You will often be able to pay a smaller deposit than for a resale property and there may be attractive deals on such things as conveyancing costs. In many countries, properties are covered by a builder's guarantee against structural problems and/or plumbing, electrical and other installations. The architect may also be responsible for some defects for a set number of years, and the developer may be backed by financial guarantees.

The downside is that you tend to get considerably less space for your money with a new home and many new properties lack character. Capital growth – the money you make on the property since the time you bought it – can be more difficult to achieve than for older properties. In some regions – such as Florida – your property may not go up in value at all.

It is important to choose the developer carefully. Many countries lack the protection buyers have in the UK and many developers are vastly underfunded and have financially precarious businesses.

Before buying, take a close look at the site. Is it tidy and well-managed? Small developments often grow into larger estates. If the development is next to open ground, check whether it has been earmarked for a later phase of building. Ask the sales people lots of questions. What are the total number of properties planned for the development? Who looks after communal areas? How long will the construction work for the whole site take?

When the property is supposedly finished, have a good look around to see that the standard of work is acceptable before paying out. For example, has everything that was in the original specification been included? Has the whole of the interior been painted well? Unless any unacceptable or outstanding items are of a minor nature, where you should get a written undertaking that they will be sorted out, you should not complete until the matter is rectified. However, don't be put off by minor cracks around the property. These usually appear when the plaster dries out, although larger cracks should be investigated.

Buying off-plan

Increasing competition for new homes has meant buying a property from the developer's plans, rather than waiting until it is built, has become common, especially in areas with a large presence of new-build developments popular with foreign buyers, such as on the Spanish *costas* and Florida.

There can be great benefits to buying this way, which is known as buying off-plan. Developers often discount properties to get sales moving at a new development, and if prices rise steeply as word gets round and as the development takes shape, you can have a real bargain on your hands.

You also often have the choice of the best plots with the most impressive views, with the bonus of gaining extra time to save and sort out a mortgage. Another advantage is that you have far more say about how your property will look if you buy off-plan. Developers often have a sizeable range of tiles, carpeting, colour schemes and kitchen and bathroom fittings you can choose from, and you may even be able to rearrange the layout – for example, changing two bedrooms into one large room, or maybe two bathrooms into one study and a bathroom.

For all its advantages, buying off-plan can be a gamble, especially abroad, and it is crucial to find a reputable, independent, experienced lawyer in the country you wish to buy in who can advise on possible pitfalls of buying off-plan. These could include the developer going bust, failing to complete in time or not building to the specifications given.

Investigate carefully to see how established and financially secure the developer is before committing to buy. In many countries, there are few controls over developers and there is little guarantee that the property, as well as communal areas and infrastructure such as electricity, swimming pools and parking areas, will ever be completed.

The sales people working on off-plan developments often earn a hefty commission and can subject potential buyers to a whole host of high-pressure sales techniques to get them to sign on the dotted line. Do not sign anything written in a language you do not understand until it has been translated fully into English. Also, do not hand over any funds, even if pressurised to do so to secure a property.

Ask the developer to arrange for you to speak to other people who have bought from the company to find out what their experience has been. A developer who is not prepared to do this should be treated with suspicion. Also bear in mind that when buying off-plan, if the property market contracts, completed homes could cost less than those previously bought off-plan.

Prepare for delays. Factors like bad weather or bureaucratic hold-ups can cause the development to run seriously behind schedule. Examine the developers' plans carefully and refer to them on completion: are neighbouring houses too close or will you have great views of the dustbins? Consider having a clause included in the contract that allows you to delay completion if there are faults in the property. And if your home is one of the first to be completed, be prepared to live on a building site for weeks or even months.

Managed developments

More and more buyers are opting for a property at a brand-new managed development rather than subjecting themselves to the hassle of converting a rambling ruin, which can be a particularly fraught process if you live abroad. In a managed development, the maintenance and security of the development will normally be taken care of.

Although the initial cost is higher, you have no security worries or mainten-ance headaches and replace worry about burglars and burst pipes with peace of mind. Often these developments have other features, such as a gymnasium, beauty salon, swimming pool or golf course.

Shared developments

Properties in shared developments, where common elements like building, land or amenities are shared, are common abroad. There can be a number of advantages. The outside of the building, communal areas and gardens are usually maintained by the managing agents and you share the costs with the other property owners. There may be added security as other home owners may keep an eye on your property in your absence.

Yet there are disadvantages. An inefficient managing agent can be a real headache, especially if there is a pressing problem that needs to be attended to and they don't appreciate the urgency. You may have little control and be lumbered with hefty maintenance charges.

Before you are committed to buy, make sure you understand the whole range of charges and fees you may be responsible for. Read any agreements (or have them translated) governing the property and go through any points you don't understand with your solicitor, who should highlight any points he thinks could cause problems. There may be important legally enforceable restrictions such as banning pets or restricting access to part of the grounds, so make sure you have understood every clause.

Service charges can be high and usually include a contribution towards things like repairs and maintenance, communal electricity and buildings insurance. Before buying, it's a good idea to ask for copies of the service charge demands for the last few years. Have the charges risen sharply or have there been a high number of costly repairs? In some countries, repairs and upgrading of the building can result in a hefty increase in fees.

Many managing agents are not regulated by any statutory body and their standards vary greatly. Before buying, try to speak to other residents to see whether there have been any problems concerning them.

If you are buying a holiday property, you may be paying for such things as water and heat throughout the year regardless of whether you are at the property or not, so check the position there.

Building a home from scratch

Another option is to build a home from scratch after buying a plot of land, either an architecturally designed one-off or to a cheaper standard design offered by a builder. You can get more for your money building this way, but in some countries, the process can be fraught with difficulty, from ensuring the land can be built on, to builders following instructions adequately.

Self-builders typically make savings of 25 to 35 per cent by building their homes themselves, although the term 'self-build' is itself rather misleading. Only about one per cent of self-builders undertake any of the building work themselves, with most employing a builder to carry out the work for them. One of the biggest obstacles a self-builder faces is finding a suitable building plot: one that is the right size, an affordable price and unencumbered by insurmountable planning permission problems. If you opt for self-build, build at least a 15 per cent contingency fund into your budget for the unexpected, which invariably will come up. Pay your builder in stages, not up-front, otherwise you won't have a hold over him if there's a dispute.

Timber-framed homes, such as those offered in kit form by self-build companies, speed up the building process. Often such self-build homes ready for assembly can be shipped anywhere in the world. The following companies supply this sort of home:

- **Acorn and Deck House** (UK), **t** (01789) 720270; **www.deckhouse.com**.
- **Border Oak Design and Construction** (UK), **t** (01568) 708752; **www.borderoak.com**.
- **Griffner Coilite** (Eire), **t** (01) 663 5201; **www.griffnerhomes.com**.
- **Huf Haus** (UK), **t** (01932) 828502; **www.huf-haus.de**.
- **Potton Homes** (UK), **t** (01767) 263300; **www.potton.co.uk**.
- **Swedish House Company** (UK), **t** (01892) 665007; **www.swedishhouses.com**.

The website **www.psa-publishers.com** lists architects around the world and **www.selfbuild.co.uk** has useful self-build information. The monthly UK self-build magazines have their own websites: *Homebuilding and Renovating* (**www.homebuilding.co.uk**), *Build It* (**www.self-build.co.uk**); *Self-Build and Design* (**www.selfbuildanddesign.com**).

Retirement accommodation

Specific sheltered accommodation for the retired has grown considerably in popularity in recent years in the UK and now there are many options. At the very least, you can buy specifically equipped, modern developments with independent living units, which are independent properties in their own right with some facilities like call systems and ramps for disabled residents as well as some communal facilities such as an on-site manager and a gardener. Schemes with more provision are usually called assisted living units, while nursing homes offer more help to residents, which may include constant nursing care.

Retirement accommodation is often complemented by such features as a social club, restaurant, bar and lounge areas, a library, therapy centre, exercise room, guest suites and organised leisure programmes. For older residents there may be an in-house clinic or adjacent nursing home, nursing staff and regular visits by doctors.

Accommodation in retirement homes and retirement developments is wheelchair-friendly and has such features as alarm systems and assistance rails. The best retirement developments are located where facilities like shops, entertainment and public transport are easily at hand.

In many countries in the world such retirement accommodation is very rare or even non-existent. Generally, the less developed the country, or the greater the tradition for the elderly to be cared for by family, the less likely it is that such accommodation will be present. Conversely, the warmer American states, like Florida, California and Arizona, have whole retirement villages geared towards the elderly, with facilities from transport to medical care all in place. Australia, New Zealand, Canada and South Africa are also countries where a good range of retirement accommodation is available.

It is important to look into the maintenance and service charges of such places as well as the likelihood of these charges increasing substantially in years to come. Some such properties can be bought outright, while others are bought on a lease, either for a fixed term, or with ownership reverting to the landlord on the resident's death. Bear in mind that many retirement developments give residents independence yet have no care facilities so that they may have to move again at a time when they are most vulnerable.

Another thing to consider is the amount of space you need. Many people downsize when they retire; will there be the room for that treasured piece of furniture? It is a good idea to check out retirement homes in the UK before moving abroad, at least to see what facilities are available or what you want from such a home abroad.

These are some of the points to consider when looking for a retirement home:

- **Can the property and the development accommodate changing needs, such as the installation of a stair lift or sit-down shower?**

- You may be mobile now, but if you later needed a wheelchair, are the doorways wide enough and could you live on the ground floor only and access the bathroom and kitchen?
- Are pets welcome?
- Bear in mind that what may at first be a pleasure, like gardening, may turn into a chore.
- What is the view like? Is the development noisy?
- Does the development seem to be well-managed?
- Would it be easy to receive visitors and is there adequate parking for them?

Companies in the UK who build retirement homes include:

- **Care Village Group** (UK), **t** (01225) 865555; **www.carevillagegroup.co.uk**.
- **McCarthy and Stone** (UK), **t** 0800 919132; **www.mccarthyandstone.co.uk**.
- **Newfield Jones Homes** (UK), **t** (01253) 820900; **www.newfieldjoneshomes.co.uk**.

Other purchase options for holiday homes

If you don't want a permanent home to retire to abroad, but would like a property that you can take regular holidays in but without the expense and worry of owning a property outright, here are some other options.

Timeshare

Often the dream of owning a holiday property abroad doesn't work out as planned. You start with good intentions of regular visits several times a year, but mounting commitments result in your visiting the property far less than you would wish. Maybe you should have dipped your toe in the water to start with, to see whether property ownership abroad was really for you. In such a situation, it can seem that a timeshare (also known as holiday or vacation ownership) may be the answer, where you purchase just a short period each year at a property, commonly a couple of weeks.

Unfortunately, in the 1980s, soon after it became popular, timeshare rapidly got a bad name due to the high-pressure sales techniques many companies applied and also because many developments did not live up to the promises the initial sales literature and banter claimed. Owners of timeshare weeks found out the hard way that rather than appreciating in value, their timeshare weeks became less and less valuable and often was impossible to sell.

This led to legislation being brought in in the early 1990s to protect customers and today timeshare has cleaned up its act. Now about one million Britons take timeshare holidays, three times as many as a decade ago. At a rate of about 16 per cent per year, it is one of the fastest-growing sectors of the travel industry, rapidly conquering new territories.

The market, worth more than US$6bn worldwide, is expanding into more and more countries. To many people, timeshare suggests resorts in Spain or America, but the UK has its own growing market, with over 120 resorts, double the number 10 years ago. There are now over 4,700 resorts worldwide in countries as diverse as Hungary, Senegal and India, though Spain remains the most popular. The swift expansion of timeshare is even more impressive when you consider the antics of early players in the market.

The idea of just buying a single unit in one block and being limited to that block for the rest of your life is now history. There are different schemes available nowadays so that you can be more flexible on the type of unit or time of year, or you can opt for a points system, a currency to exchange, rather than buy at a specific resort.

The bad stories about timeshare focused on the way the product was sold, but traditionally the properties have generally been of good quality. What you are buying is generally superior to a hotel or package holiday. Timeshares have to be better or no one would buy them. A package holiday to Spain costs a family of four typically £2,000–2,500. With timeshare, you typically pay £10,000 now and, apart from flights and an annual maintenance charge, you don't have to pay anything more for 60 years.

As the sector has put its house in order, credibility has been further enhanced by the involvement of major players like Marriott, Disney, Airtours, Hilton, Hyatt, Stakis and Four Seasons. Also, a 1997 EU Timeshares Directive giving added protection to purchasers, including a statutory 'cooling-off period', has been taken up by many European states which increases the confidence of buyers. Additionally, credit card companies Mastercard and Visa introduced a 10-day cooling-off period for holidaymakers who have put down a deposit to be able to cancel the deal if they have second thoughts.

Although timeshares offer a higher standard of accommodation than most package holidays, can save money on future holidays and save on the hassle of arranging the annual break, the spectacular expansion of timeshare is largely the result of the opportunity to exchange weeks for timeshares at other resorts. The flexibility and variety offered by the exchange system appeals to many British holidaymakers; now they can vary their holiday plans, swap weeks or try a different destination. Interval International and Resort Condominiums International (RCI), the two leading exchange companies, have over 3.2 million customers on their books.

People are retiring earlier and consequently have more time to holiday, and timeshare is ideal for this. People are taking advantage of special offers like bonus weeks and late break availability. Prices from resellers of timeshare weeks are at least 50 per cent lower than new timeshare purchase prices, sometimes just 10 per cent of the new price. Even so, for all the advantages and improvements, you can never escape the fact that a timeshare property is never actually your own. And only a few people get to buy the best weeks of the year. A place in the sun isn't an ideal place to visit in the height of winter.

Do not buy in a hurry, as there are still some sharks out there and loopholes in the system remain. Also, it is not advisable to buy off-plan, i.e. before the apartment or the development's leisure facilities have been built. There is always the possibility that it won't be completed. Always buy in a resort that has an owners' club that can represent your interests.

Lastly, the handling, community, marketing, maintenance and service charges never go away – and may go up. Timeshares can be very difficult to resell, and instead of making a profit you may have to resort to giving yours away to someone prepared to take over the maintenance contract. And remember that in essence, all you are buying is a long-term reservation on an annual holiday.

These organisations have further information:

- **Department of Trade and Industry** (UK), **t** (020) 7215 5000; **www.dti.gov.uk**: offers a leaflet, *Timeshare – Making the Right Choice*.
- **Organization for Timeshare in Europe (OTE)** (UK), **t** (020) 7821 8845; **www.ote-info.com**.
- **Association of Timeshare Owners Committees** (UK), **t** 0845 230 2430; **www.tatoc.co.uk**.
- **Timeshare Consumers' Association** (UK), **t** (01909) 591100; **www.timeshare.org.uk**.
- **Timeshare Users' Group** (USA), **t** (904) 298 3185; **www.tug2.net**.

Timeshare companies include:

- **Interval International** (UK), **t** 0870 7444 222; **www.intervalworld.com**.
- **Primeshare** (UK), **t** (01386) 47813; **www.primeshare.com**.
- **RCI** (UK), **t** 0870 609 0141; **www.rci.com**.
- **Timeshare Council** (UK), **t** (020) 7821 8845; **www.timesharecouncil.net**.
- **www.tradingplaces.com** and **www.timeshareresources.com**: resource centres for buying, selling and renting timeshares around the world.

Holiday property bond

An alternative to timeshare is the holiday property bond, where you purchase part-ownership in a holiday property for around £2,000 to £3,000, which enables you to use rent-free holiday accommodation at 27 locations around the world. You can either keep the bond for as long as you like and pass it on in your will, or after a couple of years you can sell it, almost certainly for less than you paid for it.

An advantage is that, apart from a share of maintenance charges, you have paid for future holiday accommodation and the price never increases. A disadvantage is the lack of locations.

Further details are available from the **Holiday Property Bond** (UK), **t** (01638) 660066; **www.hpb.co.uk**.

Shares in a property

Properties at some developments, especially in Florida, can be part-purchased through property companies. For example, at the Parque de Floresta scheme, near Lagos in Portugal, buyers have recently been able to purchase a quarter share of a property at £40,000, around a quarter of the full price of the property, which entitles them to stay there for 13 weeks of each year forever.

It is not like timeshare. There, you are buying a right to use someone else's property for a set period. Group ownership, on the other hand, boils down to buying shares in your own property. It is an idea that has long been established by people buying boats and aircraft without the budget to buy outright.

To get around the problem of sharing the property with complete strangers, as you do with a timeshare property, some buyers have persuaded friends and family to buy the other three shares in the property, so that it is jointly owned by them all.

Some people buy in a group privately, without the expense of an agent, allowing them to have access to a much better property than what they could normally afford. A clear, effective contract should be drawn up to protect everyone's interests. It may be advantageous in some countries, such as France, to form a company for ownership of the property so that the property is not subject to inheritance laws. A good way of ensuring fair distribution of weeks is for owners to be given priority in turn. Whoever gets first choice at dates one season or year has the last choice the next.

Group ownership can be very advantageous if you need to sell, as the other owners have first call on buying it. Therefore, it is also possible to increase your share as other parties drop out.

The **Owner Groups Company** (**t** (01628) 486350; **www.ownergroups.com**) puts together buying groups, finds properties and advises on property management. It can provide a central website for the group so that each owner can bid for the weeks they need each year.

Leaseback

Here a hotel or development company typically sells a suite or apartment at a significant discount (usually around a third off the price), so that the purchaser is entitled to stay at the property for several weeks per year for a set period, typically 20 years. For the weeks they do not use the property, the owner receives rental income when the property is used by others. Especially popular in Spain and Portugal, prices are not cheap and usually exceed £100,000. It is important to check that you gain full vacant possession at the end of the agreed term.

Searching for a property

Although buying a home abroad is easier than ever before, with new English-speaking agents setting up shop daily and new markets opening around the globe by the week, the process of buying is seldom as simple as viewing a few photos and descriptions, fixing up a weekend visit and putting a deposit down for the first property that takes your fancy.

Firstly, the property laws and customs in many countries can be unclear, even illogical and baffling, and offer many opportunities for the unwary to hit significant problems, or even in some cases be completely fleeced. The need for expert, independent advice – *before* you have paid a deposit and signed the contract – cannot be overstressed. Never rely on the advice given by someone with a financial interest in the property, such as an agent or a developer, or a professional registered with a recognised body or organisation.

Be aware that in some countries laws to protect the consumer may be inferior – non-existent even – compared to the protection you are used to in your home country. Developers may not necessarily have adequate funds to complete projects, professionals may lack indemnity insurance, and there may be no legal comeback if a service is provided wrongly and causes problems rather than solves them.

Another complication is that choice varies considerably between countries and the regions within them. France is amply represented by English-speaking, often UK-based, specialist companies with hundreds, sometimes thousands of properties to view, initially on the Internet. Yet for a British buyer buying, for example, a property in Belgium or the Netherlands, it is far more difficult to begin a search from the UK and it would be far more effective to visit local agents in the area you're interested in.

Even in countries well served with property agents geared to the UK market, like France and Spain, many companies only specialise in one small area, and if you want to buy outside the normal holiday regions favoured by the British – such as Brittany, the Dordogne and the south of France in France and the *costas* in Spain – it can be considerably more difficult, especially if you don't speak the local language.

Local estate agents

In most countries, estate agents (or real estate agents or property brokers) are regulated by law and must be professionally qualified, licensed and in possession of indemnity insurance. Choose one that is a member of a recognised professional association. Do not take details contained in the property particulars as gospel and check any measurements stated. Also check that the property is still for sale before travelling to see it.

If a deposit for a property is paid to an agent, this must go into a special protected escrow account. Check beforehand exactly what the agent's fee is and whether you will have to pay any of it if a sale goes ahead, which is normal practice in some countries.

International estate agents

You could try some of the main international estate agency chains in the UK that have a good spread of branches abroad:

- **Chesterton International, t** (020) 7201 2070; **www.chesterton.co.uk.**
- **FPD Savills, t** (020) 7499 8644; **www.fpdsavills.co.uk.**
- **Hamptons International, t** (020) 7589 8844; **www.hamptons.co.uk.**
- **Knight Frank, t** (020) 7629 8171; **www.knightfrank.com**. Sells homes in more than 30 countries on five continents.
- **Sotheby's Realty, t** (020) 7598 1600; **www.sothebysrealty.com.**
- **Strutt and Parker, t** (020) 7629 7282; **www.struttandparker.com.**

When considering using international agents, bear in mind that they usually concentrate on the luxury market, so unless you are looking for an estate in Kenya or a beachfront Caribbean villa – rather than a £19,000 studio flat in Benidorm – they may not be able to help.

The Internet

The Internet is now well-established as a useful resource when searching for UK homes, but if you're looking overseas, the process can still be fraught with difficulty. Typically, either the website hasn't been updated since the millennium, or the property descriptions are all in a bewildering foreign language.

In some countries, notably in Spain, it can be galling to see the same property on several property websites – with several different asking prices and selling fees.

Relocation agents

Property-search, buying or relocation agents can help sift out out unsuitable properties. The European Relocation Association (EURA; *see* below) can provide a directory of members.

Typically such firms charge an upfront fee of several hundred pounds, as well as a percentage of the purchase price (typically a £500–600 registration charge plus around 2–2.5 per cent of the purchase price), and if you're buying a wreck to do up in rural Greece or France, you may not think their fees are worth it, and likewise they may feel financially it's not worth their while either. Yet often the fee is soon recouped, as a good agent's understanding of the local market can help negotiate asking prices downwards. Buying agents can usually also help to arrange mortgages and legal coverage, and to recommend gardeners, builders and electricians.

European relocation agents for people looking for a European retirement or holiday home are still a very underexploited search option. They're strongest in areas where there's a big market fuelled by foreign buyers like the Costa Blanca and the Balearics. Such agents can save time guiding buyers away from unsuitable areas or those that have recently become too expensive and more to up-and-coming areas. They can consider a large area, unlike an estate agent, who is only concerned with his own small catchment area.

- **European Relocation Association, t** 08700 726727; **www.euro-relocation. com**. Details on and links to many relocation agents worldwide.

- **Association of Relocation Agents, t** 08700 737475; **www.relocation agents.com**. Details on and links to many relocation agents worldwide.

International UK-based relocation agents include

- The **Property Finders (t (01908) 218753; www.thepropertyfinders.com)**

- **County Homesearch International (t (01872) 223349; www.wefindhouses.com**.

Inspection trips

Many property companies serving the haunts popular with expatriates in Spain, and to a lesser extent, Florida, France, Italy and Portugal, offer inspection trips where you are able to see the area in detail as well as properties currently for sale. These can at first sight be very tempting; indeed, one of the biggest UK firms geared to Spanish buyers currently offers four-day inspection tours of Spanish properties for £49, including accommodation, flights, food and drink.

Yet there is no such thing as a free lunch and accepting such trips can often – although not always – open you up to incessant high-pressure sales pitches and warnings that if you leave your designated rep during your time abroad, you will be charged the full cost of the trip. Typically on these trips you will tour 10 or 12 building sites, show homes and half-completed developments each day, and be encouraged, often with the alcohol flowing, to put your name down for a property bought off-plan. There is likely to be no time to explore the area or view older properties, even if you specify an interest in these.

The current situation is reminiscent of the aggressive sales techniques that accompanied the early days of timeshare, which so quickly gave that sector such a bad name. Now timeshare is far more regulated than the property market and many former timeshare salespeople are now concentrating on hard-selling property.

Inspection trips are usually only worth considering if they only take small groups rather than whole coachloads on the trips and they put the buyer under absolutely no pressure. Unfortunately, such trips are few and far between.

Overseas property shows

If you're not set from the start on buying in a specific country, with so many enticing destinations to choose from, one of the biggest problems for those buying a home overseas is deciding where to retire. Should you opt for the sun-drenched beaches of Spain, a villa close to Disney World and the endless other theme park-type attractions of Florida, or a home on a sleepy Greek island with little more than a taverna as a distraction?

It can be very fruitful to visit one of the regular international property shows that exhibit regularly around the country and which are often advertised in the property sections of national newspapers, as well as the specialist magazines geared to buying property abroad. Whether interested in a coastal villa, country home or mountain retreat, prospective buyers are usually able to compare how far their budgets stretch in each destination and find out about travel options.

Not only do these 'trade fairs' feature property developers and agents, but often there are representatives from companies that can help in other ways, such as financial advisers, mortgage lenders geared to foreign property owner-ship and firms of solicitors who specialise in property sales abroad. Some current examples of property shows are listed below.

The Best of Southern Spain property exhibition

• **Where:** Exhibitions in venues in cities such as London, Birmingham, Manchester, Edinburgh, Brighton, Bristol, Norwich, Brighton and Harrogate.

• **When:** The last Friday to Sunday in February.

• **Details: Viva Estates**, Reserva de Alvarito, Urb Andasol, CN340, KM189, 29600 Marbella, Malaga, Spain, **t** (UK) 0800 298 9594; **www.vivaestates.com**.

• **What's there:** Up to 25 developers and agents. There is relocation, buying, legal, tax, investment, financial and mortgage advice as well as new developments showcased.

Destination Sun Homes

• **Where:** various UK venues.

• **When:** Various dates throughout the year.

• **Details: Destination Sun Homes**, 60a High Street, Ingatestone, Essex CM4 9DW, UK, **t** 0870 9911882; **www.destinationsunhomes.com**.

• **What's there:** Focuses on the Caribbean, Cyprus, Florida and Spain.

French Property exhibition

• **Where:** Typically held at venues like Olympia, London, Edgbaston Cricket Ground, Birmingham plus Harrogate and Taunton.

• **When:** A Friday, Saturday and Sunday in January (London), March (Birmingham), May (Harrogate), September (London) and November (Taunton).

• **Details: French Property News**, 6 Burgess Mews, London SW19 1UF, UK; **t** (020) 8543 3113; **www.french-property-news.com**.

• **What's there:** Probably the best French property exhibition, with around 60 exhibitors focusing on France.

The Homebuyer Show

• **Where:** ExCel, Docklands, London.

• **When:** The first Friday, Saturday and Sunday in March.

• **Details: Homebuyer Events**, Mantle House, Broomhill Road, London SW18 4JQ, UK, **t** (020) 7069 5000; **www.homebuyershow.co.uk**.

• **What's there:** This is possibly the UK's largest and most comprehensive residential property event, with more than 200 exhibitors and 22,000 visitors in 2003. Both UK and overseas property is covered, with many exhibitors and seminars, and lots of details on hotspots, investment, legal and tax issues.

Homes Overseas exhibitions

• **Where:** More than 30 annual exhibitions at major venues including the NEC, Birmingham and Olympia, London. Other cities include Manchester, Belfast, Dublin, Glasgow, Brighton, Exeter, Leeds and Liverpool.

• **When:** Generally held on a Friday, Saturday and Sunday.

• **Details:** *Homes Overseas* **magazine**, Blendon Communications, 207 Providence Square, Mill Street, London SE1 2EW, UK, **t** (UK) (020) 7939 9888, (Spain) **t** 00 34 952 76 8369; **www.homesoverseas.co.uk**.

• **What's there:** Developers, estate agents, mortgage lenders and international lawyers, with seminars covering the purchase process, pensions, investment, tax planning and inheritance. The exhibitions, organised by *Homes Overseas* magazine, provide information on new and resale property from many places such as Australia, the Balearics and Canary Islands, Brazil, Bulgaria, Canada, the Caribbean, Croatia, Cyprus, Czech Republic, Dubai, Egypt, France, Goa, Greece, Florida and other US locations, Hungary, Ireland, Italy, Malta, Monaco, Montenegro, Portugal, Romania, Sardinia, South Africa, mainland Spain, Switzerland, Turkey and Thailand.

International Property Investor Show

• **Where:** A London hotel.

• **When:** First weekend in May.

• **Details:** International Homes, **t** (01245) 358877; **www.international-homes.com/exhibitions**.

• **What's there:** Co-organised by the publications *International Homes, English Homes* and the *Wall Street Journal Europe*, thousands of homes are on offer costing from £35,000 to £6 million. Countries featured include Cyprus, France, Malta, Portugal, Spain, South Africa and the USA.

The International Property Show

• **Where:** A hotel in London and Manchester.

• **When:** The first Friday, Saturday and Sunday in February or March and October.

• **Details:** International Property Show, 7 The Soke, Alresford, Hampshire SO24 9DB, UK, **t** (01962) 736712.

• **What's there:** Usually more than 35 exhibitors have stands to show their properties from around the world including the Balearics, the Canaries, Cyprus, Florida, Gibraltar, Greece, Portugal, Spain and the Turks and Caicos islands.

The Property Investor Show

• **Where:** ExCel, London.

• **When:** A September weekend.

• **Details:** Property Investor, **t** (020) 8877 3636; **www.propertyinvestor.co.uk**.

• **What's there:** Features developers from around the world.

MGB Homes international property exhibitions

• **Where:** Hotels in towns and cities including Ashbourne, Bolton, Basingstoke, Ellesmere Port, Bromsgrove, Truro, Swindon and Stratford-upon-Avon.

• **When:** A weekend in late February.

• **Details: MGB Homes**, Centro Commercial La Campana, Punta Prima, Orihuela Costa 03189, Alicante, Spain, **t** (UK) 0808 1800 500, **t** (Spain) 00 34 965 327 804; **www.mgbhomes.com**.

• **What's there:** Focuses on the Costa Blanca, Costa Almería and Costa Cálida.

Overseas Property Expo

• **Where:** Typically at 45 venues in the UK annually including Edgbaston Cricket Ground, Birmingham and Twickenham Stadium or Lords Cricket Ground, London.

• **When:** Fridays to Sundays throughout the year.

• **Details: Overseas Property Expo**, **t** 0800 3101218; **www.overseasproperty-expo.com**.

• **What's there:** Focusing on Florida, Costa del Sol, Costa Blanca and southern France, there are seminars, buying advice, inspection trips and subsidised flights and accommodation offers.

QSD Group

• **Where:** various UK venues.

• **When:** Various dates throughout the year.

• **Details: QSD Group**, Avenida de las Naciones, 1-6-03170 Ciudad Questada, Rojales, Alicante, Spain, **t** (UK) 0800 389 8152, (Spain) **t** 00 34 965 725 410; **www.qsdgroup.com**.

Viva Espana!

• **Where:** NEC Birmingham.

• **When:** A weekend in early May.

• **Details: Viva Espana**, **t** 0870 120 0332; **www.vivaespana2004.com**.

• **What's there:** Spanish property show.

Visiting properties abroad

Once you have read up on the area you are interested in, blitzed agents with questions, studied reams of property particulars and scanned Internet sites, before long you will have a good grasp of the local property market and will hopefully be able to make a shortlist of the properties or property types you really want to see. This is the time to plan a trip.

Holiday and travel insurance

Before anything, sort out some travel insurance. Check and compare policies carefully as they vary considerably. Note inclusions and exclusions and levels of cover. Although these cover such eventualities as cancelled flights, lost baggage and delays, the most important factor is the provision of medical expenses, which can add up to many thousands of pounds in some territories, such as America. Household policies, private medical insurance policies and credit card companies all often provide holiday and travel insurance, but this is unlikely to be adequate and should be treated as a bonus. An annual policy may be suitable – and cheaper – if you go abroad frequently or for long periods.

Visit the region at different times of year

When you have narrowed things down, visit the area that interests you at different times of year. Nothing beats visiting the region you wish to buy in as often as possible, and really you should get to know the place well, at different times of year, before committing to a purchase rather than buy on the basis of a two-week summer holiday as so many people do. Does the area lose many of its attractions outside the holiday season? Is the transport network good all year round? Can the climate change dramatically from month to month? This is an increasingly important factor the further north you go.

Ask yourself, the agent and the vendor lots of questions

There are lots of questions to answer before committing to buy. Location is a good start. The north of Spain or France may be convenient for the ferry ports, but would you want to visit during a freezing winter? The south of both these countries may enjoy the most sun, but are you likely to visit regularly if it's a long trek each time? Is there an airport, a good train station, attractive town or village nearby? Is there a sizeable retired community? Is there local animosity to foreign buyers of holiday homes? Is there a good local hospital nearby? More distant destinations like Florida and South Africa may sound very enticing and offer bargain properties, but will you want to endure airports and long-haul flights and fork out the cash for the fare often enough to justify buying there?

There's also security of the property the months you're away to consider, and the expense of buildings and contents insurance.

Conveyancing costs like taxes and lawyer's fees can be substantially higher than in the UK. The **Federation of Overseas Property Developers, Agents and Consultants** (FOPDAC) estimates that on average, a buyer can expect to pay 10 or 12 per cent on top of the original purchase price when buying abroad. There may be a minimum purchase price for a property imposed on foreign buyers, as in Malta, for example (*see* p.127).

If you are buying a holiday home rather than a retirement home and need to let out the property for most of the year to finance it, what is the local rental demand like? Never assume that it will finance the venture, whatever the claims and assurances of agents and sellers, unless they provide proof. Try to be as objective as possible when choosing a property. There may be restrictions on letting your home , which is a common restriction in developments in Florida, for example. If you let out your second home, income must be declared to the Inland Revenue; this involves completing a self-assessment form, although expenses may be offset against this. You will also probably have to pay tax if you sell the property, and the position here should also be clarified.

Property laws vary enormously. Not considering in whose name the property should be bought could risk a hefty inheritance tax bill for the owner's heirs, for instance. If you haven't commissioned the services of an independent lawyer (not one nominated by the agent) with experience of foreign property trans-actions, you could find you've bought yourself a home where the local farmer has the right to drive his tractor over your front lawn whenever he pleases, or worse, where there's a question mark over ownership of the land or the prop-erty. Most importantly, don't sign any binding documents that you don't understand fully without having them checked by a suitably qualified, prefer-ably UK-based, expert first.

If you are buying in an apartment block, development complex of villas or something similar, you should be made aware of the annual share of the main-tenance and other costs you will be required to pay with the other owners as well as terms, such as the frequency of exterior painting of the properties in the complex, for which you will have to contribute an amount.

Do not allow the seller or estate agent to rush you. Ask them lots of questions. How long has the property been on the market? Has anyone else made an offer and why did the sale not proceed? How ready and able is the seller to move? Are there copies of bills showing running costs or guarantees for work done avail-able? Is there an indication of the annual running costs?

Is the property being offered at a fair price?

There are many factors that can affect the value of a home. A central location in the city, proximity to water and seclusion in the countryside, mature gardens, selling in the summer, easy access to main commuting routes, or being well sited in an attractive village or town all help to increase the value of a property.

Factors like noise from a flight path, motorway or railway line, a nearby night-club, restaurant, tower block, industrial estate or electricity pylon are among the many things that can hinder a property's value.

A greater number of bedrooms does not necessarily mean a greater price. Three double bedrooms is better than five cramped box rooms purporting to be bedrooms. Restructuring a house to reduce five bedrooms to three, if done well, could enhance profitability as the resulting light, spacious design with maybe a gallery and other novel features can be especially appealing. Added space, such as an extension, should be in keeping with the house.

Viewing

Don't disregard a property just because it does not look attractive in the photo. Appearances can be deceptive, and the cosmetics of the house can often be surprisingly easily changed – whereas the location cannot.

Unless you have an unlimited budget, you need to have a flexible approach. Still, it is easy to be seduced by a property where you're so keen to move in you overlook the disadvantages that could cause problems later on. To ensure that this doesn't happen, work through a checklist of things to look out for from the very first viewing. Make notes as you go round, especially if you are looking at other properties in the day as you can soon forget what features were in which particular house or apartment.

Although it's easy to change the wallpaper or the fitted kitchen, you won't be able to change the position of the property, its views and the light it receives, so focus on these closely and try not to be influenced by cosmetics. Look out for trees nearby that could lock out light. If the approach to the property is steep, will access be a problem in the winter? If industry or a farm is nearby, would noise, pollution or smoke be a problem? A nearby river or stream could pose a threat of flooding, and if the property is near the coast there could also be the problem of coastal erosion. Such factors could affect insurance cover.

Visit the property again at different times of day and look for possible causes of disturbance in the locality: a nearby, seemingly quiet bar may spring to life and create disturbance in the evening; a school may cause lots of noise and traffic problems at drop-off and pick-up times; it may be under a flight path; or a newsagent may get daily deliveries of papers in the early hours.

If the property looks as though it satisfies your minimum requirements at first viewing, look again in more detail. Will the layout allow you enough space for your needs? Is there adequate space for large items of furniture? Can they easily be brought into the room you plan them for? Measure large items first and check with a tape measure at the property.

What kind of heating is used? Does it look as though it may need updating? Does the electrical system look modern and are there enough power points or does it look as though you would have to consider rewiring – a costly and messy job. Is noise a problem? Open a window to hear the traffic noise.

Is the dining area or dining room convenient for the kitchen and is the layout of the kitchen suitable for your needs or simple to change? Is there space for all required appliances? Is the staircase suitable for very young or elderly visitors? If it is an older property, has it been modernised well?

Before committing yourself to buying and possibly paying for a survey, you can get a good idea of the condition of a property by looking out for certain indicators. New wallpaper or paint, for instance, could be concealing cracks or damp patches. Cracks around doors and bay windows and long, diagonal cracks across walls, which look as though they have been repaired but have again cracked, could indicate subsidence where the foundations of the property are not secure, and which can be very costly to rectify. Doors sticking or not hanging correctly, a sloping floor, bent chimney stack or uneven roof line or bulging outside walls can also indicate subsidence. To see if a wall is bulging, stand close to the end of it and look along it to see whether it is straight.

Cracked or sagging plaster ceilings in older houses can be an often under-estimated danger and messy to repair. Springy floors can be a sign that the floors themselves or joists underneath may have rotted. A musty smell and cracking in the woodwork can indicate dry rot, caused by a fungus (*serpula lacrynens*), which is usually very expensive to treat, especially as all the affected wood, down to window frames and joists, must be replaced.

Stains on ceilings and walls can indicate damp, although this may be less serious than it looks – perhaps penetrative damp caused by a leaking roof, window or gutter, which should go away once the culprit is fixed. If there is a smell of damp and you can feel moisture on walls, this may indicate rising damp, when a damp-proof course breaks down and the brick walls suck up water from the ground. Typically in this situation, you will have wet walls with damp, discoloured wallpaper on the lower portion of walls, possibly a smell of mouldy paper, flaking paintwork and crumbling plaster.

Roof tiles and slates should also be checked by moving some way from the building to have a look at the condition, ideally with binoculars. While outside, also looks at the pointing (the mortar between the bricks) because if it is in a bad condition, it can allow damp to seep into the property. Nearby trees may have roots that could undermine the property's foundations.

If you want to check the property even more thoroughly yourself, use the checklist in Appendix II, pp.287–93.

Alternatives to buying

Renting before buying

If you are not sure what kind of property or location you want, it may be worth renting property that is similar to the type you have in mind, in different seasons if possible. Renting for an extended period not only gives you the opportunity to search for the most ideal home at your leisure but also allows you the opportunity to find out what the climate, locals and facilities are like, and perhaps to hear the experiences of other foreign buyers who have already taken the plunge.

Home exchange

A cheaper alternative to renting is to exchange your home for another one over a limited period, if you have no problem with allowing strangers to move into your home in the UK.

Agencies that organise home exchanges include:

- **Green Theme International Home Exchange Holiday Service** (UK), **t** (01208) 873123; **www.gti-home-exchange.com**.

- **Home Base Holidays** (UK), **t** (020) 8886 8752; **www.homebase-hols.com**.

- **HomeExchange.com** (USA), **t** (805) 898 9660; **www.homeexchange.com**.

- **HomeLink International** (UK), **t** (01962) 886882; **www.homelink.org.uk**.

- **Intervac International Home Exchange, t** (UK) (01249) 461101, **t** (USA) (415) 435 3497; **www.intervac-online.com**.

- **The Invented City** (USA), **t** (415) 846 7588; **www.invented-city.com**.

- **Vacation Homes Unlimited** (USA), **t** 800 848 7927; **www.vacation-homes.com**.

Financing the Purchase and Financial Implications

06

Finance options

When you have found the home you want to buy, the main options to finance the purchase are buying outright, remortgaging your UK home or taking out an overseas mortgage.

Buying outright

Buying outright, where you have the capital available for the total cost of the purchase, is of course the most straightforward option, but beware of using all your funds for the purchase leaving with you little or no spare cash for any unforeseen expenses.

Remortgaging your existing home

If you are planning to retain your UK home and you have sufficient equity in it, and assuming you can satisfy the lending criteria of the lender, you could raise the required amount for the purchase by remortgaging or taking out a second mortgage. This may be cheaper, is often simpler to arrange and avoids much baffling paperwork compared to taking out a foreign mortgage. Mortgages overseas also tend to be more restrictive and have stricter lending criteria, requiring applicants to supply detailed income and expenditure details.

Yet bear in mind that sterling-based finance to fund a foreign asset is subject to currency fluctuations. Also, having bought the property, should you later need to raise money on your foreign home, this is often not possible as many foreign mortgage markets are far less flexible than that in the UK, do not permit equity release and only allow money to be lent to buy or improve a property.

Borrowing on your existing home means that you are able to present yourself as a cash buyer, which can be a bargaining tool.

Taking out a foreign mortgage

Some foreign mortgages are more expensive and restrictive than those in the UK, while others, notably many in Europe, offer better rates. Yet the process of obtaining a mortgage abroad can be far more difficult than in your home country, especially if you do not speak the language of the foreign bank you are dealing with. An international mortgage broker can help smooth the way, although there will usually be an additional fee, usually of around 1 per cent of the loan.

An increasing number of UK lenders are offering loans specifically meant for properties abroad, although a number of countries are excluded.

Taking out a mortgage in another currency

As well as the option of taking out a mortgage in the currency of the country where your foreign property is situated or your income is paid in, you can also take out a loan in another foreign currency, whether it be US dollars, Australian dollars or euros. In this situation you are exposed, however, to currency swings and devaluations that may not work in your favour.

A UK or foreign mortgage?

The advantages and disadvantages of borrowing in the UK mortgage for your property abroad or in the destination itself vary from country to country. The differences can be large.

For example, in May 2004 the Bank of England base rate was historically low at 4 per cent, yet the European Central Bank's interest rate was 2 per cent and the American Federal Reserve's most important lending rate was just 1 per cent. At this time, Japan's central bank rate was effectively zero following economic stagnation, with mortgages of just 2 per cent being widely available.

If such differences continue, in countries like Spain, France and Italy mortgage interest rates are likely to be lower than if you borrowed in the UK, although the set-up charges and administrative requirements may be more. A further point is that some countries allow tax relief against rental income for the interest on a local mortgage but will not allow this on a UK mortgage.

Fluctuating exchange rates can really alter monthly payments. According to international legal firm John Howell and Co., over the last 15 years the pound sterling has varied between 280 Spanish pesetas and 162 pesetas. This means that a mortgage of 100,000 pesetas per month would have varied in cost between £357 and £617.

Whatever option you take, you should take expert advice about how the loan could affect tax allowances and liabilities. In some countries, residents receive tax relief on their mortgages, which can mean it is financially beneficial in some circumstances to take out a mortgage if you are resident abroad, even if you can pay cash.

Equity-release schemes

Older homeowners (over 60) can ask their financial adviser about these schemes, which release capital or income earned from their homes. You should take care to check whether the Inland Revenue will consider the income released as taxable under new regulations designed to prevent the avoidance of inheritance tax.

They consist of:

- **Home income plans:** you take out a loan secured on the home and use the money to buy an annuity, which provides an income for life; the fixed interest on the loan is paid out of the income from the annuity.

- **Home reversion plans:** you sell part of the value of your property in return for an income for life; with these you can instead raise a lump sum and have the right to remain in the home as a tenant for life.

- **Cash-release schemes:** becoming more popular, these allow you to borrow a fixed percentage of the value of the home and to spend or invest.

- **Fixed-appreciation mortgages:** involve taking out a loan to buy an annuity.

- **Shared-appreciation mortgages:** allow you to take a cash loan if you agree to let the lender take a share of the future appreciation in value of the home. The loan is repaid when you die or the property is sold.

Buying a property through an offshore company

Non-resident buyers of property in some countries buy through an offshore company in order to legally avoid paying stamp duty and transfer tax, as well as capital gains, wealth and inheritance taxes. Buying via an offshore company requires expert legal advice. The practice has been common in France, Spain and Portugal.

In Spain, many homes are sold through a Gibraltar-based company to lessen the Spanish stamp duty bill. In France, setting up a company gives the buyer more control over who can inherit the property.

However, the loophole has increasingly come under threat. In Portugal, for example, the tax rules have been changed recently, so that home owners using an offshore firm are liable for a hefty tax bill.

In the UK a House of Lords ruling in 2004 brought the possibility of homes owned through a company structure being taxed as a benefit in kind, although nothing has as yet been confirmed.

Lenders and other financial companies

These companies specialise in aspects of finance associated with buying a property abroad or living abroad, such as tax planning, pensions, currency transfer, mortgages and investment:

- **Abbey France, t** (UK) 0800 44 90 90, **t** (France) (00 33) 3 20 18 18 18; **www.abbey.com**. Provides bilingual mortgage advisers and has a free guide to buying property abroad.

- **Banco Halifax Hispania** (UK), **t** (01422) 333868; **www.halifax.es**.

- **Barclays Bank Spain** (Spain), **t** (00 34) 91 336 1610; **www.barclays.es**.

- **Blevins Franks Financial Management**, Barbican House, 26–34 Old Street, London EC1V 9QQ, UK, **t** (020) 7336 1000; **www.blevinsfranks.com**. Specialises in overseas property finance and foreign exchange.

- **Conti Financial Services**, 204 Church Road, Hove, East Sussex BN3 2DJ, UK, **t** (01273) 772811; **www.mortgagesoverseas.com**. Mortgage provider for overseas buyers in more than 20 countries, including Australia, Canada, the Caribbean,Cyprus, France, Gibraltar, Greece, Ireland, Italy, Israel, Malta, Portugal, New Zealand, Spain, South Africa and the USA.

- **Expatriate Advisory Services**, 14 Gordon Road, West Bridgeford, Nottingham NG2 5LN, UK, **t** (0115) 981 6572.

- **Newcastle Building Society Gibraltar** (Gibraltar), **t** (00 350) 42136; www.newcastle.co.uk.

- **Norwich and Peterborough Spanish Home Loans** (UK), **t** (01733) 372006; **www.norwichandpeterborough.co.uk**.

- **PFK**, PO Box 296, St Peter Port, Guernsey GY1 1DZ, UK, **t** (01481) 727927; **www.pkfguernsey.com**. Specialises in France and Spain.

- **PropertyFinance4Less**, 160 Brompton Road, London SW3 1HW, UK, **t** (020) 7594 0555; **www.propertyfinance4less.com**. Specialises in overseas mortgages, foreign exchange and associated insurance products.

- **UK Expatriates Professional Advisory Services**, 84 Grange Road, Middlesborough TS1 2LS, UK, **t** (01642) 221211.

- **Wilfred T. Fry**, Crescent House, Crescent Road, Worthing, Sussex BN11 1RN, UK, **t** (01903) 231545.

Currency exchange

When you have decided on a country to buy within, it is prudent to read up on its recent financial history. Some currencies devalue and strengthen alarmingly in short periods, and buying at the wrong time can cost you thousands more pounds than just a few months before or after. Although one can't predict the future, an overall picture of the economy of a country can be a great asset.

Major events can have a big impact on exchange rates, as they can greatly affect economic confidence. For example, South Africa's rand slipped from R11 to the pound in March 2001 to R20 in December 2001 after September 11.

Exchange rates can make a very big difference, as the following examples show. If you bought an average-priced property in North America in January 2002 it would have cost $157,000 (then about £97,000). An identical property bought in January 2003 would cost $164,650 (*c.* £89,000). Even though prices rose by 5 per cent over the year, the actual cost in pounds fell by 9.5 per cent.

Conversely, buyers in Europe during the same period would have paid an average of €169,650 (then around £115,000) in 2002 and €183,380 (about £125,000) in 2003. Therefore, a British buyer would have paid around 8 per cent more in 2003 for the same property.

It is possible to forward-buy as much as 18 months ahead, with a **forward contract**, the currency that you need to purchase a property, at an agreed fixed rate. This can provide peace of mind of knowing exactly what you will have to pay, although you will lose out if the currency subsequently weakens.

You can also opt for a **spot transaction**, which allows you to transfer funds immediately, in line with the current exchange rate.

You can also place a **limit order** in the market for a desired exchange rate. The currency is purchased as soon as the market reaches your specified exchange rate, protecting you from negative exchange movements but allowing you to gain from a positive one.

For further currency-related information and online currency converters, try:

- **Currencies Direct**, Hanover House, 73–74 High Holborn, London WC1V 6LR, UK, **t** (020) 7813 0332; **www.currenciesdirect.com**.

- **Currencies4less** (UK), **t** (020) 7594 0594; **www.currencies4less.com**.

- **Moneycorp Commercial Foreign Exchange**, 2 Sloane Street, London SW1A 9LA, UK, **t** (020) 7823 7700; **www.moneycorp.com**.

Taxes

Before buying a property abroad, find out what taxes you will be liable for. These could include transfer taxes and stamp duty when you buy, annual property taxes, rates, residential taxes, real estate taxes and/or council tax once you have bought, wealth tax, inheritance tax and capital gains tax. Also worth investigating are tax incentives encouraging you to live in a certain country.

Property taxes

Annual property taxes, rates, residential taxes, real estate taxes and/or council taxes may be payable and are usually for such things as rubbish collection, road cleaning, street lighting and community services.

Prospective owners should check that there are no outstanding taxes of this sort relating to the property, especially where the new owner is responsible for unpaid property taxes and debts.

Such taxes are usually based on an assessed value of the property. Although this is usually lower than the real current value, it is important it is not more, in which case you would pay more tax than necessary, but the assessed value can affect a number of taxes, which could end up being very expensive indeed. For example, in Spain several taxes relate to the fiscal value of a property, including transfer tax, letting tax and inheritance tax.

In some countries, the owner is not necessarily sent an annual bill, and instead the onus is on the owner to find out and pay whatever taxes are due.

Many properties abroad attract other taxes. These vary from region to region within each country, but could include a surcharge in tourist areas for beach cleaning, for example.

Capital gains tax

In many countries capital gains tax is payable on the profit from the sale of property and sometimes other assets like antiques, jewellery, stocks and shares. It is a complex subject, especially in international terms, and it is advisable to check your tax position with a suitably qualified expert before committing yourself to buying abroad.

Such an expert would be able to clarify your liabilities, any gains that are exempt and capital losses that can be offset against gains. Bills associated with buying, selling, renovating or restoring the property can all be offset against capital gains tax and may be index-linked.

As far as property goes, generally the tax applies to property that is not your principal home. Therefore, if you buy a holiday home abroad the tax would apply to that property according to the tax laws of that country, but if you retain but move from a home in the UK and make a foreign home your principal residence, your UK home may be liable to the tax when you sell, instead.

Often, the longer you own a property in a country, the less you are liable for until you eventually owe nothing. In Spain this is currently a decade and in France it is 32 years.

Wealth tax

Taxes and their effects can vary greatly around the world and many countries have taxes not present in Britain. For example, in some countries a wealth tax is applied, depending on your domicile, where typically your assets (including such things as property, vehicles, shares, jewellery and business ownership) are totalled, with liabilities subtracted (such as mortgages and debts), and a tax on this is paid on assets above a certain sum. In France, the tax is exempted at below €700,000; in Spain, the exemption is €108,182 and the tax varies from 0.2 to 2.5 per cent.

Income tax, pensions and savings

Income tax is an important factor in your financial affairs mainly if you are planning to live or work abroad or let out your foreign home, as it is generally payable if you receive income from a local source in a country. In some countries, income tax and social security contributions can be very high, so it is important to clarify the taxation position early on.

As far as the UK goes, to be treated as not ordinarily resident for income tax purposes you need to spend three tax years out of the country. During that period, you should spend no more than 90 days in Britain per year. Plan comfortably in advance so that your finances are set up efficiently as possible. Contact a financial adviser who specialises in the country you are moving to.

A number of countries, such as France and Spain, have double tax agreements with the UK – agreements that mean you don't have to have to pay tax in two countries. Yet you need to know how the laws determine your tax position, and which country you are living in for tax purposes.

Bear in mind that if you are no longer resident in Britain, you give up British tax advantages. If you move abroad, for example, you cannot continue to put money into ISAs. However, as far as the Inland Revenue is concerned (Inland Revenue ISA regulations 11 and 22(2)), ISA accounts can be left open and you would continue to pay gross interest as before. Even so, some companies could require you to cash in their accounts.

You must declare any income derived from rent, even if you don't make an overall profit, and pay tax on any gain. If you have a UK business, it remains subject to UK income tax even if you are a non-resident. Interest on bank and building society accounts held in the UK remain subject to UK tax. UK pensions, whether state, occupational or personal, are subject to UK tax even if paid to you abroad.

Inheritance and gift tax

Inheritance tax, estate tax or death duty is payable in most countries on the estate of someone who dies. Whether you are a resident or non-resident, the tax is usually applicable in the country you own property in. You generally pay inheritance tax in the country the tax authorities deem is your domicile. Inheritance tax can be paid by the estate or, as in the case of Spain and France, by the beneficiaries of the estate.

Inheritance tax (and gift tax) varies greatly from country to country and can differ a lot depending on such factors as the relationship of the beneficiary to the deceased or the beneficiary's own personal wealth. A lawyer or financial adviser specialising in the taxation system of the country concerned can advise on ways to avoid or reduce inheritance tax. It is a good idea to decide how to do this before purchasing a property to avoid complications later.

Making the Purchase

07

Planning ahead

As soon as you start looking for properties, you should start to plan ahead so that everything is in place once you are ready to buy. You will need to appoint a solicitor and the sooner you find one, the better. The solicitor will check the title of the property and investigate potential problems like boundaries, rights of way or major developments that might be planned for the locality, which could affect the property. Your solicitor will oversee the transfer of funds to complete the sale and formally register the change of ownership with the authorities.

When you are buying abroad, you are often using a legal system that is completely different from what you are used to, from transferring the property through to inheritance law. There are a lot of potential problems that most buyers are unlikely to consider and which can cause far greater difficulties than they would here. This makes buying a property abroad a stressful business.

There is a great need for a suitably qualified professional to oversee the legal aspects of a purchase or sale; this person can be a lawyer (or solicitor), or in some countries, such as Britain, a licensed conveyancer. In some countries, conveyancing is carried out by a public notary, who oversees the sale on behalf of the government.

Engaging a lawyer

As property laws vary considerably abroad, and have many potential pitfalls, it is in a buyer's interests to engage an English-speaking lawyer who is familiar with the law of the country where the property is located and with the law of the country the buyer is resident in.

The legal process can be slow in many countries and hold-ups can lose you the property, so choose your solicitor with care. You will want one who has a good command of both your mother tongue and of the language of the country you are buying in. Their fees, expertise and enthusiasm can vary greatly. Obtain quotes and chat to several before making a final choice. Some charge a percentage of the purchase price while others charge by the hour. Ask whether they charge a fixed fee and, if so, whether this includes everything, down to the search and electronic bank transfer fees, postage and any local taxes. Ask what the charges will be if the sale falls through. If you only obtain a guide price, you could be charged for every fax or letter on top.

Such firms carry out the property acquisition, which involves vetting the contract to see that it is legal, clear and fair, providing translations when needed and carrying out local enquiries and searches.

The lawyer will:

- **oversee the signing of the preliminary contract and the completion of the sale where the deed of sale is signed by both parties.**

- ensure that the property has good title (i.e. that it belongs to the vendor or that he has legal authority from the owner to sell it) and is not burdened by outstanding mortgages, loans, local taxes, utilities bills or other debts.

- make sure that the property has no pre-emption rights or restrictive covenants (such as rights of way).

- find out whether there are plans for development that would adversely affect the property, such as airports, shops, retail parks or railway lines.

- check that the property has the necessary planning permission and building permits and that it was built according to such permissions.

- advise on the subject of under-declaration, where a deflated purchase price is declared to the authorities to reduce the tax liability, a common occurrence in many countries; under-declaration can carry the risk of heavy penalties.

Specialist firms can also advise about related matters, such as commissioning a survey, raising finance, converting and sending funds, property insurance, timeshare sales, emigration and retirement, setting up in business abroad, taxation and dealing with foreign inheritance laws. They should ensure that your money is protected if you have bought before the property is finished because there is always the possibility the developer could go out of business before completion, and the lawyer should ensure that there are safeguards to protect you against this.

UK solicitors specialising in foreign property conveyancing

Countries that these firms of lawyers specialise in are noted.

- **Baily Gibson**, 5 Station Parade, Beaconsfield, Buckinghamshire HP9 2PG, **t** (01494) 672661; **www.bailygibson.co.uk**. Spain.

- **Bennett and Co.**, 144 Knutsford Road, Wilmslow, Cheshire SK9 6JP, UK, **t** (01625) 586937; **www.bennet-and-co.com**. International lawyers dealing with property transactions, inheritance and taxation in Europe, the United States and the Caribbean. Associated firms are in Lisbon, Albufeira, Madrid, Marbella, Alicante, Torrevieja, Tenerife, Barcelona, Mallorca, Ibiza, Lanzarote, Paris, Athens, Marseille, Gibraltar, Cyprus and Istanbul.

- **Brooker Grindrod**, Suite 3, Dudley House, High Street, Bracknell, Berkshire RG12 1LL, **t** (01344) 456565. Spain.

- **Carter Slater and Co.**, 41 Harborough Road, Kingsthorpe, Northampton NN2 7SH, **t** (01604) 717505. Spain, Cyprus, Portugal, France.

- **Champion Miller and Honey**, 153 High Street, Tenterden, Kent TN30 6JT, **t** (01580) 762251.

- **Cornish and Co.**, 1–7 Hainault Street, Ilford, Essex IG1 4EL, **t** (020) 8478 3300; **www.cornishco.com**. Spain, France, Cyprus, Italy, Gibraltar, Malta, Greece and Portugal.

- **Croft Baker & Co.**, 95 Aldwych, London WC2B 4JF, **t** (020) 7242 3370. Spain, France, Portugal.

- **De Pinna Notaries**, 35 Piccadilly, London W1V 0PJ, **t** (020) 7208 2900; **www.depinna.co.uk**. France, Spain, Portugal, Germany, Italy.

- **Glaisyers Glickman**, 559 Barlow Moor Road, Chorlton Cum Hardy, Manchester M21 8AN, **t** (0161) 881 5371. Spain.

- **John Howell and Co.**, 17 Maiden Lane, London WC2E 7NL, **t** (020) 7420 0400; **www.europelaw.com**. France, Spain, Portugal, Italy.

- **Leathes Prior**, 74 The Close, Norwich NR1 4DR, **t** (01603) 610911; **www.leathesprior.co.uk**. Europe.

- **Lita Gale**, 43 Gower Street, London WC1E 6HH, **t** (020) 7580 2066; **www.litagale.com**. Spain, Portugal, with branches in Lisbon, Faro, Madeira and throughout Spain.

- **Neville de Rougemont**, Greentree, Ascot Road, Holyport, Maidenhead, SL6 2JB, **t** (01628) 778566; **www.nevillederougemont.com**. Portugal, with an office in Lisbon.

- **Sean O'Connor and Co.**, 2 River Walk, Tonbridge, Kent TN9 1DT, **t** (01732) 365378. France.

- **Pannone and Partners**, 123 Deansgate, Manchester M3 2BU, **t** (0161) 909 3000; www.pannone.com. Spain, France.

- **G. Pazzi-Axworthy**, Llys Eira, Birklands Lane, St Albans, Hertfordshire AL1 1EQ, **t** (01727) 823186. Italy.

- **Penningtons**, 69 Old Broad Street, London EC2M 1PE, **t** (020) 7457 3000; **www.penningtons.co.uk**. Most of the European Union, Norway, Switzerland, South Africa, Hong Kong, Denmark and Russia.

- **Prettys**, 25 Elm Street, Ipswich, Suffolk IP1 2AD, **t** (01473) 232121; **www.prettys.co.uk**. Europe.

- **Pritchard Englefield**, 14 New Street, London EC2M 4TR, **t** (020) 7972 9720; **www.pritchardenglefield.eu.com**. France, Germany.

- **Russell-Cooke Potter and Chapman**, **t** (020) 8789 9111; **www.russell-cooke.co.uk**. France.

- **Michael Soul and Associates**, 16 Old Bailey, London EC4M 7EG, **t** (020) 7597 6292; **www.spanishlawyer.co.uk**. Offices in Madrid, Malaga and Marbella.

- **Taylors**, Red Brick House, 28–32 Trippet Lane, Sheffield S1 4EL, **t** (0114) 276 6767; **www.taylorssolicitors.co.uk**. France.

- **John Venn and Sons**, 95 Aldwych, London WC2B 4JF, **t** (020) 7395 4300; **www.johnvenn.co.uk**. Spain, France, Portugal, Italy, Switzerland.

- **Withers**, 16 Old Bailey, London EC4M 7EG, **t** (020) 7936 1000; **www.withers.co.uk**. France, Spain, offices in Milan and New York.

In addition, embassies and consulates can usually provide a list of lawyers, and the **Law Society** (50 Chancery Lane, London WC2A 1SX, UK, **t** (020) 7242 1222; **www.lawsociety.org.uk**) can provide details of lawyers specialising in property sales abroad.

The notary

This public official, who is a crucial part of the conveyancing process in countries such as France, represents neither buyer nor seller but ensures that all documents are in order on behalf of the government.

There are two principal stages where the notary is involved: the signing of the preliminary contract and the completion of the sale where the deed of sale is signed by both parties. He registers the property and makes sure that all applicable state taxes are paid upon completion, and makes various other checks relating to things such as the sales contract and any developments that could directly affect the property. It is advisable to engage your own lawyer to protect your interests even when a notary is involved in a sale.

Making an offer for a property

Finding the property you want can be difficult enough, but clinching the deal can be a substantial hurdle in itself. By the time you are ready to make an offer, you should have visited the property several times to ensure that it is the property for you. You should be aware of your legal responsibilities once you have made the offer. Would you later be able to pull out from the deal should the need arise, or will you now be legally committed, so that walking away from the deal would be a very costly or difficult process?

Find out when the vendor is likely to be in a position to move. Would the property be so attractive if there were a lengthy wait for possession – for example, if you were to miss out visiting the property during the upcoming summer?

Clarify exactly what will remain and what will be removed from the property. Such things as curtains, curtain rails and tracks, carpets and built-in cookers, lampshades, wall lights, built-in cupboards, shelving, garden furniture and plants, and sheds can all be very expensive to replace all at once. Would you be interested in buying the refrigerator, dishwasher, washing machine, tumble-drier and any other such appliances on offer?

If you want to make an offer, you probably won't be taken seriously if you offer substantially less than the asking price unless you know the vendor is desperate to sell, the property has been on the market for a long time or the property has serious problems that need rectifying.

Unlike in England, Wales and Northern Ireland (not Scotland), where vendors usually realise that their property may sell for less than the 'asking price', in some countries it is almost unheard of to offer anything below the asking price; or the asking price may on the contrary be simply a starting point for discussions about the final purchase price, which everyone knows will almost certainly be higher.

Find out exactly what the traditions of property-buying in the country you are buying in are. A good knowledge of the local property market will put you in a stronger bargaining position. Establish how long the property has been on the market. The longer it is, the more likely the vendor will be receptive to bargaining. If you make a lower offer, justify it by pointing out problems that could be expensive to put right, such as ancient wiring or structural problems or problems with the location. Sell your advantages as a buyer. If you are a cash buyer, remind the vendor.

You may have to wait for a decision, or your offer may be accepted or rejected straight away. You may instead enter a period of haggling. It is probably not worth jeopardising the deal for the sake of a few hundred pounds if the vendor ups the price slightly or quibbles over the worth of the decrepit washing machine he is leaving behind. Especially in many areas popular with British buyers, it can be important to move fast to ensure that the sale goes through. If it fails because you quibbled over £500, it could cost you far more once you've had to start the home-searching process all over again.

After you have made the offer on the property you want and it has been accepted, contact your solicitor regularly to make sure your file stays at the top of their invariably large pile of clients.

Surveys

Regardless of whether or not it is common practice locally to commission a survey before buying, in most cases you will want a survey to ascertain the condition of the property. Buildings standards vary greatly around the world and some regions offer considerable threats to the stability of a building, such as an increased risk of earthquakes or hurricanes, or wood-boring insects like termites, or poor building land resulting in an increased risk of subsidence. Obviously, the older and more unusual a property is, and worse the condition, the more useful a survey will be. This can be carried out by a surveyor, engineer or technical architect.

Even if the property has a low asking price, a survey may still be needed as the cost of repairing serious defects can far exceed the cost of purchase.

If a property has been restored, ask to see bills detailing works done. Are there guarantees for such things as damp proofing?

Whether you commission a survey or not, there are many things you can check yourself before buying. See **Finding a Property**, pp.232–3 and **Appendix II**, pp.287–93 for further details. It is worth testing things such as electrical sockets, light switches, doors and windows, taps and drains. Just because they are there doesn't mean that they are in good repair.

The stages of buying

Before committing yourself to buying, ensure that an independent, English-speaking lawyer specialising in the conveyancing process of the country you wish to buy in has checked that all matters relating to the property, such as boundaries, access, connection to utilities and current ownership of the property, are clear and satisfactory.

• **Are there any restrictions on things such as further building on the property, making structural alterations, running a business or letting the property out?**

• **Have you had an independent survey carried out by a suitably qualified surveyor? Do you know about all the tax implications of owning a property in the country in question, and of the local inheritance laws?**

• **Is the contract to buy satisfactory, stating the correct requirements, such as guaranteed vacant possession on the agreed completion date? Obtain professional advice about property tax, inheritance tax, capital gains tax and other financial matters relating to your purchase.**

• **Do ensure that you have sufficient funds to cover all fees and expenses relating to the purchase. Don't pay anything until your lawyer says so.**

The preliminary contract

The first stage of buying is normally to sign a purchase contract indicating your intention to buy. It is advisable to have the contract checked by a lawyer before signing. If the contract requires translating, it is important to be aware that the translation may be inaccurate and is not legally binding.

Be wary of being tied to **conditions** you may not be able to keep to, such as completing within a specified time or a short period from signing the preliminary contract. Some contracts specify that simply losing your deposit is not an option should you wish to pull out of the sale, but you are instead legally compelled to go ahead with the sale whatever the circumstances.

Ask your lawyer to insert clauses to cover you against circumstances out of your control, the most common being a clause releasing you from the contract should you fail to obtain a mortgage. You usually pay a deposit of between 5 and 10 per cent of the purchase price on signing the contract. Make sure you know on which terms you could lose your deposit or have it returned.

Paying for your home

Your solicitor will be able to advise of the best form of payment for the balance owing on the property before completion. The transfer of large sums should be at the commercial rate of exchange rather than the higher tourist rate. *See* 'Currency exchange', p.239.

Importing and exporting money

Most countries present few or no barriers to the import or export of funds, although it is common for countries to require foreigners to declare the importation or exportation of funds over a set amount. There may be a limit to the amount of cash that can be brought on or taken out of many countries. If required, it is important to declare funds used for buying a home as otherwise they could later be confiscated.

Payment methods

- **Personal cheque:** These can take considerable time to clear abroad.
- **Bank draft:** These should always be sent by registered or recorded mail and the disadvantage is that if a draft is lost or stolen it cannot be cancelled. Some banks treat them as normal cheques and the recipient has to wait for the draft to clear.
- **International money transfers:** In today's electronic age, making international money transfers (also known as swift transfers) is usually quick; normally they are processed within three days, and are relatively inexpensive. Most banks and building societies can arrange them and usually either charge a percentage of the amount you are moving (for example 0.25 per cent is charged by Lloyds TSB) and others charge a flat fee (Nationwide charges £20). Ask your bank how it calculates exchange rates and whether the rate is fixed for the day of transfer.

Completion

When it comes to signing the deed of sale, of which you receive a copy, you should check that the property is in the same condition as it was when you agreed to buy. You should be clear about the capital gains tax and inheritance tax consequences of signing the deed.

Properties in some countries do not have title deeds, and in this case ownership is shown by registration of the property at the land registry.

Moving In and Settling Down

Removals

Getting quotations

Charges by professional removal firms vary considerably, so shop around for an experienced firm that can offer a competitive quote. Use a removal firm accredited to a recognised trade association. You may be tempted to do it all yourself, but be aware that this could be a false economy when you take into account time off work, the cost of materials, van hire and labour costs. There could also be risks of damage and unforeseen hitches.

Ask at least three companies for a written quotation that includes the company's full terms and conditions and ask them to supply a quote free of charge and without obligation. Will the items be moved by boat, air or road? Is packing included or will you be required to pack everything, and if so, will boxes be provided free of charge? Does the quote include items in the attic, basement, garage and garden shed? Is insurance included and is this for 'all risks' to the replacement value of all goods?

Ask removal firms whether there is a charge for loan of boxes and other packaging. How much work are you required to do in preparation? Many removal firms will not accept a booking until contracts have been exchanged in case the sale falls through.

Will the van be able to access your street? Ensure there is adequate parking and inform the removal firm of any parking restrictions, poor access, spiral staircases and other potential difficulties in advance. Removers are not permitted to interfere with mains services, so contact gas, electricity and water companies well in advance of the move.

When the removal company comes to quote for the work, be sure to show everything that is to be moved. It's easy to forget an attic or garden shed stuffed with boxes, and it can be an unwelcome shock if the extra cost for these only emerges on moving day. Homes that have been altered so that furniture that originally went in can't be removed easily, and cumbersome, heavy objects like a piano on the first floor, will bump up the price.

Do you want removers to take down curtains, dismantle self-assembly beds and furniture, and fixtures and fittings? These usually need to be quoted for and will cost extra. Do you have unstraightforward items like antiques, pets, plants or a wine collection?

The more details about the move you can supply the removal firm, about both the old property and the new one, the more accurate their quote will be and the less likelihood there is of nasty financial extras on completion of the move. Is the property an easily accessed bungalow or a cramped apartment on the sixth floor with no lift? Are you moving to an island with infrequent ferries or is the property sited just off the highway?

• **British Association of Removers Overseas,** 3 Churchill Court, 58 Station Road, North Harrow HA2 7SA, UK, **t** (020) 8861 3331, **www.barmovers.com**. Can provide lists of removal companies specialising in international relocation.

• **International Federation of International Furniture Removers,** 69 Rue Picard B5, 1080 Brussels, Belgium, **t** 32 2 426 51 60, **www.fidi.com**. Can also put you in touch with removal firms and shipping companies.

Deciding what to take

Think carefully about exactly what you need to transport. It is sometimes cost-effective to buy items again at your destination rather than transport existing ones. If you intend to bring furniture, household goods and other items to furnish your home, check that there are no restrictions on importation.

Also, some electrical items may not be compatible, either in terms of voltage (which could entail the need for a transformer) or format; for example, videos suitable for a UK video player may not work in an American one.

It could be cheaper and easier to buy things locally for your home abroad, and availability of spares, servicing and repairs may not be good for items that are not commonly available in the country in question.

UK furniture may not be suitable in the style of your home abroad or for the climate there. You may find it a good chance to replace older furniture once you arrive rather than pay to transport it and then change your mind once there.

What will you do with any goods you are leaving behind? Will they remain in the home you are leaving and renting out; should you put them in storage or dispose of them?

Planning the move

You will need to have someone available to oversee what is being moved at both addresses. A clear plan showing where you want furniture placed allows the removers to put it exactly where you want it rather than leaving you with another job to do.

Removals insurance

Check that the removal firm, if you are using one, is insuring your possessions. It is a good idea to also contact your own insurance company to try and get temporary cover through your contents insurance policy, or even a temporary policy for the move.

Insurance for the move will generally cost about 10 per cent above the total moving cost but is recommended.

Check the small print in the policy: is 'new for old' cover offered or only indemnity cover? Items you pack yourself will generally not be covered. It is worth making a photographic record of your belongings in the event of a claim.

Moving in

The days leading up to the move

If you are relocating abroad rather than buying a second home, the process leading up to the move could go something like this.

In good time

- If you live in rented accommodation you will have to give your landlord notice that you intend to leave.
- Check that your passports don't need to be renewed.
- Start obtaining quotes from removal companies.
- Check whether there are any special entry requirements such as visas, permits or inoculations.
- If you have a pet, find out about inoculations or quarantine.
- Check the procedure for shipping your belongings and arrange health, travel, buildings, contents and other insurances as necessary.
- Organise the opening of a bank account in your new country of residence.

With a month to go

- Book the removal firm if applicable, obtaining packing boxes and starting to fill them – with clear labelling on the outside; put books in small boxes as large ones will be difficult to lift.
- Chuck out or sell unwanted goods; clear rubbish from the loft or garage and organise a car boot sale.
- Arrange your final utility bills at your old home.

With a week to go

- Arrange for professional disconnection of appliances you are removing.
- Arrange for final readings of gas, water and electricity supplies.
- Notify your local authority that you are leaving – you may get a refund of council tax.
- Check whether you are due for a rebate on your tax or social security contributions.
- Cancel direct debits and standing orders connected with your old home (such as gas, electricity and mortgage).

- Begin new ones at the place you are moving to.
- Cancel milk or newspaper deliveries and pay the final bills.
- Return library books and other borrowed items.
- Remove fitted items like mirrors, pictures, shelves, etc. and pack them carefully.
- Clear out rubbish from the loft or garage.
- Inform the following organisations and companies in the UK of your change of address: utilities companies; insurance companies; bank and building societies; doctor, dentist and optician; employer; pension provider; loan companies; credit and store card companies; Driver and Vehicle Licensing Authority (DVLA); council tax department; national savings and premium bonds, TV licensing department; electoral register; schools, Inland Revenue, Department of Social Security; lawyer; accountant; organisations you have subscriptions with.

Just before the move at your old home

- Disconnect the cooker and washing machine.
- Defrost the freezer.
- Check that your solicitor has arranged for the new owner to take over the council tax bill.

On moving day

- Take electricity, gas and water meter readings.
- Ask for a final telephone bill.
- Leave a set of keys with your estate agent at your old property and label the spares.
- Make sure all important documents and any emergency numbers are acccessible.
- Leave pre-addressed labels so that new owners can send on any mail that hasn't been redirected.
- Lock all windows and doors before leaving.
- In many countries, it is an unwritten rule not to remove things like light-bulbs and light fittings, doorhandles, fireplaces, fitted cupboards or anything cemented down or planted in the garden, but in others many such things are routinely removed, so be prepared.
- Leave the property in the condition in which the buyer first saw it, but cleared of all the items that were not included in the purchase price or bought separately by the purchaser. Be careful not to leave anything, as the new owner would be able to claim it belongs to them, making it diffi-cult to recover.

• Arrange connection of gas and electricity at your new address. Are there any guarantees or service agreements relating to the property that you will be taking over? Will you be receiving keys for all of the locks in the property, from front door to garden shed?

Soon after arrival

• In some countries, foreigners are required to register with the police and it may be a good idea in some destinations to register with your local embassy or consulate after taking up residence abroad. Also register with your local social security office.

• Once you have moved in, transfer all the utilities services to your name if you haven't already done so. You may have to pay a deposit or arrange for periodic access to the meters to be read for billing.

• Arrange household insurance (*see* below).

Insurance and security

Usually you should insure your property abroad the moment you own it, for buildings, contents and third-party liability cover. In some countries this can be even more necessary than in the UK, where risks like flooding, hurricanes, earthquakes and storms can be significant.

It is often cheaper to arrange insurance for your home abroad with a local company but if the documentation is not in English, unless you understand it or can easily get it translated, it may be better to pay extra for a policy originating in the UK. And a domestic insurer may provide better cover, claiming may be easier and you may have better protection under UK law. Currently UK insurers that cover homes abroad include Andrew Copeland International, Hiscox, Norwich Union and Saga – the latter with preferential rates for retirees.

Insurance policies vary greatly, even when you're getting identical cover, so be sure to get several quotes for each type of insurance. Be sure to check the small print of any policies you consider. Definitions and cover can vary greatly.

It is important to ascertain conditions your insurer may attach to periods when the property is not occupied. You may be required to switch off the water, electricity and gas, and not doing so could cause the insurance to be void. Typically, cover for hazards such as theft may lapse after 30, 60 or 90 days of unoccupancy. You may be able to extend this period to six months or more. Check how 'unoccupancy' is defined. It does not necessarily mean that someone has to be living at the property full-time. Weekly visits by a local agent may be enough to define it as occupied.

If your property will have paying guests, check that the policy covers this. Many policies only cover friends and family. Check that you have sufficient legal liability cover against being sued should someone injure themselves in your home, especially if you are taking out a local rather than UK policy.

There are two main types of household insurance – buildings and contents. Buildings insurance covers the building itself, its fixtures and fittings, garden walls and fences. Contents insurance covers everything else, things that you would normally take with you if you moved.

Your mortgage deal may include a condition that you buy the lender's insurance; otherwise buy directly from an insurance company or an insurance broker. There may be a small insurance tax added to the premium.

By increasing the excess (the amount you pay on any claim) slightly, the cost of insurance policies can reduce surprisingly, so ask how much the premium would be if you took the highest excess. Combining buildings and contents insurance may attract a discount. Policies ideally should be linked to inflation.

Many countries also require third-party cover against financial liability for injuries or accidents to third parties on your property.

Buildings insurance

Not only is it extremely unwise to omit to take out buildings insurance – which pays for repairing or rebuilding your home should it be destroyed in a fire or other calamity – but you will be required to have this insurance if you have a mortgage. Your mortgage lender may offer to provide this insurance, and sometimes, though less and less frequently, it may insist you take out its cover. The insurance should begin before you take ownership of the property.

The cost of the premium relates to the cost of rebuilding your home from scratch. Buildings insurance is for the rebuilding cost rather than for the value of the property, which may be very different. This can be difficult to work out but your lender will state how much to insure for, otherwise there may be a figure in your survey if you had one done, or your insurance company may be able to help. Otherwise consult a local builder or surveyor. Although the UK has strict building controls and regulations, construction methods can be very different abroad and this can be reflected in the rebuilding costs. The rebuilding cost for a very old property, especially, may be very difficult to assess and could be much more than the market value of the property.

In some countries, a proportion of the insurance premium goes to the state insurance fund. In Spain, for example, the *consorcio* provides cover against natural disasters such as floods, and if you were to claim in such a situation, you would be claiming against the *consorcio* rather than your insurance company. A similar system operates in France. In some countries, notably Greece, Turkey and Italy, earthquake cover is important. Local policies may only provide you with half the sum insured for this risk, so check before taking out the cover. If you underinsure, any claim is likely to be reduced.

Policies generally cover eventualities like flood, fire and water damage and may include malicious acts, like vandalism. You can add on extras like accidental damage and legal protection, covering legal fees in the event of a legal dispute. For the policy to remain valid, it is important to fulfil all the requirements of the policy, which may be very specific: for example, fitting a certain standard of lock. Check the strength of the door or window that locks are fitted to – a good lock on rotten wood is useless. Regions prone to subsidence may incur higher insurance costs.

If you buy a flat or apartment block, there may be a communal insurance policy covering the whole building, for which you pay a share.

Contents insurance

Contents insurance can be of two types. The cheaper is **indemnity cover**, where your contents are insured for their current worth. Therefore a camera would be valued as being second-hand. **New for old cover** is pricier, where your contents are insured for what it would cost to replace them. You can pay extra for **accidental cover**, which includes anything you break yourself, and you can also pay extra for **all-risks cover** to insure possessions outside the home.

Make a detailed **inventory** of everything you own and try to work out the value as accurately as possible: if you are underinsured, your claims will not be met in full; if you overinsure, you are wasting money.

Particularly valuable items will usually have to be specified on the policy, otherwise only a proportion of their worth will be covered. You may need to use a professional valuer to obtain a price the insurance company will be happy with if you have items like antiques or collectables, which could be difficult to value.

There are lots of add-ons you can buy, covering such things as family legal expenses, garden furniture, freezer contents, plants, cash and replacement of lost or stolen keys and having locks changed.

Securing your home

Crime prevention has advanced greatly in recent years, with increasingly sophisticated alarms coming as standard. As well as alarms that are monitored 24hrs a day, there are even systems that allow you to monitor your property remotely from another country using a computer link. If you have valuable furniture or antiques, microchips linked to tracking systems can be injected into upholstery or into a tiny hole drilled into the back of a picture frame.

Although you can never make your home completely secure, you can make it so much trouble that the casual thief will move on to the next property. Sensored external security lights, prickly bushes, noisy gravel and cumbersome, large window boxes with big plants can all help deter a burglar. Ladders, tools and climbing frames left around the garden can help a thief.

As far as fire prevention and protection goes, at the very least fit a smoke alarm on each floor. These are a legal requirement in some countries. The cheapest, ionisation alarms, are sensitive to smoke from flaming fires, while optical alarms are better at detecting smouldering fires.

Managing finance

Appointing a local financial professional such as an accountant or a tax adviser to deal with your local financial affairs is sensible, and in some cases mandatory, for example in Spain, where a fiscal representative is required by the government to be appointed by non-resident property owners to deal with their taxation matters.

Local bank accounts

Although many owners of homes abroad get by using a combination of travellers' cheques, credit cards and cash exchanged at a *bureau de change*, in the long term this is less secure, more expensive and more troublesome than opening a local bank account, which may be necessary anyway for paying utility and tax bills. Be aware that in many countries overdrawing on a bank account is not treated as lightly as it often is in the UK, but is considered a criminal offence and can greatly hinder your credit rating and financial dealings abroad in the future.

You may be able to open a foreign account with a bank that has branches in your home country. For example, an increasing number of British high street banks have a presence abroad, notably in France and Spain. Some banks abroad offer a multilingual service.

Financial companies

Some financial companies offer convenient services that organise currency transfers for regular payments like overseas mortgage payments, repatriating foreign income, spending money and pension transfers. It takes the hassle out of regularly buying currency to settle monthly financial commitments, which can be time-consuming and also make efficient budgeting impossible due to currency fluctuations. They generally make their money on the exchange rate and do not charge fees or commissions like the international transfer fees and commissions charged by banks. Rates can usually be fixed for a set period, such as six months or two years.

• **HIFX**, 59–60 Thames Street, Windsor, Berkshire SL4 1TX, UK, **t** (01753) 859159; **www.hifx.co.uk/mpa**. Offers a 'monthly payments abroad' service, managing regular overseas financial payments.

Letting and Selling Your Property

09

Letting

If you are not intending to live at your home abroad full-time, its costs could be partly offset by renting it out. But be aware that, although letting can offset some of the costs of financing and maintaining the property, it is rare for it to completely cover costs – never buy if rental income has to cover all of your costs, as this can never be guaranteed.

It is important to thoroughly assess the local rental market before buying, noting the sorts of things that attract renters, such as good access to transport links like airports and motorways, and plenty of tourist attractions nearby. It is a good idea to visit agents and pose as a potential renter yourself before buying a property, to see the current situation of the rental market first-hand, rather than relying on the word of a local letting agent. You may be presented with scores of properties available to rent at far less than you were hoping to receive for your property.

It is imperative to check that you are actually permitted to let the property out at all. Some countries (there are widespread limits to letting in the USA, the Republic of Cyprus and Malta, for example) and councils within countries have restrictions on letting and special zoned areas, and many apartment blocks and property complexes have restrictions.

You have to ask yourself whether, once you have moved in and made the place your own, you will be happy renting out to strangers. Many novice letters assume that their friends and family will flock to rent the property, too, but this often does not happen, and it can also be difficult charging people you know rent, even at a discounted rate.

If you are not organising lets yourself, choose the letting agent carefully, as in the past many have ceased trading in debt to their clients. Typically, agents charge 20 per cent of the rental income for their fee, although this can vary greatly from country to country and depends on whether a full management service is required. Rental income is taxable in most countries and an annual tax return has to be filed. All property-related expenses are usually deductible against income.

Don't forget the extra costs, should you decide to let: safeguarding valuables and insuring them against the possibility of breakages, keeping the place in an immaculate condition, ensuring that all appliances work properly, furnishing the property to a standard that meets the local safety regulations, paying for someone to deal with daily maintenance, possibly paying for professional management of the property, and paying for an accountant to calculate the tax you would have to pay on rental income.

Unfortunately, often the times of highest letting potential are also the times that you are most likely to want to spend time at the property yourself.

Selling

If you decide to sell your home abroad, invest some time in investigating the local property market. There are too many factors at work in the sale of a property for there to be a definitive, ideal time to sell your home, but if you are a vendor it is probably best to follow the pack: the best time to sell is likely to be when the majority of other sellers are trying to, when the market is strong and prices are rising.

If, on the other hand, there is a property slump and prices are falling, it may be better to ride out the storm if you are able to, letting out your home long-term until the market has picked up.

Estate agents

In spite of the the negative view so many people have of estate agents, the overwhelming majority of buyers and sellers still use them both in the UK and abroad.

If your home is at the luxury end of the market, you may be able to use the services of one of the big, well-known, international agents who can all give access to wealthy buyers around the world:

- **Chesterton International, t** (020) 7201 2070; **www.chesterton.co.uk.**
- **FPD Savills, t** (020) 7499 8644; **www.fpdsavills.co.uk.**
- **Hamptons International, t** (020) 7589 8844; **www.hamptons.co.uk.**
- **Knight Frank, t** (020) 7629 8171; **www.knightfrank.com.**
- **Sotheby's Realty, t** (020) 7598 1600; **www.sothebysrealty.com.**

But most people will have the option of a local agent in the country the property is located in or in areas popular with foreign buyers, or a British-based agent who specialises in selling foreign properties to Brits.

Take care in choosing an agent, especially as in many countries there are few legal constraints and a high proportion of unscrupulous operators, who usually congregate in resorts and other areas popular with foreign buyers. You could initially pose as a buyer and then ask the agent lots of questions. Test their knowledge of the area and see what other types of property they have on their books. Some may specialise in expensive homes, others may consistently deal with the cheapest ones or properties in need of modernisation.

Experience counts for a lot. You want an agent who can successfully combine assessing what's been selling recently, seeing where the market is now, and reading how the market will be over the next few months when the property will be on the market.

Note that commission rates can vary widely from country to country; indeed, commission rates in the UK are among the lowest in the world. If you think the rate of commission is too high you could try haggling, especially if the agent has few properties on its books, but bear in mind that an agent's expertise can often get the vendor a better price that more than compensates for the commission charged.

Be clear about what is included in the package. Do you have to pay extra for advertisements in property magazines or the local press or for a glossy brochure? Ask the agency to confirm in writing its fees and what will be included. You will be given an agreement to sign. Look carefully at the clauses.

Check the estate agent's details. The photographs of your property should be in colour and taken during daylight, ideally in the summer. Good-quality interior shots can also help a lot. Check that the agents' descriptions of the property are accurate. Ensure that easily overlooked features that could make your property more attractive or saleable are mentioned.

It is important to obtain several valuations from different agents, which can vary considerably. Ask each agent to back up their valuation with an explanation of how they reached that figure. For a quick sale, it is important to have your home priced accurately. Too high, and you could put off potential buyers, and being forced to make a price drop a few weeks on could discourage them further.

Bear in mind that some agents go to great lengths to get your business. If one substantially undervalues your home, he may simply want to stimulate a quick sale for high turnover of commission, and if you are given a high figure, he may instead be trying to flatter you to get your business, with the intention of dropping the price to a realistic figure a few weeks on.

Selling your home yourself

If you have a particularly attractive home and the market is strong, you could consider selling it yourself, thereby avoiding paying an invariably large commission to an estate agent.

When a sale goes well, an agent can seem invaluable: preparing accurate, effective sales details, looking after all the viewings, weeding out unsuitable buyers and negotiating the best possible price. Yet many house sales don't go like that, and vendors are instead left to conduct most of the viewings by potential buyers, who have been enticed by inaccurate, imaginative property particulars and who are looking for something completely different.

To have a chance of selling the property yourself, you need plenty of time, energy and good negotiating skills. You can advertise on an Internet site dedicated to selling homes privately, or even construct your own website solely for selling your home. You could advertise in specialist magazines geared to property-buyers abroad, or within property sections of national newspapers.

Selling privately is likely to involve considerable legwork, including arranging valuations so that you can decide on an asking price, drawing up particulars, answering enquiries, arranging and carrying out viewings and negotiating. When you find a buyer, the process should then be handed over to your solicitor, who should make sure that the buyer's solicitor sends a formal letter with confirmation of the offer.

It is important, when selling privately, to ensure that all sale particulars are accurate, as incorrect statements could result in being sued for damages or cancellation of the contract, or both.

Encouraging a quick sale

Your buyer is likely to have made an initial decision to buy within the first few seconds of arriving at your property for the first time. Therefore making a good first impression is vital when you come to sell: keep the house as spotless as possible, make sure the doorbell works, get rid of any clutter and carry out any redecorating that is necessary.

If you live in an apartment block, ensure that the communal areas are looking as good as possible. Brighten your property's hallway, maybe sanding the floorboards or installing a neutral carpet and adding extra lighting. If the place is small, keep the doors open when you show people around as it makes the rooms look bigger.

By all means bake bread, grind some coffee beans, make a real fire, use soft lighting, put soothing music on and place fresh flowers around the place when prospective buyers come to view, but it is more important to ensure your home is clean, tidy, aired and uncluttered. Salivating, growling dogs, grumpy teenagers and demanding children can be a real turn-off. Don't have a bath or shower before viewers arrive, as the bathroom will be steamy and may suggest a condensation problem.

The overall impression should be clean, light, and simple, using lots of neutral, natural materials. Highly patterned wallpapers and fabrics should be kept to a minimum but the odd splash of colour is welcome. Cover dated or worn sofas and chairs with large throws in a neutral colour and cover carpet stains with neutral-coloured rugs. Paint tiles white with tile paint and regrout if the grout is grubby. The general effect should be calm, comfortable and not fussy.

Bear in mind that some initiatives could be a complete waste of money. It's seldom worth splashing out on an expensive new kitchen or bathroom, for instance, as there's little guarantee that potential buyers will like your taste or that it will add value to the property. Complete redecoration is seldom necessary and may prompt suspicion of your trying to hide hidden faults like damp patches or cracks.

Any evidence of faults spells neglect, so eradicate leaking gutters, loose door handles and dripping taps. Things that may be very cheap to put right can put off buyers because it can suggest the possibility of more serious problems. A slate missing from the roof could be rectified easily but if left may suggest to the buyer that the whole roof needs replacing. A few suspect cracks in the walls could simply need filling with a dab of plaster, but they may also suggest that there are serious structural problems like subsidence. Many potential buyers don't want to take the risk, or the cost and trouble, to find out how serious the problem is. It's well worth looking into the cost of every repair and improvement before putting the property on the market.

Have utility and maintenance bills, invoices for work done such as rewiring as well as damp-proofing, timber treatment guarantees and similar paperwork to show potential buyers. Do not hover behind viewers as they look around, but give them ample chance to inspect the property at their own pace.

If your property has some interesting aspect to it – maybe it is unusual architecturally or someone famous has lived in it, for example – it may be worth approaching the local or even a national paper, which may be interested in featuring your home.

Further Information

10

Organisations

- **Age Concern**, Adastral House, 126 London Road, London SW16 4ER, UK, t (020) 8765 7200; **www.ageconcern.org.uk**. Publishes *A Buyer's Guide to Retirement Housing*, plus there is also a useful website.

- **Airpets Oceanic**, Willowslea Farm Kennels, Spout Lane North, Stanwell Moor, Staines, Middlesex TW19 6BW, UK, t (01753) 685571. A travel agency for pets.

- **American Association of Retired Persons**, 601 East Street NW, Washington DC 20049, USA, t 800 424 3410; **www.aarp.org**.

- **American Citizens Abroad**, 5 bis, rue Liotard, CH-1202 Geneva, Switzerland, t (00 41) 22 340 0233; **www.aca.ch**.

- **American Citizens Abroad**, 1051 North George Mason Drive, Arlington, VA 22205, USA.

- **Animal Aunts** (UK), t (01730) 821529; **www.animalaunts.co.uk**. Pet and property-minding service.

- **Assist-Card**, t (212) 752 2788 (USA). Card members can be helped with travel-related problems like theft, illness and legal difficulties.

- **Association of Americans Resident Overseas**, BP 127, 92154 Suresnes Cedex, France, t (00 33) 1 42 04 09 38; **www.aaro-intl.org**.

- **Association of Retired People**, Greencoat House, Francis Street, London SW1P 1DZ, UK, t (020) 7895 8880.

- **Benefits Agency, Overseas Department**, Benton Park Road, Newcastle-on-Tyne NE98 1YX, UK, t (0191) 213 5000.

- **British Association of Removers Overseas**, 3 Churchill Court, 58 Station Road, North Harrow HA2 7SA, UK, t (020) 8861 3331.

- **British Australian Pensioners Association**, PO Box 35, Christie's Beach, South Australia 5165, Australia.

- **British Council**, 10 Spring Gardens, London SW1A 2BN, UK, t (020) 7930 8466; **www.britishcouncil.org**.

- **British Retirement Pensioners Society**, PO Box 165, Cramerview 2060, South Africa, t (00 27) 11 792 8160.

- **Canadian Alliance of British Pensioners**, 605 Royal York Road, Suite 202, Toronto, Ontario M8Y 4G5, Canada.

- **Department of the Environment, Food and Rural Affairs, Export of Cats and Dogs Section**, 1a Page Street, London SW1P 4PQ, UK, t (020) 7904 6347.

- **The Elderly Accommodation Counsel**, 3rd Floor, 89 Albert Embankment, London SE1 7TP, UK, t (020) 7820 1343; **www.housingcare.org**. Has a UK database of all types of accommodation for older people.

- **Federation of Overseas Property Developers, Agents and Consultants (FOPDAC)**, 95 Aldwych, London WC2B 4JF, UK, **t** (020) 8941 5588; **www.fopdac.com**. Trade federation that unites agents, developers and specialist consultants in the international property markets who wish to protect the interests of those buying and selling overseas.

- **Four Corners Emigration** (UK), **t** (0161) 608 1608; **www.4corners.com**. Worldwide emigration and resettlement service for Australia, New Zealand, Canada, South Africa and the USA.

- **Golden Arrow Shippers**, Horsford Kennels, Lydbury North, Shropshire SY 8AY, UK, **t** (01588) 680240. Pet transport.

- **Help the Aged**, St James's Walk, London EC1R 0BE, UK, **t** (020) 7253 0253.

- **Homesitters**, Buckland Wharf, Aylesbury, Buckinghamshire HP22 5LQ, UK, **t** (01279) 777049; **www.homesitters.co.uk**. Home and pet-minding service.

- **International Pensions Centre** (UK), **t** (0191) 218 7777; **www.dss.gov.uk**.

- **Passport Agency**, Clive House, 70 Petty France, London SW1H 9HD, UK, **t** 0870 521 0410.

- **Pensions Information Line** (UK), **t** 0845 7731 3233.

- **Property Finders International** (UK), **t** 0845 330 1449; **www.newskys.co.uk**.

- **Social Security Agency**, Overseas Branch, Lindsay House, 8–14 Callender Street, Belfast BT1 5DP, UK.

- **Society of Pensions Consultants**, 92 Fleet Street, London EC4 9PQ, UK, **t** (020) 7353 1688.

Magazines

The websites for many of these publications have online features, property listings, travel information and plenty of links.

Best Retirement Spots
Published by Best Retirement Spots, 17101 East Baltic Drive, Aurora, Colorado, USA, **t** (303) 358 0512; **www.bestretirementspots.com**.

Emigrate
Published by Outbound Newspapers, 1 Commercial Rd, Eastbourne, East Sussex BN21 3XQ, UK, **t** (01323) 726040; **www.outboundnewspapers.com**.

France magazine
Published bimonthly by Archant Life, Archant House, Oriel Road, Cheltenham, Glos GL50 1BB, UK, **t** (01858) 438832; **www.francemag.com**. Lots of features on all things French: travel, food and drink as well as property.

French Magazine

Published bimonthly by Merricks Media, Charlotte House, 12 Charlotte Street, Bath BA1 2NE, UK, t (01225) 786845; **www.frenchmagazine.co.uk**. Lots of features on all things French: travel, food and drink as well as property. Again.

French Property News

Published monthly by French Property News, 6 Burgess Mews, London SW19 1UF, UK, t (020) 8543 3113; **www.french-property-news.com**. *French Property News* has more than 400 advertisers in each edition, giving access to tens of thousands of properties throughout France as well as access to specialist solicitors, surveyors, removal companies, builders and other services. The company also stages five French property exhibitions throughout Britain (*see* p.227).

Holiday Villas magazine

Published by Merrick Publishing, Wessex Buildings, Somerton Business Park, Somerton, Somerset TA11 6SB, UK, t (01458) 274447; **www.holidayvillasmagazine. co.uk**. Property owners wishing to let out their homes can be included.

Homes Overseas

Published monthly by Blendon Communications, 207 Providence Square, Mill Street, London SE1 2EW, UK, t (020) 7939 9888; **www.homesoverseas.co.uk**. Long-established magazine on all aspects of buying abroad in many countries; regular features on finance, removals and legal issues. *Homes Overseas*, the UK's best-selling specialist international real estate magazine, has independent advice and ideas on all aspects of the overseas property purchase.

International Homes

Published bimonthly by International Homes, 3 St John's Court, Moulsham Street, Chelmsford, Essex CM2 0JD, UK, t (01245) 358877; **www.international-homes.com/exhibitions**. Features about countries around the world.

Italy Magazine

Published bimonthly by Poundbury Publishing, Agriculture House, Dorchester, Dorset DT1 1EF, UK, t (01305) 266360; **www.italymag.co.uk**. The magazine for lovers of all things Italian: people, places, style, culture, food and property.

Living France magazine

Published monthly by Archant Life, Archant House, Oriel Road, Cheltenham, Glos GL50 1BB, UK, t (01242) 216050; **www.livingfrance.com**. Lots of features on French life, culture, wine and gastronomy, property, home interiors and celebrity interviews, plus an in-depth feature on a particular region of France.

Nexus Expatriate magazine

Published by Expat Network, 500 Purley Way, Croydon CR10 4NZ, UK, t (020) 8760 5100; **www.expatnetwork.co.uk**.

A Place in the Sun magazine

Published 13 times a year by Brooklands Media, Medway House, Lower Road, Forest Row, East Sussex RH18 5HE, UK, **t** (01342) 828700; **www.aplaceinthesun mag.co.uk**. A companion to the Channel 4 television programme, it has country profiles, features and celebrity interviews on a wide range of regions.

Private Villas

Published by DaltonsHolidays.com, 8th Floor, CI Tower, St George's Square, New Malden, Surrey KT3 4JA, UK, **t** (020) 8329 0222; **www.privatevillas.co.uk**. Property owners wishing to rent out their homes can be included.

Residence

Published four times per year by Mosaic Magazines, 129–131 City Road, London EC1V 1JB, UK, **t** (020) 7250 3007; **www.residence-int.com**. Rich in photographs, this magazine features a handful of countries around the globe each issue.

Resident Abroad

Published by Resident Abroad, 149 Tottenham Court Road, London W1P 9LL, UK, **t** (020) 7896 2525; **www.ra.st.com**. Aimed at British expatriates, with features on finance, property, employment opportunities and living conditions in countries with substantial British expatriate populations.

Spain Magazine

Published monthly by The Media Company Publications, 21 Royal Circus, Edinburgh EH3 6TL, UK, **t** (0131) 226 7766; **www.spainmagazine.info**. Features on all things Spanish: travel, food, drink, style and property.

Spanish Homes magazine

Published quarterly by Spanish Homes Magazine, 116 Greenwich South Street, London SE10 8UN, UK, **t** (020) 8469 4381; **www.spanishhomesmagazine.com**. Magazine on all things Spanish: property, cuisine, fashion and travel.

Transitions Abroad

Published bimonthly by Transitions Abroad, PO Box 1300, Amherst, MA 1004-1300, USA, **t** (413) 256 3414; **www.transitionsabroad.com**. Articles on living, working and retiring abroad.

Unique Homes

Published by Unique Homes, 327 Wall Street, Princeton, NJ 08540, USA; **www. uniquehomes.com**. This American publication focuses on the luxury market, with anything from European castles to modern oceanfront villas.

World of Property

Published six times per year by Outbound Publishing, 1 Commercial Road, Eastbourne, East Sussex, BN21 3QX, UK, **t** (01323) 726040.

Travel bookshops

UK

- **Blackwell's Map and Travel Shop**, 50 Broad Street, Oxford OX1 3BQ, t (01865) 793550.
- **Daunt Books**, 83 Marylebone High Street, London W1M 4AL, t (020) 7224 2295.
- **John Smith and Sons**, 57–61 St Vincent Street, Glasgow G2 5TB, t (0141) 221 7472; **www.johnsmith.co.uk**.
- **Stanfords**, 12–14 Long Acre, London WC2E 9LP, t (020) 7836 1321.
- **The Travel Bookshop**, 13–15 Blenheim Crescent, London W11 2EE, t (020) 7229 5260; **www.thetravelbookshop.co.uk**.

Republic of Ireland

- **Eason's**, 40 O'Connell Street, Dublin 1, t (01) 858 3881; **www.eason.ie**.

North America

- **The Complete Traveler Bookstore**, 199 Madison Ave, New York, NY 10019.
- **Globe Corner Bookstore**, 28 Church Street, Cambridge, MA 02138, t 800 358 6013; **www.globecorner.com**.
- **The Literate Traveller**, 8306 Wilshire Boulevard, Suite 591, Beverly Hills, CA 90211, Los Angeles, t 800 850 2665; **www.literatetraveller.com**.

Health and travel guides

Eurotunnel (t 08705 353535/08457 697397; **www.eurotunnel.com**) offers 7 free regional 'Discover' guides: *Pas-de-Calais*; *Lille and the Nord*; *Seine Maritime*; *Champagne-Ardenne*; *Flemish Coast*; *Wartime Memories*; *Cities of Flanders*.

Dawood, Dr Richard, *Travellers' Health* (OUP, 2003). A very comprehensive yet readable book on the subject.

Hatt, John, *The Tropical Traveller* (Penguin 1993). A well-written, absorbing and entertaining book full of advice on most aspects of travelling in the tropics, anything from money to flying, health, culture shock, animal and human hazards.

Schroeder, Dick, *Staying Healthy in Asia, Africa and Latin America* (Moon Publications). A detailed, good all-round guide.

Wilson-Howarth, Dr Jane, *Bugs, Bites & Bowels* (Cadogan Guides). Now in its third edition, this excellent book offers practical health advice. Indispensable.

Websites

Websites with a good selection of properties around the world include the sites for the international estate agency chains, such as **www.fpdsavills.co.uk**, **www.hamptons.co.uk**, **www.sothebysrealty.com**, **www.chesterton.co.uk** and **www.knightfrank.com**. Website **www.newskys.co.uk** is the site of **Property Finders International**, with almost 12,000 properties worldwide. **www.viviun. com** has around 3,500 properties from every corner of the world, including more unusual markets, such as Brazil, Costa Rica, the Dominican Republic, Panama, the Philippines, Slovakia and Thailand. It also has sections on hotels, castles and islands for sale. **www.escapeartist.com** is a website with international property listings.

Government advice is available from the **British Foreign and Commonwealth Office** (**www.fco.gov.uk**), the **US Department of State Travel Advisory Dept** (**www.travel.state.gov**), the **Australian Dept of Foreign Affairs** (**www.dfat.gov. au**) and the **Canadian Dept of Foreign Affairs** (**www.dfait-maeci.gc.ca**).

The UK **Department of Health**'s site, **www.dh.gov.uk/travellers**, lists countries with reciprocal agreements and gives lots of further useful information. The **Department of Work and Pensions** is **www.dwp.gov.uk**. The **Inland Revenue International** website (**www.inlandrevenue.gov.uk/international**) has information on international tax issues.

The **European Commission**'s website (**www.citizens.eu.int**) contains country guides and fact sheets. **www.embassy.org** has links to all the embassies in Washington DC, USA.

Try these:

- **www.50plus.com**: Canadian website for retirees.
- **www.50connect.co.uk**: British website for people aged 50+.
- **www.adrian-barrett.co.uk**: advice on building works.
- **www.britishexpat.com**: website for UK expatriates.
- **www.britishinamerica.com**: website for UK expats in America.
- **www.cibfarnham.com**: courses for expatriates.
- **www.countrylife.co.uk**: features upmarket property.
- **www.countrynet.com**, **www.livingabroad.com** and **www.liveabroad.com**: information on living in various countries.
- **www.directmoving.com**: expatriate information and advice.
- **www.elderhostel.org**, **www.seniornews.com/travel**, **www.seniority. co.uk** and **www.thirdage.com**: information specifically for retirees.
- **www.escapeartist.com**: comprehensive site for expatriates plus property.
- **www.expataccess.com**: information on moving abroad.

- **www.expatexchange.com**: website for expatriates with a big network and features on relocation.

- **www.expatica.com**: website for English-speaking expatriates living in European countries.

- **www.expatnetwork.com**, **www.expatboards.com**, **www.expatworld.net**, **www.peoplegoingglobal.com**, **www.expatfocus.com** and **www.expatexpert.com**: expatriate advice and guides.

- **www.expatshopping.com** can be used for ordering goods from your home country while **www.expatforum.com** provides cost-of-living comparisons around the world.

- **www.expatspouse.com**: information about working abroad.

- **www.fawco.org**: the Federation of American Women's Clubs Overseas.

- **www.fnworldwide.com**: information about relocation.

- **www.globalnetwork.co.uk**: information for English-speaking expats.

- **www.informer.it**: information on Italy.

- **www.kiplinger.com/retreport**: informative website on retiring abroad.

- **www.outpostexpat.nl**: information on different countries.

- **www.overseasdigest.com**, **www.peoplegoingglobal.com**, **www.planetexpat.com** and **transabroad.com**: informative websites for expatriates.

- **www.realpostreports.com**: relocation services and accounts by people who have moved abroad.

- **www.siphealth.com**: information on private healthcare.

- **www.tckworld.com**: website geared to the children of expatriates.

- **www.the-retirement-site.co.uk** and **www.retirement-matters.co.uk**: websites with information specifically for retirees.

- **www.tradepartners.gov.uk**: investment and trade information.

- **www.wheretoretire.com**, **www.familyhaven.com/retirement** and **www.wwseniors.com**: information on retirement internationally.

- **www.womanabroad.com**: advice on family and career matters.

- **www.worldwide-tax.com**: compares taxation rates around the world.

- **www.wtgonline.com**: worldwide travel information.

Appendix I:
Further Countries

11

There isn't the room in this book to examine the property markets of every country in the world, but here is some information on some other countries where you might be interested in retiring to.

Belgium

Although France is still in many areas astoundingly cheap when compared with Britain, some areas are drowning in Brits. To escape your countrymen, head for Belgium, so often overlooked and which offers far more than simply beer, chocolates, Poirot, Tintin and the European Parliament. It boasts a great coast, and the resort of Knokke is particularly popular with buyers of holiday homes. The area enjoys easy access to four fabulous Belgian cities – Antwerp, Bruges, Brussels and Ghent – all bristling with cafés, restaurants, shops and culture. Belgium is also ideally located for visiting the Netherlands, Luxembourg and northern France. Coastal properties suitable as holiday homes tend to be in the form of apartments. There is a far better choice of houses when you focus further inland. For the coast many buyers focus on Knokke-Heist, De Haan and Ostend, while Antwerp, Bruges, Brussels and Ghent are ideal for city-lovers.

But beware. Belgian property can be considerably more expensive than neighbouring France. In 2004 around Knokke, a four-bedroom villa near the sea is around £350,000; a three-bedroom apartment by the sea is about £125,000; and a modern studio near the coast starts at £70,000 or so. Prices in the best areas of cities like Antwerp and Brussels can almost be on a par with Mayfair or Belgravia in London. The property market is steady and secure in Belgium, and in both 2002 and 2003 prices rose by about 7 per cent.

Access to the UK is good. As well as ferries from Dover to Ostend, there is easy access to Belgium via the Eurotunnel and the Calais ferries, whose continental ports are little more than an hour's drive away. For northern Brits, two routes to the Netherlands – Stena Lines' Harwich–Hook of Holland service and DFDS Seaways' Newcastle–Amsterdam – are another possible option.

Belgium is one of few remaining EU countries that do not tax private capital gains. The requirements for non-EU citizens to become Belgian residents are relatively strict.

Further information

- **Belgium: t** (00 32)
- **Belgian Tourist Office, Brussels and Wallonia**, 217 Marsh Wall, London E14 9FJ, UK, **t** 0906 3020 245; **www.belgiumtheplaceto.be**.
- **Belgian Tourist Office, Brussels and Flanders**, 1a Cavendish Square, London W1G 0LD, UK, **t** (020) 7867 0311; **www.visitflanders.co.uk**.

Estate agents

All are in Belgium.

- **Adviesbureau Dewaele, t** 5044 4999. For properties around Bruges.

- **Agence Agimobel, t** 5060 3299. Coastal estate agent based at Knokke-Heist, selling mainly apartments.

- **Century 21 Group Agimmo, t** 2425 0803. For properties in Brussels.

- **FPD Savills, t** 2646 2550. Coastal and city properties are on offer from this international agent.

Chile

The South American country of Chile has a superb, untouched coastline, coupled with the dramatic Andes Mountains and the rainforest, while the lakes region has numerous tranquil retreats. It has one of the most varied landscapes in South America. Although it has had a troubled past, stability has taken hold, the economy is improving, the government democratic, and the future is optimistic. Prices at this Latin American beauty spot aren't necessarily cheap, and houses of interest to a foreign buyer typically start at around £150,000 at least.

Further information

- **Chile: t** (00 56)

Estate agents

- **Invest in Chile, www.investinchile.com.**

- **www.escapeartists.com:** property listings for Chile.

Costa Rica

This Central American delight sandwiched between Nicaragua and Panama has a gorgeous climate, beautiful flora and fauna, imposing volcanoes and two coastlines with palm-fringed beaches. Both tourism and foreign investment are booming due to a buoyant economy, improving infrastructure and a democratic government. The cost of living is low and people friendly. What more could one want? Apartments start at just under £100,000 and a really splendid home can be had for less than £400,000.

Further information

- **Costa Rica: t** (00 506)

Estate agents

- **Dominical Realty** (Costa Rica), **t** 787 0223; **www.dominicalrealty.com**.

India

The former Portuguese colony of Goa on India's west coast is considered a beautiful place to live. Prices, along with the rest of the country, are low compared with Europe. With land prices and salaries in India a fraction of their UK counterparts, you can buy a sizeable piece of land and build a luxurious residence for £50,000, or buy a former colonial residence in need of renovation for less.

The Goan resort of Candolim on the Arabian Sea is popular with the British and houses are available for less than £10,000, while newly built one-bedroom apartments with a communal swimming pool, are available for £12,000 or so. Calangute and Baga are also popular areas. Prices in Goa are expected to rise as foreign investment rises. The Indian government is also considering granting citizenship to non-resident Indians, which would greatly increase the number of people who would consider investing there, further raising prices.

Another popular area is Kerala in southern India, which has been an increasingly popular tourist destination in recent years. A large modern villa at Ernakulam or Thruvanamthapuram costs from £35,000.

The cost of living is cheap too – it is possible to have a three-course meal out for an amazing 50p. Flights from the UK typically start at £300.

The Indian conveyancing process and attendant bureaucracy is quite a maze, and includes a requirement for foreign purchasers to obtain a one- to five-year resident visa. To do this they need to spend at least 182 days (not necessarily in one stretch) in the country in the financial year (1 April to 31 March) previous to the purchase. The deeds for the property cannot be registered until after 1 April of the year in question. Also foreign purchasers must obtain approval to buy from the local authorities and the Reserve Bank of India before a property purchase can commence. Rental rates are lower than in Europe and the money earned cannot be taken out of the country.

Further information

- **India: t** (00 91)
- **High Commission for India**, India House, Aldwych, London WC2B 4NA, UK.

Estate agents

All are in India.

- **Prazeres Resorts, t** 832 277 064.
- **Homes and Estates, t** 832 250 115.
- **Kerala Property, t** 484 235 8947; **www.keralaproperty.com.**

Japan

Japanese property is seldom viewed as an investment, as homes are not built to last and prices have fallen for 13 consecutive years. Therefore the value of properties falls rapidly over the course of several decades, and a building that is 50 years old is generally considered to be almost worthless and ready for demolishing.

More positively, the lengthy recession the country has suffered means that the Bank of Japan currently is adhering to a zero interest policy resulting in mortgages as low as 2 per cent.

Latvia

The Baltic state of Latvia joined the EU on 1 May 2004, which will ensure that its economy will flourish even more than it has done since gaining its independence from Russia in 1991. Latvia is one of the least costly and least spoilt countries in Europe. It boasts beautiful countryside and property prices are exceptionally low as a result of low owner-occupation and years of a sluggish economy. Yet EU membership in 2004 will change this, with large-scale EU investment improving infrastructure, and mortgage finance becoming increasingly available to locals, causing prices to shoot up. Early investors will be able to rent or sell at a good profit.

Although average earnings are a quarter of an average EU salary, Latvia currently has the highest annual growth in GDP in Europe. In early 2004, city apartments were already rising by 20 per cent per year and rental yields were very strong. But as with the other Baltic states, Lithuania and Estonia, investment here is seen to be more of a risk than more familiar Eastern European countries like Poland, Hungary and Croatia. It is also not for sun-worshippers: from October to March, the country is generally very cold and dark.

For a small country such as this, there is a wide variety of property types, from city apartment blocks to tall merchant houses, country manor houses and wooden homes in the forests and chalets by the sea. The attractive capital, Riga, is as cheap to live in as it is to buy in. Elsewhere, property prices plummet.

Further information

- **Latvia: t** (00 371)

Estate agents

- **Ober Haus** (Latvia), **t** 728 4544; **www.ober-haus.ee**.

The Netherlands (Holland)

Curiously, extremely few Brits buy property in the Netherlands, popularly known as Holland. Its uncrowded road network is excellent for visiting the attractive towns and cities including the beautiful, fairytale city of Amsterdam, and Delft, Den Haag, Haarlem and Rotterdam.

The country is generally thinly populated and has plenty of pretty, relatively unspoilt towns and villages to choose from. Many areas are suitable, especially along the coast, such as around the coastal resort of Zandvoort. The coastal region has numerous wild stretches of dune and beach. The unspoilt region around the delightful, quiet town of Oudewater, near Gouda, is well located for the most popular towns and cities, as well as many of the country's attractions.

The Netherlands has experienced property boom-and-bust in recent years. Prices fell in the early 1990s, but then there was a property boom on a par with the UK culminating in a 20 per cent rise in prices in 1999. Since then the property market has been stable, and is likely to be a reasonably good investment over the long term. In 2002 and 2003, prices rose by about 2 per cent per year. Prices are relatively high compared with, say, France or Italy, but substantially cheaper than the UK. Prices for a pretty canal-side property, such as a gabled three-bedroom house in the centre of Oudewater near Gouda, start at under £200,000, and apartments typically start at under £120,000. A bijou pad in the centre of Amsterdam would typically start at around £180,000.

Stena Lines' Harwich–Hook of Holland route, and DFDS Seaways' Newcastle–Amsterdam service, are the ferries of choice for the Netherlands.

Further information

- **The Netherlands: t** (00 31)
- **Netherlands Tourist Office**, PO Box 30783, London WC2B 6DH, UK, **t** 0906 871 7777; **www.holland.com**.

Estate agents

All are in the Netherlands.

- **Groene Hart Huizen, t** 348 564711. **Estate agent that specialises in the Oudewater region near Gouda.**
- **Prismaat, t** 20 662 6364; **www.prismaat.nl.**
- **Ter Haar, t** 20 573 6000; **www.terhaarmakelaars.com.**

Nicaragua

Nicaragua offers beautiful, untouched beaches, elegant, inexpensive colonial houses, cattle ranches at London apartment prices, and islands that are also for sale at very low prices. The country has shaken off its troubled past and now, peaceful and democratic, it shows encouraging signs; increased tourism and investment from large hotel chains such as Holiday Inn and Radisson are causing buyers of holiday homes, retirement homes and tourist-related businesses to snowball. Prices remain very low, even by the ocean. Many buyers are buying colonial homes at Granada on Lake Nicaragua, which start at around £25,000, and a very good example with four bedrooms could be bought for £200,000. One-bed flats are available in Granada for under £10,000. Flights from Miami take just over two hours.

Further information

- **Nicaragua: t** (00 505)

Estate agents

- **Nicaragua Properties** (Nicaragua), **t** 552 3199; **www.nicaraguaproperty.com.**

Russia

Russia's property market, especially in the big cities, has been experiencing a boom as a result of Russia's improving economy and growing confidence. But potential buyers should be aware that the legal system is unreliable, conveyancing a minefield and clear land-ownership laws are still evolving, although property is far more secure than even just five years ago.

New moneyed Russians (*novy Russky*) flush with Siberian oil money have been buying up swanky city apartments and grand old dachas with gay abandon, pushing up prices significantly as they do so. The demand for decent properties and a lack of good housing stock has pushed prices up further. Prices have soared in Moscow, by 100 per cent in 2002–2004, and are expected to continue to rise. A two-bedroom flat in the 'Golden Triangle' would now be over £450,000. A one-bedroom flat in a neighbourhood like Park Kultury in central Moscow would set you back about £150,000. But on the outskirts of the city prices plunge to a starting price of about £50,000, although you could easily pay £1 million for a large, traditional home just outside Moscow. A steady stream of affluent foreign tenants is keeping the Moscow lettings market very buoyant.

Move away from Moscow and prices can be amazingly low. In the south of Ukraine and around the Black Sea Port of Odessa a small dacha could be yours for under £15,000. But avoid looking north of Kiev as it is closer to Chernobyl.

As far as borrowing is concerned, local mortgages are very rare – less than 5 per cent of property purchases in the country are made using mortgages and most people deal in cash – but have become increasingly available. Currently only a handful of banks offer mortgages and interest rates are high, but it is predicted that soon the mortgage market will greatly enlarge, with most Russian banks offering loans, competition bringing down rates, and the availability of mortgages driving up prices further.

Further information

- **Russia: t** (00 7)
- **Russian Tourist Office**, 70 Piccadilly, London W1J 8HP, UK, **t** (020) 7495 7555.

Estate agents

- **Beatrix** (Russia), **t** 095 792 5922; **www.beatrix.ru**.
- **Jones East 8**, **www.joneseast8.com.ua**.
- **Knight Frank** (UK), **t** (020) 7629 8171; **www.knightfrank.com**.
- **Penny Lane Realty** (Russia), **t** 095 232 0099; **www.pennylane.ru**.
- **Sotheby's Realty** (Germany), **t** 892 280 2894; **www.sothebysrealty.com**.

Slovakia

Attention has increasingly focused on Slovakia since the country obtained European Union membership in May 2004. Access is good now the country has cheap flights. Slovakia is not as 'westernised' as some European countries, which would put off some buyers, although attract others.

Property in the capital, Bratislava, is about 50 per cent cheaper than in Prague, although prices are set to rise now Slovakia has joined the EU, which will increasingly see Bratislava residents commuting to Vienna, just 40 miles away in Austria. Prices start at about £30,000 for older flats, and £65,000 for a new-build two-bed apartment. Houses in the countryside start at about £15,000.

You need to set up a local company to buy property here, and this can usually be arranged by the estate agent or property consultant. The company is subject to tax in the Slovakia but also corporation tax has to be paid in the UK on any company profits, ie when you sell or from rental income. Currently UK corporation tax is 23.75 per cent on profits of between £10,001 and £50,000. However, tax paid on the property overseas can usually be offset against your British tax bill.

Further information

- **Slovakia: t** (00 421)
- **Slovak Embassy**, 25 Kensington Park Gardens, London W8 4QY, UK, t (020) 7313 6470; **www.slovak-embassy.co.uk**.

Estate agents

- **www.en.redo.sk** and **www.sak.sk** have properties for sale in Slovakia.

Sri Lanka

More than two years after the ceasefire by the Tamil Tigers, the beautiful island of Sri Lanka is a good source of property bargains, although prices have been rising of late in response to increasing foreign interest. Yet prices are still appreciably lower than popular Asian spots like Bali and Thailand. Direct flights are available from the UK to the capital, Colombo. Rich in unspoilt countryside and coastline, former British and Dutch colonial properties abound. One area foreign buyers are focusing on is Galle, on the southern tip of the island. It boasts an imposing fort by the sea, which is a UNESCO World Heritage Site. With houses starting at £120,000 here, it has Sri Lanka's most expensive real estate. Just a few miles away, prices drop to a fraction of that. Unspoilt beaches with land available to build on abound at Matara and Tangalla further up the coast.

As well as the unstable political situation, land ownership disputes are common and it is important to employ an experienced local lawyer to unearth any possible problems before a purchase. At the time of writing, the Sri Lankan government was considering the possible introduction of a 100 per cent duty on land and property purchased by foreigners and stricter regulation of foreign purchases.

Further information

- **Sri Lanka: t** (00 94)

Estate agents

- **Eden Villas, www.villasinsrilanka.com.**
- **Lanka Real Estate, www.lankarealestate.com.**

Sweden

Sweden is stunningly beautiful and one of the finest wilderness areas in Europe, with endless opportunities for fishing, hunting, boating, hiking and skiing. You get a lot for your money in a country widely perceived as astronomically expensive to live in. A restored large rural farmhouse with lake frontage set in several acres would typically cost around £150,000.

Stockholm has a lot to offer, including slick city apartments and easygoing island retreats. Small apartments in the centre, such as the Kungsholmen district, are available for less than £75,000 with country properties a few kilometres from the centre commonly for around £135,000.

Further information

- **Sweden: t** (00 46)
- **Swedish Tourist Office**, Swiss Centre, 10 Wardour Street, London W1D 6QF, UK, **t** 0800 100 200 30; **www.mysweden.com.**

Estate agents

- **Homes in Sweden** (UK), **t** (0131) 663 7605/0777 424 1177 (mobile); **www.homesinsweden.com.**
- **Notar** (Sweden), **t** 8 545 815 13; **www.notar.se.**

Thailand

More and more people are considering retiring to Thailand. Medical facilities are relatively good here and the cost of living is low. Yet properties aren't cheap.

Property types vary from simple village homes going for a song to luxury beachfront villas. For example, Knight Frank was recently selling brand-new

£1.5 million spacious, five-bedroom, five-bathroom properties with swimming pools in landscaped gardens overlooking the Andaman Sea at Kamala Bay, Phuket.

Expect to pay from around £650,000 to over £2 million for the most luxurious villas; from about £350,000 to £650,000 for mid-range villas; and under £350,000 for smaller villas and apartments. Despite the market crashing in the 1997 Asian financial crisis, it has recovered and generally prices have risen by more than 50 per cent in the past three years. Even so, there is plenty of cheaper accommodation, with village houses of a good standard easily available for less than £100,000.

Popular areas for foreign buyers include the capital, Bangkok, the island of Samui and around the northern city of Chiang Mai and the Mekong. This area provides the true Thai experience of exotic temples and elephants, although it is far less geared to expatriates. Bangkok, on the other hand, is congested, polluted and chaotic.

Most popular among international buyers is the resort of Phuket, in southern Thailand, which provided the setting for the Bond film *The Man With the Golden Gun*. It is the country's biggest island and is considered to have the best beaches. It is not the most authentic part of the country but has the largest expatriate population outside the capital.

Pattaya, a two-hour drive south of Bangkok, is a resort that has become overrun by tourism, pollution and prostitution, although in recent years, it has been cleaning up its act.

Buyers should engage a reputable English-speaking lawyer experienced in the Thai conveyancing system and able to organise reliable translations of all documents. Your lawyer will need to check the title deed, definition of boundaries and whether there are any outstanding encumbrances against the property. When a purchase price is agreed, both parties sign a preliminary contract binding both to the sale at the agreed price.

Foreigners are only permitted to hold 30-year leases for villas and houses, although they may hold full title in perpetuity in the case of apartments and condominiums. Thai banks do not organise mortgages for foreigners, so finance needs to be arranged elsewhere. Foreign currency to pay for the transaction is transferred to the receiving bank, which then issues a certificate confirming inportation of the funds. This document is known as a *thor tor 3* and is required by the land registry before the final contract can be signed.

In 2001, the Thai government relaxed immigration procedures for people wishing to retire in Thailand. Potential retirees must be at least 50 years of age, and provide legally authenticated proof that they do not have a criminal record in their home country, are not seeking a work permit and have no contagious diseases. Proof, for example by providing a bank statement, of an income of about £10,000 per year or £10,000 on deposit, is also required. Retirement visas are renewable annually.

The Thai bhat is a volatile currency and the market less stable than many regions; Thai property is unlikely to perform as well as in western Europe.

Further information

- **Thailand: t (00 66)**

Estate agents

All agents are in Thailand.

- **Andaman Island Group Partnership, t 76 355 330; www.andamanproperty.com.**
- **Andrew Park, t 76 354 016; www.andrewpark.com.**
- **Katamanda, t 22 538 528; www.katamanda.com.**
- **Knight Frank; www.knightfrankthailand.com.**
- **Phuket Land, t 76 340 207; www.phuketland.com.**
- **www.phuket-estate.com also has properties for sale.**

Appendix II

Checklist – Do-it-yourself Inspection of Property 288

Checklist: Do-it-yourself Inspection of Property

Task ✓

Title – check that the property corresponds with its description in the title:
Number of rooms
Plot size

Plot
Identify the physical boundaries of the plot
Is there any dispute with anyone over these boundaries?
Are there any obvious foreign elements on your plot such as pipes, cables, drainage ditches, water tanks, etc.?
Are there any signs of anyone else having rights over the property – footpaths, access ways, cartridges from hunting, etc.?
Are any parts of what you are buying physically separated from the rest of the property – e.g. a storage area or parking area in a basement several floors below an apartment or a garage on a plot on the other side of the road from the house which it serves?

Garden/Terrace
Are any plants, ornaments, etc. on site not being sold with the property?

Pool – is there a pool? If so:
What size is it?
Is it clean and algae-free?
Do the pumps work?
How old is the machinery?
Who maintains it?
What is the annual cost of maintenance?
Does it appear to be in good condition?

Walls – stand back from property and inspect from outside:
Any signs of subsidence?
Walls vertical?
Any obvious cracks in the walls?
Are the walls well pointed?
Any obvious damp patches?
Any new repairs to walls or signs of re-pointing?

Roof – inspect from outside property:
Does the roof sag?
Are there any missing/slipped tiles?
Do all faces of the roof join squarely?
If there is lead flashing, is the lead present and in good order?

Task   ✓

Guttering and Downpipes – inspect from outside property:
- All present?
- Do they seem to be in good order?
- Securely attached?
- Fall of the guttering constant?
- Any obvious leaks?
- Any signs of recent repairs?

Enter Property
- Does it smell of damp?
- Does it smell 'musty'?
- Does it smell of dry rot?
- Any other strange smells?

Doors
- Any signs of rot?
- Close properly – without catching?
- Provide a proper seal?
- All locks work?

Windows
- Any signs of rot?
- Open and close properly – without catching?
- Provide a proper seal?
- Window catches work?
- Any security locks? Do they work?
- Any sign of excessive condensation?

Floor
- Can you see it all?
- If you can't see it all, will a surveyor be able to get access to the invisible parts easily?
- Does it appear in good condition?
- Is there any sign of cracked or rotten boards, tiles or concrete?

Under Floor
- Can you get access under the floor?
- If so, is it ventilated?
- Any sign of rot?
- What are the joists made of?
- What is the size (section) of the joists?
- How close are the joists?
- Are joist ends in good condition where they go into walls?
- What is maximum unsupported length of joist run?
- Any sign of damp or standing water?

Task   ✓

Roof Void

Is it accessible?

Is there sign of water entry?

Can you see daylight through the roof?

Is there an underlining between the tiles and the void?

Any sign of rot in timbers?

Horizontal distance between roof timbers?

Size of roof timbers (section)?

Maximum unsupported length of roof timbers?

Is roof insulated – if so, what is the depth and type of insulation?

General Woodwork

Any signs of rot?

Any signs of wood-boring insects?

Is it dry?

Interior Walls

Any significant cracks?

Any obvious damp problems?

Any signs of recent repair/redecoration?

Electricity

Is the property connected to mains electricity?

If not, how far away is the nearest mains electricity?

Check electricity meter:

How old is it?

What is its rated capacity?

Check all visible wiring:

What type is it?

Does it appear to be in good physical condition?

Check all plugs:

Is there power to the plug?

Does a plug tester show good earth and show 'OK'?

Are there enough plugs?

Lighting:

Do all lights work?

Which light fittings are included in sale?

Water

Is the property connected to mains water?

If not, what is the size of the storage tank?

If not connected to the water supply, how near is the nearest
    mains water supply?

Do all hot and cold taps work?

Task   ✓

Water (*cont'd*)

    Is flow adequate?

    Do taps drip?

    Is there a security cut-off on all taps between the mains and tap?

    Do they seem in good condition?

    Are pipes insulated?

Hot Water

    Is hot water 'on'? If so, does it work at all taps, showers, etc?

    What type of hot water system is fitted?

    Age?

Gas – is the property fitted with city (piped) gas? If so:

    Age of meter?

    Does installation appear in good order?

    Is there any smell of gas?

    If the property is not fitted with city gas, is it in an area covered by city gas?

    If it is in an area covered by city gas, how far away is the nearest gas supply?

    Is the property fitted with bottled gas? If so:

    Who is the supplier?

    If there is a safety certificate, when does it expire?

    Where are bottles stored?

    Is the storage area ventilated to outside of premises?

Central Heating – is the property fitted with central heating? If so:

    Is it 'on'?

    Will it turn on?

    What type is it?

    Is there heat at all radiators/outlets?

    Do any thermostats appear to work?

    Are there any signs of leaks?

    How old is the system?

    When was it last serviced?

    If it is oil-fired, what capacity is the storage tank?

Fireplaces

    Is property fitted with any solid fuel heaters? If so:

    Is there any sign of blow-back from the chimneys?

    Do the chimneys (outside) show stains from leakage?

    Do the chimneys seem in good order?

Task   ✓

Air-Conditioning
Which rooms are air-conditioned?
Are the units included in the sale?
Do the units work (deliver cold air)?
If the units are intended also to deliver heat, do they?
What type of air-conditioning is it?
How old is it?
When was it last serviced?

Phone
Is there a phone?
What type of line is it?
How many lines are there?
Is there an ADSL line?
Does it all work?
Number?

Satellite TV
Is there satellite TV?
If not, is the property within the footprint of satellite TV?
Who is the local supplier?
Does it work?
Is it included in the sale?

Drainage
What type of drainage does the property have?
If septic tank, how old is it?
Who maintains it?
When was it last maintained?
Is there any smell of drainage problems in bathrooms and toilets?
Does water drain away rapidly from all sinks, showers and toilets?
Is there any inspection access through which you can see
     drainage taking place?
Is there any sign of plant ingress to drains?
Do drains appear to be in good condition and well pointed?

Kitchen
Do all cupboards open/close properly?
Any sign of rot?
Tiling secure and in good order?
Enough plugs?
What appliances are included in sale?
Do they work?
Age of appliances included?

Task   ✓

Bathroom
Security and condition of tiling?
Is there a bath?
Is there a shower?
Is there a bidet?
Age and condition of fittings?
Adequate ventilation?

Appliances
What appliances generally are included in sale?
What is not included in the sale?

Furniture
What furniture is included in sale?
What is not included in the sale?

Repairs/Improvements/Additions
What repairs have been carried out in the last two years?
What improvements have been carried out in last two/10 years?
What additions have been made to the property in last two/10 years?
Do they have builders' receipts/guarantees?
Do they have building consent/planning permission for any
     additions or alterations?
Are any repairs needed? If so, what, and at what projected cost?

Lifts
Are there any lifts forming part of your own property?
How old are they?
When were they last maintained?
Do they appear to be in good condition?

Common Areas
What are the common areas belonging jointly to you and other
     people on the complex?
Are any repairs needed to those areas?
Have any repairs already been approved by the community?
If so, what and at what cost?

Disputes and Defects
Is the seller aware of any disputes in relation to the property?
Is the seller aware of any defects in the property?

Index